I SURVIVED
AUSCHWITZ

There is always the danger that we will forget things that are best not forgotten. Certainly, some things should be permanently recorded so that posterity will remember what we would prefer to erase from our memories.

This is the story of a woman who was imprisoned for a number of years in Auschwitz, the notorious death camp. What she saw there makes medieval genocides look like child's play.

This is her memoir, and she shows not only her own courage but also her fellow prisoners' fierce will to live. Half-starved, suffering from lice, scabies and dysentery and mowed down by typhus and pneumonia, they worked in fields of icy slush and mud and registered new arrivals——hundreds of thousands of women from Holland, Greece, Italy and Hungary, who did not know where they were or why they had been seized.

That she survived and finally managed to escape to tell the tale is one of many reasons why this book should be published and widely read. Most of her companions were murdered so that they could not bear witness.

KRYSTYNA ŻYWULSKA

I SURVIVED AUSCHWITZ

doM wYdawniczy tCHu
in cooperation with
Państwowe Muzeum Auschwitz-Birkenau

I Survived Auschwitz

© Copyright for the English edition by tCHu, Warszawa 2004-2011.

© Copyright by Jacek and Tadeusz Andrzejewski, Warszawa 2004-2011.

Ⓛ Copyleft—partial reproduction of this book (excluding photographs) is permitted for non-profit purposes. Any modification must be approved by the © Copyright holders.

The work is translated from the Polish, *Przeżyłam Oświęcim*,
by Lech Czerski and Sheila Callahan
based on an initial translation by Krystyna Cenkalska.

The publisher sincerely thanks the translators: Lech Czerski and Sheila Callahan for their invaluable input during the course of producing this unabridged edition.

The publisher kindly thanks Yad Vashem. The Holocaust Martyrs' and Heroes' Remembrance Authority in Jerusalem, Israel for permission to use photographs from its collection (*The Auschwitz Album* of Lilly Jacob-Zelmanovic Meier). Copyright © Yad Vashem.

The publisher wishes to thank Narodowe Archiwum Cyfrowe, the National Digital Archives, (NAC) for permission to use in the book photographs from its collection. NAC holds the Copyright (©) for them.

This book was edited in cooperation with Państwowe Muzeum Auschwitz-Birkenau, Auschwitz-Birkenau State Museum, which holds the Copyright (©) for the pictures from its archives.

The photo on page 347 is by Stanisław Mucha. The image on page 59 comes from the private archive of Mirosław Ganobis.

The publisher sincerely thanks Ms. Katarzyna Horna and Ms. Barbara Milewski for their invaluable help in preparing this extended and enriched edition.

Book design, cover photo by Lech Robakiewicz.

Editors—Lech Robakiewicz, Max Bojarski and Katherine Craddy.

Revised and Expanded Edition

tCHu, doM wYdawniczy
[tCHu pUblishing houSe]
PL 00-227 Warszawa, ul. Freta 3M3, Poland.
www.tchu.com.pl   dom@tchu.com.pl

Warsaw 2011

ISBN 978-83-89782-51-9

Printed in Poland

Contents

For My Mother

Part One

INTRODUCTION TO AUSCHWITZ

Chapter One

The First Day

The fortune-teller flipped her greasy cards and looked up at me, gloating over the effect of her prophecy. "Yes, officials, a journey, a cross."

The cards had foretold the same future for each one of us in cell 44 of Pawiak prison. We stared at them forebodingly, thinking of just one thing, the transport to Auschwitz.[1] We had become accustomed to Pawiak. Here there were fleas, beatings, even executions; we were afraid of them but we were horribly afraid of the transport.

At times when it was quiet at Pawiak, we could hear the distant sounds of wheels, the clang of the streetcar, echoes of the city. At Pawiak we received messages from home and, although we who had been arrested by the Gestapo never really believed that we would be released, we were aware that freedom was only one step away. But if they should take us to Auschwitz—we could not picture it. Not one of us knew what it really was, and not one of us wanted to know. Of one thing we were certain—from Auschwitz no one ever returned.

---

[1] Auschwitz was the German name given to the Polish city of Oswiecim and was also used for the concentration camp established there on H. Himmler's order in 1940, as well as for the series of camps which came to operate under the same administration: Auschwitz II-Birkenau, Auschwitz III-Monowitz (Buna, situated in the village of Monowice next to Oswiecim) and over forty sub-camps.

The grating of a turning key shattered the silence. An SS[2] man, Wylup, one of the terrors of Pawiak, was standing in the doorway, his face like a death skull. Our apprehension and the fortune-teller's words were already coming true. Names were read; mine was the third on the list. Stiff-legged, I walked out of the cell, followed by the sighs of those who remained. Zosia, white-lipped, stood at my side. I tried to smile.

"Well, we're not dead yet."

"We're not dead, but we'll suffer and that's worse."

"Did you think you'd go free? After all, people do stay alive there. Anyway, it's good we're going together. Cheer up. The others are looking at us. Don't look sad."

"You're right. I was only... at first... because my family wrote that they were trying... "

"Did you think it would work?"

"I sort of thought it would."

"Well, let's believe that we'll come back. It depends a little on us."

"I think a lot depends on us." She said this mechanically. "Smile!"

Zosia smiled and when her face lit up she charmed me as she had that first day. Was it a year ago when I offered her identification papers that both she and I knew were

[2] SS—the abbreviation for "Schutzstaffel"—Nazi NSDAP (National Socialist German Workers' Party) protection squads formed in 1925 initially to defend party gatherings and to fight against supporters of the Communist Party (KPD) and the Socialist Party (SPD) and for abolishing fractions within the party (eg, SA). In time, after Adolf Hitler rose to power in 1933, the role of the SS in Germany (especially in the armed forces) grew. By the 1940s the SS had become the most influential body of the Third Reich. It consisted of the most fanatical Nazis, and its leaders (including Reichsführer H. Himmler) further increased that fanaticism by establishing secret rituals.) The SS is responsible for creating and overseeing the operation of the death camps; the genocide of Jews, Gypsies and Slavs; and for inhumane medical experiments, slave labor in Germany and for many other of the Third Reich's most bestial crimes.

false, and she had accepted without a word? Zosia was the superintendent of an apartment house and I had needed an apartment. This slim, dark young woman with the delicate face not only protected me from the police but joined me in working for the underground. The Gestapo had arrested us at the same time and we had been lucky enough to remain together. Now her smile, a warm good-humored smile that never could show a belief in bad fortune, said to me, "You'll see. It won't be so terrible."

At that moment Wylup passed. He looked as if he would strike her, but he too seemed a little surprised by her bright face. He dropped his arm and walked on.

They crowded us into the transport cell. There we met women from other cells and floors—women who came from solitary and quarantine, women who had been at Pawiak for a whole year and who thought they had been forgotten, and those who had arrived a month ago and still bore signs of the free outdoors, traces of the sun which never showed itself in Pawiak's cells.

In the transport cell some of the women began to pray. Others tried to recall everything they knew about Auschwitz and about concentration camps in general. Others still found release in banter.

"They'll give you a beautiful haircut." We knew our heads would be shaved.

"They'll give you a number so you won't get lost."

"You'll live in virtue. You can't even talk to men... "

"Shut up," Stefa snapped. Her black eyes flared beneath smooth hair that combed Madonna-like, gave a deceptively placid appearance to her nervous, sensitive face. She bit her lips to fight back the tears—she was always on the verge of tears. She pressed my hand and began to talk about the young son she had left at home. She could not believe that she might never see him again. His eyes haunted her. She felt that he was blaming her because she had allowed them to take her away—because she, his wise mother, had been helpless against this worthless trash.

"What is he doing now?" she kept repeating tearfully. "My little one, he's waiting for me. Oh God, when my family finds out that I've been transported..."

I could not listen to her. A lump was rising in my throat. "Stefa[3], we really shouldn't cry—we're not the first ones... there's a war going on!"

Nothing helped. I looked around the cell. The jokes and the lively talk had died down. More and more of us began to cry until one deep spasm shook us all. It seemed that this sob would burst the prison wall, giving us back our freedom and—Warsaw.

But the walls did not burst. No miracle happened. Mrs. Pawlicz from cell 43 had an attack of hysteria. She jumped to the middle of the cell and began to flail her arms and legs. Her lips twisted in a frightful grin.

"Do you know where we're going? We're going to a party. You never saw such a party. I'm wearing my new hat. Look at all the pretty young women who are coming to the party. You'll dance to their music. You'll see."

She frothed at the mouth and her eyes rolled back into her head. We placed her on a bunk. She called out wildly at intervals and then grew silent.

"Well, girls, let's pray and then get some sleep," somebody said. We knelt down. A chorus of evening prayer reached us from another cell. The damp August evening looked in through the small grating above. Somewhere, so near and yet so far, people were walking along the Vistula. Stefa's little son was sleeping. My mother was keeping a wakeful watch.

Not many of us slept that night.

At six in the morning, Wylup came in and told us to get out as soon as we stood up.

[3] Pronunciation and equivalents of Polish names and their English equivalents — see the dictionary: page 366.

14

We were counted and our names were read from the transport list. Everything was in order. We were led out immediately after. The Pawiak dogs barked angrily. Not one of us had taken either bread or clothing. Wylup had told us we would return. He said they would only count us. Everything we had accumulated—the food given to us by those who stayed behind—everything was left in the transport cell.

Frightened, sleepy and tired, we walked to the Pawiak courtyard. Pale-faced men looked through the windows; about eight hundred of them were going in the same transport, the largest ever to leave the prison.

Obese SS men, counting, pushing and shouting, arranged us in columns of five. I tried not to show my nervousness but to no avail. Finally the trucks arrived and we were taken to the station.

We raced through the city under the escort of helmeted guards armed with machine guns. People on their way to work glanced fearfully at the crowded trucks and tried to recognize friends. I looked for someone I knew, perhaps someone who would hail me but never saw a familiar face. They loaded us into cattle trucks and secured all the openings.

"We're buried alive," someone groaned.

They shunted us from one track to another, to and fro, backwards and forwards until finally the wheels began to spin and the train moved forward. I don't know how it happened, but suddenly from all corners of the car our voices rose in a spontaneous song: "Land of Our Fathers, We'll not abandon Thee."

The train moved faster and drowned out the melody and the words. It tapped out the dreadful truth that lay at the end of our journey: Auschwitz—Auschwitz. At ten in the evening we stopped in an open field.

"*Aussteigen!* [4]—Our car was opened. There were dogs again, a large number of them, barking, howling and straining towards us.

[4] Get Out.

And again in columns of five the SS drove us on. We walked in silence.

The camp lay ahead of us. We moved closer and closer. The electric-charged wire fence gleamed through the darkness, and the sentry boxes made tall silhouettes against the sky. Each measured step echoed in our brains.

"So that's it, that's how it looks," I thought, glancing at Zosia. She knew I was looking at her but was afraid to return my glance. Her head was held high and her lips were tightly closed. Just then we entered the camp. I turned around and calmly told myself, "I'm in the camp. This is Auschwitz, *vernichtungslager*[5]—there is no return from here."

"We've entered hell," Zosia spoke in a quiet, distant voice. Then she added bitterly, "Do you think we'll roast?"

"I think we'll die in some other way. I don't know how. Don't look up. Don't look at the wire fence. Look at the barracks—look how many there are. People like us are sleeping in them. There will be work in the morning. Think about it. Maybe the war will end. We will try to survive. Perhaps even one day on a night like this you will wake up and there will be no dogs or wires or barracks. There will be a forest or a city, some location far away. For such time in the future, isn't it worth it to suffer? Isn't it worth it to wait for their downfall?

"It is, but so little will depend on us!"

"We'll see, Zosia. We have to promise each other that we won't let anything break us—anything, only death, perhaps."

We were pushed into a hut and we lay down on the floor— Zosias, Stefas, Hankas—we, Pawiak prisoners, united until our death by terror, pain, fear and friendship. One thought kept revolving in our heads and we could not sleep or lie quietly because of it: What would tomorrow bring?

---

[5] Death camp. All German terms are defined in the dictionary starting on page 360.

The Auschwitz gate. All photos are from the war unless otherwise indicated.

* * *

During our childhood all of us had listened to fairytales. In every fairytale there was always a bad spirit—a witch on a broom. If this witch were to appear before us in the flesh, she probably would have looked like the German woman with the black *winkel*.[6] The *winkel* was a triangular badge bearing a prisoner's number, nationality and criminal offence. For

[6] *Winkels* were triangular badges showing the prisoners' number, nationality and the reason for their internment. Political prisoners were marked by a red triangle, criminals by a green one, black for prisoners judged to be "asocial," violet for Jehovah's Witnesses prisoners and pink ones for homosexuals. A badge in the shape of a six pointed star, made by putting together a yellow triangle and one of the above mentioned triangles, was used for the Jews who, from 1943 on, were the most numerous group. From mid-1944, instead of a star, they had to wear a triangle with a yellow stripe over it.

instance, a red *winkel* with the letter P signified a Pole with a political offence. In many instances the red *winkel* was given for smuggling or sneaking across the border. It depended on the local Gestapo. Jewish women wore a star. Green *winkels* were for criminals; black *winkels*, called "Aso," were for the "asocial." Prostitutes and women convicted for work absenteeism belonged to this class. Later, women absent from work for even a few days, or women who did not return to work immediately after their vacations were sentenced to six weeks in the camp and were called reform-prisoners. Very few Polish women wore the black *winkel.*

The German woman who wore the black *winkel* made an immediately unpleasant impression on me. She sat on a small stool in our barrack, her legs wide apart—stocky, podgy and alien, a stick in her fist. Finally someone bravely asked in German:

"Do we get some food?"

Each one of us would have asked the same question. We were all very hungry.

The German woman did not hear or pretended not to hear. Someone repeated a little louder,

"When do we eat?"

The witch scratched herself under the arm with an animal-like gesture, shifted the stick to the other hand (a few women moved, just in case) and began to laugh or rather howl in a deep voice, "Ha ha, you want to 'eat' *verfluchte Schweine!* [7] What's the hurry? Maybe you want cocoa, rolls and butter? I haven't eaten for years, and I'm still laughing."

She continued to scratch herself and to wave the stick. In the dim light of the lamp she suddenly seemed unreal.

Zosia blinked so funny that I laughed.

"Pinch me," said Zosia. "Maybe I'm dreaming. What's this? A woman?"

---

[7] Damn pigs!

"It must be... maybe she was once normal—had a house—maybe she became this way here."

"Do you mean to say that we'll become like that too?"

"No, we cannot become like that, and that's why we have to die."

I didn't know then that I was not far from the truth in thinking that only this type could manage to survive.

Our brave friend, undaunted, asked the next question:

"Do we die here immediately?"

"Why? I've been locked up for eight years already. I was locked up before the war and I'm still alive—but I'm the only one and there were over eighty of us."

Her voice sounded almost human. We were shaken. Each of us thought the same thing, "There are a hundred and ninety of us. How many will be still alive a year or two years from now?"

"What did they die of?"

She gave her interrogator a dull look: "A cold, *du dummes Arschloch.*"[8] Suddenly she rose and began to shout, "*Auf Tod*[9]. In a concentration camp you die of death, understand? You don't understand, but you will understand when you kick the bucket."

Zosia covered her eyes. She got the general drift, even though she did not understand the language. I shuddered and felt as if someone had struck me. The witch sat down, mumbling under her breath. We did not ask her any more questions. We didn't dare.

"So...we now know a little," I said out loud. "If everything will be like the beginning, we can survive two weeks with ease."

Nobody talked until the morning.

In the morning the hut door was opened. We looked up at the morning light with tired and hungry eyes. Strange, striped figures with shaved heads peered into our hut. They moved

[8] You stupid asshole.
[9] Of death.

away, dragging their large Dutch clogs. They asked in Polish whether we came from Pawiak. Did we know such and such a person? Someone came in and drove the striped shadows away. We would look like that. We knew that without speaking.

"Are you nervous?" I asked Zosia. "Are you worried about losing your hair?" It was the deep urge to survive which made me and all the others try to speak light-heartedly.

"I'm not worried about anything. I'm hungry. Will they ever give us some food?"

They lined us up for the tattooing. A few fainted. Some screamed. My turn came.

I knew that this pain would pale compared to that which awaited us. What is pain that lasts a minute compared to pain that endures for years?

A political prisoner with a very low number wearing a red *winkel* without the *P*, a *volksdeutsch*[10], took my arm and began to tattoo the number 55908.[11]

---

[10] Literally, "Ethnic German," people who signed the *Volksliste* declared themselves to be of German ancestry and part of the German nation, though living outside its borders. In the part of Poland incorporated into Germany in 1941 it was practically mandatory to sign. Not doing so was seen as a betrayal of the race and was associated with displacement or being sent to a concentration camp. During the so-called "General Government" which began in 1940, signing provided huge privileges from the occupier and often resulted in stigmatization by Polish society. (Often envoys of the Resistance shaved the heads of volksdeutsch women). Volksdeutschers were deemed zealous collaborators (denunciators, spies and informers) and faced a death sentence from AK (Polish Home Army) tribunals, the dominant Polish resistance movement.

[11] Auschwitz was the only camp where prisoners received tattoos during registration. The first prisoners to be tattooed were Soviet POWs sent in autumn 1941. In March 1942 prisoners in Birkenau were also tattooed. From spring 1943 onward, all prisoners were tattooed, both the newly imprisoned as well as those already registered in the camp. (The exceptions were German prisoners, criminals, those arrested by the Gestapo and people brought via transports from Pruszkow <a town of 30,000 population about 15 kilometers or 10 miles, west of Warsaw> after the Warsaw Uprising.)

I felt she was tattooing my heart and not my arm.

From that moment I ceased to be human. I stopped feeling, stopped remembering. Freedom, mom, friends, houses, trees—died. I did not have a name or address anymore. I was *häftling*[12] No. 55908. In that one minute, with every prick of the needle, a period of my life vanished and the madness in which I was suppose to live as a number began.

* * *

The *sauna* was a building through which every internee had to pass. The camp authorities took it for granted that every person, whether brought from a prison or not, must be deloused. We were not familiar as yet with the *lager*[13] terminology. We heard the word *sauna* repeated over and over again until they took us there. Prisoners with low numbers were sitting at the table. They had hair and wore black aprons. They wrote down our names and took our papers and clothes. Suddenly a shaved head appeared in the window and we recognized one of our companions from Pawiak. She had arrived in the previous transport.

"Sweater," she said softly but clearly.

"What does she want?" Zosia asked.

"She wants us to give her a sweater. They'll take it away from us anyway, and she must be cold."

Zosia quickly took off her sweater and handed it through the window. At that moment a hand struck her on the cheek. A German *aufseherin*[14] in an SS uniform was standing in front of us. She was already holding the sweater in her hand, shaking it at us.

"When you leave, you'll raise hell about your things," she

[12] Prisoner.
[13] Camp.
[14] Overseer.

21

shouted. "You..." She unleashed a flood of incomprehensible names at us.

Zosia did not understand a word. She held her reddened cheek; her eyes gleamed dangerously.

"Zosia, calm down," I said. "She said, 'when you leave'. That means it's possible."

"Oh, Krysia, did she really say that?"

"As I hope to live, she did."

Zosia laughed. "Well, you see, your cheeks have to get used to it. It wasn't the last one, was it? Anyway, it didn't hurt at all."

"It didn't hurt," I thought, "but it sure would be great to be able to hit this green monkey with a skull back one day."

We undressed. Someone threw our things into sacks. Someone else asked for our names, and another someone pushed us forward. Zosia was sitting in front of me—half her hair was shaved off. On the other side of her head, her hair fell in soft curls. A young girl was flashing a razor above her head.

"Don't look", Zosia begged.

My turn came shortly after, and my hair swiftly fell away. Zosia looked down at me.

"You look lovely, only your nose is twice as long. I'm afraid it will be a long time before anyone will fall for your golden locks again."

We tried to joke about it, but we looked like scarecrows. We all looked alike. I never imagined that hair added so much personality. It was difficult for me to recognize the others; when I entered the room, laughter greeted me. I felt offended.

"Why are you laughing? You think you are prettier? If did it to Greta Garbo, she would lose a bit of her charm too."

"I'd rather be a shaved Greta Garbo sitting in Hollywood right now."

"Oh yes," Zosia moaned. "There they would surely have given us at least something to eat."

* * *

We had had no food, not even a drop of water, for two days and two nights.

Somewhere close by we heard running water. I approached one of the workers.

"Excuse me, is that drinking water?"

"You can drink it, but you can also get *durchfall*." [15]

"What's that?"

"You'd be too smart if you knew everything. Be patient, you'll learn! One thing at a time."

We finally got to the water. It came from the shower. We drank it as we washed ourselves, without soap of course. The shower lasted three minutes. Then they drove us into another room. There were no towels in sight. Shirts and striped dresses were handed out. I got a shirt stained with yellow streaks which I learned were dead lice. I threw the shirt away with distaste and had my hands slapped.

"Put it on you fool, even with it you'll freeze at roll call."

"I won't freeze in August."

You crazy *zugang*,[16] you'll see how you can freeze at night, even in August."

I picked it up and asked, "Could you maybe change it?"

"Take this one. You won't live very long anyway, so it doesn't matter which shirt you get."

She gave me a better shirt. At least I didn't notice any lice. My "striper" was too long—Zosia's too short. We exchanged and Zosia exclaimed with satisfaction, "You see, it's not so bad. You got another shirt, our stripes fit perfectly! If we could only get a piece of string to tie them in the middle."

They threw out some clogs. We did not know how to put them on. Zosia was untiring in her humor. "In these, our legs

[15] Dysentery; bloody diarrhea.
[16] Literally, "admission," a new prisoner brought into camp.

will look as well as they do in the cork-soled shoes of Warsaw. You'll get used to them."

We shuffled off in full prison regalia. We examined our numbers and our feet. We touched our naked heads.

After hours of standing, being counted and lined up in fives and being pushed and beaten, we received a portion of bread, just four ounces, and soup. The soup was made from frozen turnips and some other thick substance. They explained that the soup was our dinner and the bread was our supper and breakfast. The next meal, the same soup, would be served the following day at noon.

Right then we couldn't think that far ahead. We gulped our soup and bolted our bread. As I looked up at the others I realized that within twenty-four hours they had transformed us into animals. It was difficult to realize that we had ever eaten at a table.

We marched to the barracks in which we were to be quarantined in columns of five. I looked around the camp and everywhere I saw prison-stripes like our own. A woman with a black *winkel* yelled at two women walking slowly bearing carry cots on which lay a few bricks, "*Los weiter, verflucht, noch einmal!*"[17]

Others were pushing a cart filled with excrement down the center of the *Lagerstrasse*,[18] followed by another woman wearing a black *winkel.* This was Aunt Clara, a German prisoner who was given the title *kapo*, the camp term for a prisoner vested with police powers. This was reminiscent of the Middle Ages. She was shaking her stick and bawling in a deep, hoarse voice:

"*Komm, komm, du alte Zitrone!* [19] It's still dirty here, pick up *das Dreck!* [20]"

[17] Keep moving, damn you, one more time!
[18] Camp road.
[19] Come on, come on, you old hag (literally: you old lemon)...
[20] The dirt.

24

Women declared fit to work after undergoing admission at Birkenau. May 1944.

One of the women turned and bent to pick up something. The stick belabored her back.

"Don't you like your job?" Aunt Clara continued, "Perhaps it stinks. I'll order you some Coty perfume, you—"

"I wouldn't want to work for her," Zosia said.

We approached a hut and were ordered to stop. A Jewish woman wearing a red armband with the number Bl.21 came toward us. The woman who had led us there reported how many of us were present and went away.

I found out later that the block-seniors were mostly Slovakian Jews. They also held other positions. They arrived in one of the first transports and built the camp.[21] When they first arrived there were only ditches, mud and a few huts. They built the road, the washrooms and the latrines. Out of fifty

[21] The first transport of 999 Slovakian Jewish women arrived at KL Auschwitz on March 26th 1942. From 1942–1944 some 7,200 Slovakian Jewish women were registered in the camp.

thousand, less than a hundred remained. And these naturally held positions of importance. They no longer remembered that they ever had a home. They felt at home in the camp and looked at the *zugangs* with lofty indifference. What could we know of their suffering? Obviously nothing—nothing then.

Dinner was being dished out in front of the block. We had received our portion in the *sauna*. Big fat Jozka from the kitchen detail, who seemed more pig than human, ladled the soup out of a barrel with a pot and measured it out to each woman standing in the queue.

"Move up you bastards, hurry! What are you holding your dish out for, you clumsy oaf? What are you waiting for? Didn't you get enough? Move or I'll land you one. Your boyfriend won't recognize you." She was a Polish woman with a black *winkel*.

"You filthy intelligentsia!" Jozka roared again. "Excuse me, please!" she mimicked. "Can't you talk like a human being? Your mother's a bitch, so learn."

Suddenly a familiar face went by. I recognized Hanka— beautiful Hanka from Pawiak. She had arrived in the previous transport. We missed her liveliness, her optimism and bouncing energy. She had seemed so full of life, so happy that it was difficult to believe she worked in the underground.

"How are you Hanka? Don't gobble so fast or you'll choke!"

"You have to learn the local language," I explained to Zosia.

"Krysia! Zosia!" Hanka shouted. She rushed up to us and began to smother us with kisses.

"Who else came with you? Are Stefa and Marysia with you?"

"They are."

"That's wonderful!" When she heard that they were, she laughed.

"Is it really that wonderful?"

"The more the merrier. It's not so horrible. Do I look bad?

I'm out in the fields every day. Look at my tan. There's good news—the war's going to end soon."

Though she no longer had her lovely blond hair, Hanka was the only one who managed to look well with her head shaved. Her hair was already about an inch long. She looked like a handsome boy, jabbering away in her pleasant, resonant and carefree voice. Zosia and I were surprised. How could she be so cheerful and possess this astonishing optimism?

"You know, the hardest are the roll calls. But we will keep 'our five' together and we'll try to talk. To get grub will be worse, but because we are working on Tuesdays and Fridays there is bread and sausage *zulage*.[22]"

"When will we be able to write home?"

"They say in a month. The devil knows when."

"In a month...so when will the first package arrive?"

"They'll guess where you are. They'll know to send one without getting a letter. You'll see. You don't need to know the number, simply the name and the camp. I will certainly get a package, if only they are smart and send onions. You know with onions you can bribe the block room-leaders, and manage some vitamins for yourself too."

After a moment, she remembered something.

"And how's everything at Pawiak? A lot of killings? Who died?"

"They killed Hanka and several of our friends. People are being killed there every day, you know."

"Yes, I know. And just because that, here is better than in the cell," she told us. "Not so stuffy. I tell you, it's good in the fields outside the wire. We pick nettles for soup. It burns your hands but you get used to it. They don't shout at us here. Just look around. There are no Germans about. Our own people, the prisoners, beat us. Just don't let them. No one's hit me yet. Just let them try."

[22] Food bonus for harder working prisoners.

Zosia listened intently. I saw her absorbing these "camp instructions".

"Naturally, you do not have to give in. Today, I was beaten by an SS woman, but they do not hit me."

"When are we going to be allowed to enter the barracks?" I asked. "When will we lie down? We're awfully tired."

"Oh, this is worse. You spend a full day on the *wiese*. It's a meadow where you can sit if it's dry. Only later, after the evening roll call, will they let you into the barracks. Try to find a place next to our bunk."

"What is that?"

"It's the place where you sleep. It's not too comfortable, but soldiers sleep in trenches with bullets flying over them. It could always be worse, you know. That's the motto here."

"Yes, this I've already learned. How many women are in this hut?"

"It's over eight hundred now. When it gets to be a thousand, the quarantine hut will be full. Every week they do anti-typhoid injections. Actually, besides that there is nothing to do during quarantine. They can grab you from the hut or from the *wiese* to do casual work within the camp. After the quarantine period passes you are moved through the gate to the so-called *lager* B, and there you work. You go outside the barbed wire... in the field on the *aussen*[23]."

"And what gets done in the fields?"

"You dig trenches, till the soil, plant beets—everything around here belongs to the camp. The camp must be self-sufficient. They tell us to do a lot of senseless things in order for us to suffer, but we are in a *konzentrationslager*.[24] They did not bring us here for a treatment... Well, see you later girls, at the evening roll call."

She talked to us until we were driven behind the huts

[23] Outside the camp.
[24] Concentration camp.

to the *wiese*, the meadow. I couldn't understand why it was called a meadow, perhaps because it once had been a meadow. Now *häftlings*, the "stripes" and the *zugangs* from quarantine were standing or sitting there in groups. Zosia and I wandered about the *wiese*. Fragments of conversation reached us. It was always the same.

"Where are you from? When did you get here? What do you think? Can we manage somehow? How is our block-senior? Does she beat you much? Do you go to work?"

We found our Pawiak group—Nata, Marysia, Stefa and Janka. "It's strange," said Janka. "After a month in solitary at Pawiak I feel good here. I can talk. There are no Germans. I don't even feel humiliated. We all look the same."

Nata, who also had been in solitary, agreed. I was not surprised. Day after day, Nata had been taken to the examination board. She was brought back beaten and unconscious. Every morning I would put my ear to the opening in our cell and hear them calling her out for interrogation. All the prisoners listened and knew that they had taken Nata away again. Would she return? What would be her condition? But she always returned, and in spite of the bruises and her swollen face, she always smiled. Hers was an unusually gentle and radiant smile. She would always say, "Everything's fine," that one phrase. What could be fine, when everything was bad? We couldn't understand. But we believed her. She was our idol, this quiet, middle-aged woman whose endurance was beyond our understanding. She believed that she would survive, that she was indestructible, and we, listening to her, absorbed some of her courage. Now again she said, "Everything's fine," with that same smile.

Janka, who was not cast in Nata's heroic mold, had cut her veins with a piece of glass in Pawiak. She had lost a lot of blood but she did not die. In the morning, when the door of solitary was opened, she was found in a semi-conscious state. They saved her in the hospital and sent her with our transport.

She was happy that the investigation was over—that they had not found her husband who was in hiding and that her little daughter was in good hands.

"You know, Krysia," she said, "I don't know why I did it. That was weak on my part. I wouldn't do it again. Just think, I can still return to my little girl, to my husband."

"We'll manage somehow," promised Alinka, our bride. She and all her wedding guests had been arrested at the church and she had been brought to Pawiak still wearing her wedding gown and carrying her bouquet. She was quiet and seldom expressed an opinion but it was always a pleasure to look at her and each of her words had its importance.

"Well, if Alinka says we'll manage, then I'll stop crying," said Stefa, who had not stopped crying from the moment they had taken us away.

"Stefa, stop it," we all begged her. "See how we stick together. We are full of good thoughts. We will learn to live the camp life. This is the way to do it. Others elsewhere have to cope without us, and here it is our duty to endure."

"You're right, but I cannot, believe me, I cannot stop. Be patient, I will come out of it."

Maria, a friend of Stefa, also from the "wedding", stroked her head and reassured her like a child.

"Well, shame on you, so big yourself and you have already a big son, and you weep, shh... shh..."

The sun was strong. The rough striped uniform chafed and irritated my skin. We had not yet learned to sit on the ground. We were constantly squirming.

Zosia sighed. "When will we have roll call, when can we lay down?"

"Let's be patient," Nata smiled. "They will call us."

We looked around the *wiese*. All languages were spoken here—Greek, French, German, Polish.

A girl approached us.

"Do you need a headscarf?" she asked.

"What do you want for it?"

"A portion of bread."

Zosia showed interest. "Is it for sale?"

"If you have enough willpower not to eat your supper bread or if you get a parcel, you'll be able to buy many things on the *wiese*. We Jews don't receive parcels. We're not allowed to, besides we don't have anyone anymore. They've murdered everybody, gassed them. And yet, we want to live. Surprised, aren't you?"

"No, no, we're not surprised," we assured her. "You're still young, and besides, you will probably become shocked very easily here and your instinct for life weakened, but there are no forces to put an end to this either. You are just quietly waiting for death."

"Yes, but you become very tired. It is easier for you, you have hope, waiting for a package or a letter, and we are to wait for what? We go through selections, we know that in the end we all have to die, but we are trying to postpone our death, prolonging our agony."

"What's your name?"

"Maryla."

"Where are you from?"

"From Bedzin."

The girl turned away from us. "I see you're *zugangs*. You don't get parcels yet. When you have more bread, you'll find me on the *wiese*."

She went. I recalled Hanka's principle: "Remember, it could always be worse." Just then, I thought how well off I was.

Business was transacted everywhere on the *wiese*. Bread, onions and garlic were exchanged for all kinds of rags, slips and panties. One of the women even had a sweater. This was the most expensive item. It cost two portions of bread.

"How long must one not eat to buy a sweater?" Zosia wondered. "Silly, this is still August, and we won't need a sweater in September. But it's much harder to do without a headscarf, and we need a towel. That's if they let us wash."

But Zosia was already figuring out something. She called to one of the traders.

"Look, where do you get these things?"

"It depends. We don't have a warehouse. I got this sweater because I work at the fumigator, that's where they bring them. I stole it."

"I will also steal one," Zosia decided without batting an eye. "I'm sure a lot here depends on how clever you are. At most they'll smack me on the cheek again. We'll try to work somewhere where we can steal something."

I looked at Zosia, the elegant society woman from Warsaw. Here she sat, with her bald head, dreaming about stealing.

Suddenly I heard a whistle and a shout, "*Zählappell! Zählappell!* [25]. Block twenty one, fall in!"

We jumped up and ran to the block. They began to line us up. I was most afraid of Jozka. If I should happen to say, "Excuse me," I would be told about the "filthy intelligentsia." I resolved to harden myself, to change my manner of speaking.

The first roll call in the camp was not bad. We stood together, Zosia, Nata, Janka and Stefa. Others from Pawiak were beside us. To my surprise I realized I had already grown accustomed to the sight of stripes and bald heads. The only difficulty was walking in the clogs. Bread was distributed during the evening roll call. We had received our portion in the *sauna*, but we thought they would forget. They remembered, however. We were already hungry and we would have to wait until the following evening.

We must have been standing about an hour. The block-senior appeared. Someone had stolen a pot again. Another had torn off a piece of blanket from the bunk.

---

[25] Roll call, roll call! Call, during which the prisoners were counted.

"If I catch any one of you again, you'll all kneel for two hours, you dirty swine."

"You want me to stick up for you! Not a chance! Keep distance now, and not a word. *Achtung!*"[26]

They took the roll call. An *aufseherin*, a charming blonde of not more than twenty, walked slowly in front of the first formation of fives. She seemed the most gentle of all those who were allowed to shout at us.

Our block was located in the first line of the blocks on the *lagerstrasse*. The *aufseherins* from the whole camp, after they had counted their blocks, took their places near the desk, just as though we were in school.

Again, "*Achtung!*" An SS man rode up to the desk on a bicycle.

One of the "old ones" informed us that this was Taube, the worst hangman in the camp. He was taking the roll call.

This news spread instantly, causing alarm and dread.

Finally, he rode away. The *aufseherins* mounted their bicycles. The roll call was over. Everything must have been in order. No one had escaped.

"Sometimes it takes a few hours," I heard somebody saying. "Today it lasted only a short time."

They began to allow us into the hut. We were among the last to enter. We were struck by the stagnant air, the noise, the squabbles, the curses and the din and bustle.

"God, what's going on?" Janka was behind me.

"No wonder. There are more than eight hundred people in this hut."

How were we going to stand it? Terrified, we remained at the entrance.

They pushed us to the left and told us to get into the lower bunk. Zosia and I scrambled in and instantly I felt as if I had been nailed in a coffin. It was impossible to lift one's head and

[26] Attention!

it was difficult to breath. Besides the two of us, there were six other striped figures sitting on the bunk, all of them hostile to we intruders.

"How many more are they going to give us? We're packed like sardines."

"But we'll suffocate," Zosia said with alarm.

"You won't suffocate. Don't think it's that easy to die."

"Where are you from?" I asked my bunk neighbors politely.

One growled, "From Sieradz." The other said, "None of your damn business."

Others talked among themselves.

Zosia and I tried to stretch out on the bunk. We huddled together in order to occupy as little space as possible. Zosia put her arm under my head when she noticed that I did not know what to do with it. I covered my ears. We wanted some quiet. We were trying to forget that we were resting on boards without pillows, when one of our companions nudged me. I sat up with a start.

A panorama of Auschwitz.

"What do you want?"

"Take your clogs on the bunk, or they'll be stolen."

"Clogs? But everybody has them."

"Not everybody. You can do what you want. You'll be better off if you listen to someone who has experience."

I got off the bunk and found only one pair of clogs. Either mine or Zosia's had been stolen.

"You see," the one who had warned me laughed, "They're gone already. They steal everything here."

"Zosia, we have only one pair of clogs," I wailed, and Zosia sat up quickly and struck her head.

"Bother. But we don't need clogs. It's more comfortable to go barefoot. You won't have to struggle to keep them on your feet."

I took the clogs on the bunk. Just then Jozka, the block-senior, was passing by. She placed her hands on her hips:

"Put them back, you stinking... did you take your shoes to bed at home too? Who brought you up? From Warsaw maybe? Ha, you—"

She spat with contempt and left us.

I placed one clog under my head. Zosia took the other. We covered our ears again. When you took off your hand, the noise hit your eardrums; your head buzzed. I clung to Zosia. I took off my hand, someone shouted:

"*Lagerruhe*,[27] sleep, you miserable shit. Tomorrow we'll see how you will come to the roll call. Shut your mouths! There will be enough time to talk before you die. *Lagerruhe!*

The noise subsided. I asked our companions for a piece of the blanket. They gave us one corner. I began to pull, but the blanket did not reach us. We heard women wrangling for the blanket on every bunk.

"You want it all for yourself, you damn countess! Give me the blanket or I'll call Jozka."

I don't give a shit about Jozka or you either."

"Quiet, quiet," they begged from all sides. This lasted for some time. The first day in camp was over. Finally, I don't know how, but we fell asleep. For a moment before I fell asleep I was deluded by a vision of my mom, a normal apartment in Warsaw, bed.... Oh God, it's better to imagine that there are no beds in the world. Everywhere are berths— there were always just berths.

[27] Camp Silence.

Chapter Two

Quarantine

"*Aufstehen!* Get up!" I sprang up terrified and of course hit my head. Somebody swore. My tongue seemed to thicken, my head was reeling and my heart was pounding. I stretched out again to calm down. I knew that the awakening would be the worst.

"They're giving us herbs," my bunk neighbor announced. "Get up! We have to fold the blanket and take the herbs. You can't lie around here."

I knew she was speaking to me. I couldn't move. I tried to get used to the thought of what was in store for us, but I couldn't. I wanted to cry, to shout. I wanted to go home to bed. I wanted to sleep. I wanted to not think. But would this help? Anyway, I won't give up. We promised this to one other on the first day.

If I didn't get up, I would disgrace myself in front of Zosia, on the first day too. It was because of her that at last I got up.

They gave us herbs floating in water. Horrible. We screwed up our faces in disgust. Why didn't they just give us water? Even hot water would have made it slightly more palatable.

"They are adding something to it," somebody said from one of the berths.

We drank it, however, because it was a hot fluid.

"*Zählappell.* Roll call. Out, you skinny bitches. Out, step on it!" We walked through the narrow corridor between the bunks from which other women were descending. I carried our one pair of clogs. We went out in front of the block. The night was cold. None of us knew the time. Later we were told that they woke us up at two o'clock. It was about two-thirty. Barefoot, uncomfortable and cold, Zosia clung to my hand so we would not lose each other.

We remained somewhere in the crowd, and decided that each of us would wear one clog. We tried to huddle together in order to keep warm but they dispersed as and told us to line up in fives. Block-seniors like Jozka were arranging us, all speaking in much the same manner. Shivering, our teeth chattering, we were blue with cold and fatigue. It was difficult to realize that this was just the second day and the first roll call. Already, we hardly looked human. In the half-light, one could make out eyes wide with suffering and fear.

This was only August. The unbelievably starry, deep blue sky arched above us in mockery. Why do we, the cattle with stripes, need so many stars? It, after all, evokes nostalgia even more...

Dawn was breaking. The lighter it grew, the more grey we became. Our feet and heads were the coldest. We kept repeating to ourselves although no one listened, "I hope they let us go. I hope this ends, that they let us go back to the bunk."

At this moment the bunk appeared to be the most ideal resting-place—at least it was warm.

But the roll call ended at six and we were not allowed to return to our hut. Instead, they drove us to the *wiese*. There again we began to huddle close together. Each one wanted to be in the center.

Then the sun rose and began to warm us. It was a little less cold at last, but we were already hungry. So many hours before we were to get our soup. As the sun grew hot, we began to scatter. It turned out that one of the huts on the *wiese* was a latrine. At Pawiak we had grown accustomed to the fact that nothing could be done in private. There were four such places at Pawiak.

The Auschwitz latrine had fifty holes on each side so that people sat back to back. There was a passage through the middle between the holes. That was where the latrine *kapo* ran back and forth beating us over our heads with a stick.

"Enough! Get off! No resting! This is not a café."

"Why, you'd let even a dog finish. How can she?" all of us protested indignantly.

At the center of the latrine stood a stove with a pot of soup on it. Two of the women who worked in the latrine were eating out of the pot with their spoons. They were not disturbed by the stench, the sounds or by what they saw. They ate with gusto. Nowhere had I felt so humiliated. We went out as quickly as possible.

"Maybe it's better, to 'visit' the *waschraum*"[28], proposed Zosia.

We moved to the next hut, but you were not allowed to enter. Some of our friends were already standing there, some with pots and bottles. In front of the *waschraum* some with a black *winkel* was hitting and screaming as everywhere else.

"Why are they called *waschraums*?" I asked a passing person, "If you are not allow to wash or drink?"

"I don't know, but it seems to me that they expect an international inspection. For some reason they clean up blocks every day, and we must not enter the interiors. There is always talk about an inspection. There are always rumors, for example, that authority over the camp will pass into the hands of the Wehrmacht[29]."

"And when will we bathe?"

"God knows. You may be taken to the *sauna*, and sometimes the block supervisor will bring you to *waschraum*. The first time I bathed was after a month."

"Listen. What do you do when you are sick, when you are menstruating?"

[28] Washroom.
[29] The unified armed forces of Nazi Germany from 1935 to 1945.

"Don't worry, you will not have it here. Trust me."

"And when you get sick with something else, what then?"

"A fever under 102 degrees doesn't count here. If you have at least that much, you will be taken to the hospital. It's the same as other huts, but you are with the sick, and you do not go to roll call."

"How about medical care?"

"There are doctors among the prisoners. They behave differently depending on what their conscience dictates. No one usually pays them and no one controls them. However, even the best have nothing to cure with. Do not count on the hospital. This is usually the last resort and you rarely return to the camp from there."

"Besides there is the continuous threat of selection[30]."

"Even among Aryan women?"

"Yes, the seriously ill are sent to the crematory as well. You can never predict what is in their head. The hospital should be avoided."

Soon I found out everything there was to know. At least that's what I thought. I knew how we slept. I knew about the latrines, the authorities and their attitude toward us. I knew what could be exchanged for bread. I knew that I would always be hungry and that no one could do anything about that. I knew that I would not take bathe soon, and that you could not get sick. I knew that I would get colder as winter approached. I knew that home—Warsaw—was somewhere, far, far away, maybe on another planet. I did not know how I was going to live through the next hour, the next day or the next month.

Still, days and months passed.

Waking up in the morning was the worst. The moment I

[30] From July 1941 until the end of April 1943 all prisoners were subject to selections and then physical liquidation. In August 1943 selections of Jewish prisoners resumed.

realized where I was, I needed courage to rise and start the new day, to freeze for hours during the roll call and afterwards on the *wiese*, to listen to curses, groans, and complaints, to suffer from the most hellish hunger.

We ate our supper bread during the evening roll call. Not one of us had enough will power to save even the smallest piece for the next day. By ten in the morning, the hunger was almost beyond endurance. On the *wiese* we tried to forget about it by starting all kinds of discussions.

We told each other why we had been arrested. We spoke of the hearings, of our "work" under the occupation, about its goals and prospects. There were always some who had the latest news: "Someone from the men's camp said that the end of the war is a matter of weeks."

A few skilled workmen used to come to the women's camp accompanied by *posten*[31]. They worked on the barracks as joiners or carpenters. Sometimes there would be a bricklayer or a locksmith among them. The most attractive men worked in the women's *scheisskommando*[32]. They came in a sanitary truck and would dawdle in the latrines for hours. They stretched this work endlessly. All the men agreed on the speed of work. After "repairs" were finished, the latrines would work two days at the most. Then there would be a breakdown and the boys would have to be called in again. They organized it beautifully—the repairs and the breakdowns. He who came to the women's camp once used all his skill and effort to return as often as possible. It was always possible to escape the watchful eye of the *posten* and disappear for about half an hour with some block-senior or her *vertreter*[33].

The block-seniors had private rooms in the barracks. These were the only places in the camp that resembled a

[31] SS guard.
[32] Literally, "shit unit;" the unit engaged in latrine cleaning and litter dumping.
[33] Block-senior assistant.

"home." The block-seniors received the daily ration of food for the block. They could have more margarine than the ordinary *häftling* and could be bribed. They received onions and potatoes from the camp kitchen in exchange for favors. As a rule they had long hair and civilian dresses and were the older and more experienced *häftlings*.

When a man went to a block-senior's room, *torwache*[34], a watcher would be placed in front of the door to warn the occupants of the approach of anybody with higher authority. The senior fed him potato pancakes. He ate them, smacked his lips and probably said that the war would not last long, that "you women have nothing to fear. If anything should happen we won't let anyone harm you—we are organized." He would wink significantly.

Usually the senior would make some attempt to act as though she were a model, not suspecting that to men who had been in the camp for a few years, every woman with hair was glamorous. In this manner the "boyfriend" did not find it difficult to convince the block-senior that the war would come to an end in three weeks. She would take his kisses like a drug, trying to fortify herself with new strength for the things to come.

We, however, did not count at all. Only those who had a brother or an old friend in the men's camp could expect help. Nevertheless there were cases of "disinterested" love. A man would smuggle in a "cube of margarine" (ten supper portions) and they would sing in the latrines:

> *For a cube of margarine*
> *He kissed her thirty minutes*

The cube of margarine was a token, just as flowers were on the outside. It was sometimes necessary to fight for the favors

[34] Gate-guard: a prisoner serving as a guard at the gate.

of some women. The victor was the one who had a friend in the men's kitchen. The fortunate possessor of margarine, as always and everywhere, would become the object of jealousy and gossip. Those who didn't have a chance or any possibility would say, hungry and embittered, "What does she see in that idiot? How can she? The gold-digger!"

Actually, each one dreamed of someone who would console her and say that the war would end soon, someone who would kiss her and in parting leave a cube of margarine.

Men would also bring and take messages for their friends. Risking the search at the gate or punishment in the "bunker" if they were found out, they carried messages in their shoes or sewed inside their stripes.

After three weeks or a month, camp life became all-absorbing. All thoughts and attention were focused on the immediate problems: How to get ("organize") a spoon so as not to wait until someone had finished with theirs; how to "organize" a sweater or warmer panties; where to hide from the black *winkel* whether at work in the fields or in the camp; how to get to the latrine without being beaten; how to wash a bit. After two weeks we still did not know what the *waschraum* looked like on the inside. Once, when passing a barrack window, I glanced at my reflection. I was horrified— there was a long black smudge across my forehead. Together with my bald head it looked frightful.

"Zosia, why didn't you tell me that I'm so dirty?"

"What could you do about it, if I did tell you?"

"Let's not drink the herbs today, we can wash our teeth and our faces a bit." It was only then that I noticed that Zosia was black with dirt.

As we were going out to the roll call, Zosia bent down and pulled out something from under a bunk.

"What have you got there?"

"Clogs. I won't go barefoot any longer."

"But Zosia, that means that someone else won't have any."

Zosia was so decisive that it would have been useless to argue. "She can steal them from someone else; mine were stolen!" After the roll call we went to our work. Not far behind our hut a machine was set up in which sweaters were fumigated. They were supposed to issue stockings and sweaters on November 1st. I asked where these sweaters came from. It turned out that they came from the Jewish transports.

While the things were being fumigated, we sat behind the hut. As always our legs felt the cold most. Some girls cried from the cold. We longed for the sun. Cloudy days were unbearable. Fortunately, September took pity on us. It was beautiful. When the deloused blankets were thrown out of the boiler, we took them, stinking, hot and damp, on our backs, and carried them to Camp B, to the so-called *unterkunft* [35] stores from which they were distributed according to the requirements among the huts.

As I piled some blankets on my back, I felt a sharp blow. I turned around. In front of me stood the *kapo* of the squad in which we worked—a German woman.

"Why?" I asked. I straightened up and asked again, "Why?" She struck me in the face.

The blankets tumbled off my back. My fists were clenched. The third blow fell as I heard, "Because you're *frech.*" [36]

Zosia was standing behind the *kapo* and was imploring to me not to react. I picked up the blankets and walked away.

At noon on the same day Zosia concealed a sweater inside her striper. An overseer jumped out of the *sauna* and beat her up. It was the same one who had struck her the first time when we had just arrived at the camp.

She must have been watching us. As we were going to dinner I asked Zosia, "Why did you do it?"

"I can't bear to see you freeze."

[35] Accommodation.
[36] Impudent.

44

"And you?"

"I'm not cold. I can stand more than you. I'll try again tomorrow."

"You'll be beaten again."

"And you were beaten, even though you took nothing. So you never know when you're going to get it and for what. I'd rather get it when I know the reason."

More and more often Zosia would tell stories about her endurance. "I'm not hungry—you eat it." "I'm not thirsty."

"Why do you lie? I won't eat your food and I won't drink your portion, either. Who would believe that you're not hungry now?"

She would then turn away in silence, her eyes filled with tears. She hadn't realized her own hunger.

Once because of a downpour they allowed us into the huts after roll call. Dripping wet and shivering, we sat on our bunks like chickens in a roost.

Our friends, Hanka, Elza, Stefa and Marysia came to our bunk.

"What is the point of our life?" Elza asked hopelessly.

"Don't ask stupid questions. Be glad that you're not dead yet. We are already here almost a month," Stefa said.

"Yes, but it's getting colder, sadder, dirtier. We don't know what's happening outside the camp, and there's no hope for any auspicious change. On the contrary, when the quarantine is over, work on the *aussen* begins—digging ditches on a day like today for example. Why should I be content?"

"You should be happy that this is only the first rain. Usually September is beautiful."

"And that so far none of us has gone to the hospital," I added.

"And that we have not been separated yet," added Marysia.

"So I should rejoice knowing that it will get worse, that the weather will become uglier, the job harder and that some of us will get sick and that they will separate us."

"You have to be happy, because those in the field and the Jewish woman whose parents were burned in the crematory today have it even worse. Remember that we are in a *konzentrationslager*."

But I was also not happy. Last night I put a piece of bread that Zosia and I had saved from two *zulage* and one dinner to buy a sweater under my head and it was stolen from the bunk. I couldn't understand how it happened. Zosia didn't say a thing, but I knew how she felt.

No losses on the outside could have caused us such sorrow. Suddenly a block-senior called out Hanka's number and name. She ran up to the block-senior and returned smiling with a huge box in her arms.

"Oh God! A parcel!" we all cried out.

A parcel from home—what joy! That meant someone in Warsaw had bought things in a store, packed and mailed them—surely it couldn't be true.

Hanka scrambled onto the bunk and began to cry. That was the first time I had seen her cry. We, of course, joined in. I didn't know then that you always cry when you receive your first parcel. Stefa cried every time she got one. We opened the parcel with ceremony.

"Onions!" Hanka cried out. "Bread! Oh God! Lard!" Never before had there been such cries of rapture.

Everyone received a piece of "free" bread with onions. What a delicacy! We ate in silence. This feast was not disturbed by one unnecessary word. Hanka sat over her box, proud and happy,.

"Well, I told you I'd get it. My mother must have turned Pawiak upside down to find out where I was. Now I'll keep getting them. With the camp bread I can buy underwear and maybe even shoes. I'll give the onions to Jozka so she'll stop hurrying me out to roll call every morning. Thank God for the parcel!"

The news spread to all the bunks. This was a very important event—a parcel from home. We became more hopeful. Perhaps we would also get packages. Maybe it will get easier.

Chapter Three

The River

One morning after roll call the block-senior announced, "Those who want to work outside the wire will get shoes." We consulted with each other. Shoes were important. Although they were wooden-soled, at least they weren't as bad as clogs. Besides they could grab us here too—Aunt Clara, or someone else. What could be worse than standing around on the *wiese*? Zosia and I and a few others from Pawiak were taken to one side. There were only twenty volunteers in our group. The shoes were distributed. There were between a hundred and two hundred people in the other group. We didn't know which was better or worse.

Our *anweiserin*[37] supervisor looked quite pleasant—the first black *winkel* who behaved like a human being and who spoke normally.

"Who speaks German?"

"I do," I spoke up.

"Good. You'll stay with me and translate for your friends. Is this your first time in the fields?"

"Yes, what are we going to do?"

"Oh, nothing difficult. You'll see." Then, wonder of wonders, she smiled. Of course we all smiled back. "That's good." I heard Hanka's voice. "She's nice."

---

[37] A prisoner who supervised the work of others, also known as a *Vorarbeiterin*.

We walked toward the gate—the same gate we entered the camp through on the first day.

"It's possible to walk out of here," someone said in an awestruck voice.

"Remember, march in step through the gate. Don't make any mistakes. Listen to the drum," our *anweiserin* advised us.

I had never suspected that going to the *aussen* was such a ceremony. We stood inside the gate waiting for the signal. Opposite our gate was another one leading to Camp B. The *aussenkommandos*[38] went out to work through that gate. An *anweiserin* led each squad, called a "ten". They carried cards with the numbers of the ten girls under their supervision. An *anweiserin* and a *posten*, leading a dog behind each squad, were responsible for the whole group.

"*Links, links, links und links*"[39] the camp warden, standing at the gate, commanded, and we passed through the gate.

"Squad 116 with twenty," our *anweiserin* reported to the *rapportschreiberin*[40] who recorded the departing squads.

We turned to the right according to the rules. We were all frightfully nervous. To the right of the *blockführerstube*[41] stood the camp authorities—Taube, the *oberaufseherin*[42], the *aufseherins* Hase and Drexler. Taube and Hase all looked like symbols of death, they only needed scythes in their hands to make the picture complete. The *oberaufseherin*, popularly known as Oberka, was a woman of unusual beauty.

Her beauty was like marble, pale and cold. It would be difficult to imagine her smiling, though they said she had a charming laugh.

---

[38] Outside squads, groups of prisoners going to work outside the camp.

[39] Left, left, left and left.

[40] Reporting clerk, a prisoner responsible for preparing reports showing the number of prisoners in the women's camp.

[41] Guardhouse, SS barracks at the camp gate; literally, "block leaders' office."

[42] The chief overseer or senior SS supervisor. This corresponded to the head of the camp in the men's camp.

The Auschwitz fence.

"Alraune[43]", I thought.

A band made up of *häftlings* played near the *blockführerstube*. The drum was the loudest, beating the tune—left, left.

"*Links, links*," chanted the young girls, *läufers*,[44] messengers sitting on the gate.

The worst was over. Thank God I did not fall out of step. Walking in shoes was so different.

Once outside the wire, I took a deep breath. The *posten*, a young boy who looked quite harmless, walked at our side. "Here long?" the *anweiserin* asked.

[43] The heroine of a famous novel by Hans Heinz Ewers; also: the root of the mandrake plant. It resembles a human form and possesses therapeutic and—according a centuries-old belief—very magical properties.
[44] Runners.

I was stunned by this normal, personal question coming from the lips of a black *winkel*.

"A month," I answered. "I'm so happy you talk like a human being. I haven't washed once," I added.

She smiled. "I know how the other *anweiserins* and *kapos* are. They like me here. What's your name?"

"Krysia."

"Mine is Hilda. Call me by my name. This is my fourth year."

"What are you here for?"

"I ran away from work. I was in Ravensbrück, then they moved me here."

"How wonderful it smells here," I said. "And there are no wires. For the first time in a month we are walking 'free.' I was at Pawiak during the most beautiful summer months."

"Breathe while you have a chance. The weather is good today. It's lovely where we are going."

I turned to my companions and translated our conversation. The day was off to a good start.

"Let's sing," I suggested. We started *The Weeping Willows Rustled*.

Hilda smiled with satisfaction.

After walking three miles we turned into a village—a normal village with cows, chickens and a well. People ran away at the sight of us. We understood how we looked in their eyes. We had gotten used to our appearance. I remembered how after her return from Lublin my sister told me that she once saw prisoners from Majdanek[45] on the streets—"I tell you, in stripes, barefoot, heads shaven, shivering, and there they were, walking alongside women dressed normally. I'd rather die than become, or have someone from my family and friends become, like that."

[45] Majdanek, a Nazi concentration camp located near the town of Lublin, in the southeast part of German-occupied Poland.

If only you saw me now, my dear sister, as people flee from me. If you had seen me at night during roll call... How fortunate that I am here, not you or anyone close to me.

"We must look beautiful," Hanka joked.

"That's not it," Hilda answered. "They're afraid to come in contact with prisoners, that's why they run away."

How tactful she was, I thought. It was really not important how we looked. The surroundings were becoming more beautiful. Hilda explained that we were going to the Sola River to cut osier reeds for baskets. The sun rose. The sky was without a cloud. We felt wonderful.

"How little we now need to be happy," Zosia sighed.

"Little. If they would only allow us to go this way ahead, without a *posten*."

"I no longer even think about it, only to be satiated, not hungry. That's all. I stopped dreaming about liberty."

We walked under the bridge. The Sola, a tributary of the Vistula, flowed in front of us. A few civilians were moving on the opposite bank. One of them carrying a fishing rod waved at us. It must be a dream—so near the camp and so absolutely different. Here, one could not even imagine that there was a war. The air was entirely different. In the camp the smell of the latrine and corpses hung in the air. Here, there was a real meadow and real water. I had not seen water for a long time.

Hilda handed out knives.

"Go into the shrubs and cut the osiers. Place the reeds here. Later some men will come with a cart to fetch them. Don't hurry, but don't run away. Remember that I answer with my head for you. They'll bring dinner about twelve."

We disappeared in the brush. It was so thick that we immediately lost sight of each other, and we had to call each other.

"Krysia." I heard a shout after a while.

"What, Hanka?"

"I'm so glad we came. You see, I told you, it's not so bad."

"Tell me that the war will end soon!" I shouted.

"The war will end in two weeks and when they ask us at home how it was in the camp, I'll tell them that it was wonderful, that I was sunbathing on the banks of the Sola."

"Are you really sunbathing?"

"Naturally. Hilda and the picket went into the bushes. She's not at all concerned with our work. You heard; she distinctly said 'don't hurry.'"

"You're right, I'm going to take a look at the surroundings."

I went toward the river. One of the girls, Elza, was singing a sentimental song in the willows. One day like this, and you wanted to live again.

I looked around. A civilian on the other side was making signs. I could make a break, I thought. I could swim across the river. Then someone would hide me.

I returned to Zosia. She was obviously thinking the same thing. "Yes," I gave voice to my thoughts. "And what then? You're tattooed. You're wearing stripes. You have no hair, no papers, and what if no one hides us? Remember that people in the vicinity of the camp are all scared. Who would take the chance?"

"Perhaps we could find some brave people. They'd only need to notify Warsaw and they would come for us and pay."

"Yes, but if we make a break, we endanger the rest of the girls and Hilda who has served four years in the camp."

"I don't care about Hilda. She's a German."

"A German, but a prisoner—she suffered a great deal, and she's against this fascist system just like we are."

"If we're going to think about that then we must be finished."

"If we didn't think about 'that' we wouldn't be here. If we must perish then we will.'"

We cut some osiers for the sake of showing willingness and then I went to the river again.

Something was moving in my direction from the bridge,

a barge, a barge with coal and people. At first I wanted to run away but decided to remain. The barge stopped. One of the civilians spoke to me:

"Polish?"

"Yes."

"How long have you been in the camp?"

"A month. Who are you?"

"Don't be afraid, we're friends. Is Hilda here?"

"Our *anweiserin*? Yes, she is."

"Wait—take something to her."

They brought out two bottles of vodka, sausage and white bread.

"Go! Don't let your friends see you."

"And the picket?"

"It's all right if the picket sees you and come back quickly."

I ran with my load to where I thought Hilda might be. I realized that this smuggling was not taking place for the first time. I found Hilda reclining against the *posten's* shoulder. The rifle was cast aside. They sprang up.

"Here, Hilda, nobody saw."

I handed her the food.

"Oh *schön*—lovely, are they still there?"

"Yes."

"I'll go with you. Here—take this."

She broke off a piece of bread and sausage and handed it to me. She then took my hand and we ran back together.

I thought, "I'm in on a big secret—I have bread and sausage and no one is shouting at me. And the picket was smiling. Unbelievable!"

I returned to Zosia. She looked at me and rubbed her eyes. She could not have been more surprised had I stood on my head.

"Who gave it to you?"

"A friend."

"Give me some! You've no idea how hungry I am, Oh God! White bread and sausage!"

"At last you admit that you're hungry." We ate the bread shouting in glee.

Suddenly I was struck by an idea. "Wait here," I said and ran to the riverbank.

The barge was still there. Hilda was talking to the civilians.

"Hilda," I began excitedly, "Please, may I ask them to notify my family where I am? I'll write a card."

One of the civilians was ready with a notebook and pencil. "Write quickly."

"Zosia and I are in Auschwitz. My number is 55908. Send me a parcel immediately. The bearer will tell you the rest."

I wrote the message and addressed it while Hilda kept watch. "Try to get this to Warsaw," I said. "Tell them that we can't last long here. Tell them to send us packages or to come to an understanding with you and you can take us to Cracow in this barge."

"Fine, we'll deliver the message and talk to them. Cheer up!"

Zosia waited in suspense. She was checking on me from afar.

"Well, Zosia," I said, "A ray of hope at last. I wrote home. If our family is smart and if we can work here, we can take that barge home in two weeks."

"Too good to be true."

"We'll get a parcel anyway."

"That's possible."

A few minutes later, overcome by so many emotions, I stretched out in the thick brush. It was about one o'clock. The sun was very hot. I closed my eyes imagining that I was lying on a beach dressed in a bathing suit instead of that awful rough prison dress. I imagined that I had long flowing hair instead of that rough brush. As if in a dream I heard the rustle of parting branches. I didn't move or open my eyes.

"A woman?" a male voice said in Polish.

"Once a woman," I answered lazily.

Someone standing in the bushes began to laugh, a loud and hearty laugh.

I opened one eye. Nothing mattered, I was dreaming anyway.

Everything that happened here was unreal.

"You don't even want to look at me." I heard close above my head.

"If you had heard my voice and if you then wanted to look at me, how disappointed you would be," I said this slowly, as if to myself. My eyes were still closed.

"Excuse me, you are a lady? May I introduce myself?"

"That's not necessary."

"My name is Andrzej—and yours?"

"Does it matter?"

"Put your headscarf on your head," he pleaded.

"I don't know where it is."

He found my headscarf and covered my head. If I only had some hair, I thought sadly. I realized how dirty I must look in the full noon light. I turned away and hid my face. The stranger turned my head toward him. I would not open my eyes.

"Please don't touch me, and please go away. Don't you know that we're not allowed to speak to men?"

He laughed again. Suddenly he leaned over and kissed me on the mouth. I felt weak and then I sprang up.

"Are you mad? I haven't washed my face or my teeth for a month. Are you blind? How can you kiss me? You haven't a penny's worth of good taste."

He looked at me very gravely and very sadly. I wanted to cry. "Why did you come? I felt so good. I had forgotten that it could be any different... that..."

"I also had forgotten," he said slowly and sadly. "Today, for the first time in three years, I've come near a woman. Please understand."

I looked at him. His voice was shaking. There were tears in his eyes.

"I'm young. Do you know what it means to be locked up in a camp for three years? That damned helplessness! I didn't want to offend you."

"I know. I'm not angry. I was only surprised. I've only been here a month and it seems like ages, as if there never had been anything else."

"Don't worry. Your hair will grow again. Some day you'll put on a real dress and take a bath. You'll be yourself again. Then you'll kiss me," he added after a while.

"Of course," I smiled back.

"Give me your hand to show that you're not angry. You're very nice, though very dirty."

I stretched out my hand with some misgiving. Again he wanted to pull me toward him.

At that moment the whistle sounded, followed by voices. "She escaped—she escaped—look for her."

Hanka appeared. She looked astonished. Andrzej greeted her. "We came for the osiers from the men's camp. What happened?"

"They say one of ours escaped."

"Which one?"

"An older woman. I don't remember her."

"She must be sleeping in the brush."

Hanka went to look.

"Are you hungry?" Andrzej asked me.

"No."

"I have no bread today, I didn't know. I'll bring you some tomorrow. You'll be here, won't you?"

"I don't know. We are substituting today. We're quarantined. But if she really escaped then we won't come again."

"Let's look for her."

I looked in the shrubs and behind them. I called her but I could not find her. I could not even remember how she looked. Andrzej approached me again.

"You didn't tell me your name. How will I find you?"

"Krysia."

"Pretty. I'll come here with some bread tomorrow, Krysia. You needn't be hungry if you're in quarantine. Well, chin up. Good luck, Krysia! Be sure to come," he turned to me again.

As if it depended on me—making a date as if we were in Warsaw. Funny man.

If we could only be in this squad permanently and come here for the osiers! Contact with the barge was important. I felt that we were in an exceptional position as far as the camp was concerned, that we had possibilities here no one in the camp could dream of, but now an escape.

I found Hilda. She was desperate. The *posten* said to me, "This is a fine mess. See what happens when we trust you. I'll be sent to the bunker or to the front, and Hilda to the *Strafkommando*[46], the punishment-squad or even worse."

I knew they felt guilty because they had not watched. My brain began to work as if I stood before the Gestapo. The woman had made a break; that was certain. But what excuse could we produce? They were already waiting for us at the camp. Hilda was crying. She was afraid to go back. She was afraid of the chief. I stood looking at the river. In the morning Hilda had said that she would let us bathe before leaving and now it's gone. What could we do? Suddenly I had a brilliant idea.

"Hilda, I've got an idea."

"What?" she asked through her tears.

"We'll tell them that she drowned."

"How?"

"We'll say that we were counted at four and that we were all here. Then one of the women asked if she could wash her feet in the water. She went under the bridge and drowned herself. I'll tell them that she was talking about suicide all morning and that she wasn't quite normal."

---

[46] Criminal unit.

57

Hilda listened attentively. The picket nodded.

"Not a bad idea. Anyway that's far better than our oversight. And the others, will they know what to do?"

"They'll say that we were counted at four and there were twenty of us. They don't know any more. I'll take care of that."

Hilda nodded her head in complete resignation. I went to the others.

"What now?"

"We were counted at four. If anyone asks, say that there were twenty of us and you know nothing else. You understand?"

"Of course."

"Remember, any one of us can be questioned at Auschwitz. The fate of all of us depends on what one will say."

"We understand."

We marched back. It was past the roll call hour. Hilda held my hand. Her head was lowered. She was very frightened. A motorcycle stopped on the road. The *aufseherin* Hase came toward us.

"*Na, was, warum so spat,*[47] It's after roll call." She was taking sarcastically and gravely.

"One is missing." Hilda reported.

"Such a small squad and she escaped? Is that how you watch them?

"She didn't escape, she committed suicide."

"How?"

"She drowned."

"Who saw her?"

I stepped forward.

"I did. From early morning she kept saying that she had had enough, that she'd rather die than go on suffering like this."

"What kind of suffering?"

"I don't know—that's what she said."

[47] Well, what, why so late?

An Auschwitz warning placard.

"Go back to camp. We'll look in the river."

We moved on. The camp-commandant came by in an automobile.

A similar conversation ensued. It was Kramer, a known monster. His small eyes bored through each one in turn.

"Well, if you're lying..." he shouted from the automobile as he drove away.

"What will happen if they don't find the body?" Hilda was worried.

"They won't look."

"What happens if they find her on the camp grounds and bring her back?"

"They won't catch her. We must believe in her and our luck."

Fat Katia,[48] the *rapportschreiberin*, ran out to the camp gate. She was a Slovakian Jew, a favorite of the *aufseherin's*

---

[48] Katia Singer, the prisoner who held the position of roll call Reporting Clerk from January 1943.

and *oberaufseherin* Oberka's. The authorities were trying to find Aryan ancestors for Katia so that they could change her star for a *winkel*. It was not right to acknowledge and like a Jew. Katia had been called several times to the Political Department in the city of Oswiecim. Katia, as the older *häftlings* told us, was responsible for the fact that the roll calls were in order—that we stood for such a short time. Before that, they were always wrong. *Häftlings* stood for hours. She, herself, took care of the transfers from one block to another.

"Well, Hilda, what is it?" she asked.

Hilda repeated our story. Katia smiled craftily. I realized that she saw through our scheme.

"Very good," she said more to herself than to us. "*Selbstmord, schade*,[49] she was still so young."

I didn't then understand how much irony was concealed in that phrase.

"Give me her number."

Hilda gave it to her and remained at the gate for further explanation. She only succeeded in whispering "thank you" to me.

"If it ends well take us with you tomorrow," I begged.

"I would but they won't allow that. They'll send Jews. Aryans escape. Maybe after the quarantine when you're moved to camp B, look for me then..."

We went to the barracks. The roll call lasted longer because of us. Everyone asked what had happened. We all repeated the same thing: She drowned. I told them how she was waving her hands in the water. Hanka blinked at me roguishly.

We got in to our "coffin", which was dark and stuffy. Zosia said, "After day like this, in here feels even more like hell. Over there was a foretaste of freedom."

I told her about Andrzej. "Think Zosia, in times of peace I could have met him at a ball, for example. How different our

[49] Suicide, what a pity.

conversation could have been. Poor boy, he has already been living here three years."

As expected we never went back to the river Sola. They supposedly believed Hilda and she went back with the same *posten* but with a different unit. The weather was beautiful. We terribly missed the charming nook, the barge, Andrzej and the bread, but what could we do? Had anything pleasant lasted for long in the *konzentrationslager*?

Chapter Four

Aussen

At ten in the morning the whistle sounded. The *lagerka-po*,[50] a Polish prostitute from Kielce, whistled and shouted in a hoarse voice, "*Lagersperre, Lagersperre, alles auf Block!*[51] Everybody inside! Everybody inside!"

We were driven into our block. What was going to happen? We were all terrified. No one knew. Most probably a "selection," someone concluded.

"Who, us?"

"I don't know."

"*Zählappell*, get out," we heard after a while.

A roll call at eleven in the morning? What could that mean? Stefa stood at my side as white as a sheet.

"Are we to go out too?"

"Stay here you skinny devils, only the Jewish blocks. Just try going out. The buckets are inside but don't you dare crap, remember that."

Through the small window we saw the Jewish women going out from the neighboring block to roll call. They were looking around in a frenzy trying to hide behind each other. Some were pinching their cheeks, to draw blood into them

---

[50] Camp *kapo*, the *kapo* overseeing the organization of work throughout the whole camp.

[51] Closing the camp, closing the camp, everybody inside the huts! The time when the camp remained closed and the prisoners could not leave the living quarters.

and supposedly look better. They were squabbling as to who should stand in the first row—the most noticeable position. They pushed one another to the front as if that would help. When life is at stake nothing matters but to save it. They finally lined up.

Taube, the *lagerkapo* and the *aufseherin* put in an appearance.

He faced the first line and pointed at someone with his cane. She undressed. He motioned her with his cane to the right. She went. She was of normal size and had a few boils and sores, but after having been in the camp for some time everyone had sores. Therefore, no one knew whether the right side meant life or death. The next one undressed—she was completely covered with boils. He also motioned her to the right with his cane. He was drunk; his eyes were clouded and his feet unsteady, but he watched carefully to see that each one went where he ordered.

About fifty went to the right—only a handful, those with fewer sores, stood on the left side. We understood. The right side meant death. Those chosen to die also understood. They began to look around half-conscious and rigid with fear. Where—how could they escape? A cordon of their companions surrounded them. No one could slip through it.

We watched in disbelief. Dead silence reigned over the block. You would never believe a thousand women occupied it. The sun shone on the selection square. Those designated to live a "temporary" life were very few. Out of four hundred women in the hut, three hundred twenty were selected to die. They moved in front of us—naked, crouching and almost abnormal. They moved, driven by the camp *kapo*, a prisoner just like themselves. They moved in the sun toward the death block. Each one of us knew what they must feel. Mothers and daughters walked together, sisters and friends of those who remained in the camp. We could not comprehend the fact that not so long ago each one of them had a home and parents,

A Hasidic group at the end of the road in front of the gas chamber fence.

was healthy, wore silk dresses and lived in Thessaloniki or in Amsterdam. Among them were laborers, students, doctors and society ladies. We could not comprehend the fact that these monstrous bodies, with their protruding bones and pendulous breasts with festering sores, are people who here and now, at this time, are parting with their lives.

Block 25 was the death block. There the human derelicts, segregated by a "selection", were packed. No food was allocated to this block. It was a reception room for the crematory.

After a few hours, moans coming from the block could be heard throughout the camp.

"Mother—water, water—Give me some water, I'm dying!"

64

No one approached the death block. No one brought water. We had no water, and even if we did have it, no one would take it to a strange Greek Jew. "She'll die anyway in a few minutes or in an hour." With this sentence we drowned out any feeling of duty toward our neighbor. But these cries gave us no peace. It was impossible to shut them out. They stung our hearts and our brains.

After the *lagersperre* was finished we were allowed outside. In Block 25 the condemned stretched out their hands through the grating. We could not hide from them. It was impossible not to hear the voices coming from there:

"Why? Oh God! Give us some water. Why must I die?"

Dusk fell and the wires were lit. As if hypnotized, I stared at the death block. I saw nothing but hands, hands stretching into infinity in a supplicating helpless, innocent, gesture.

At first they hung in a vacuum and after a while they shrank into terrifying, ominous fists.

That night was unusually quiet. Our hut knew that those in the death compound would be taken to the crematory. We all strained our ears. After a while the trucks arrived. Headlights lit up our hut. They stopped in front of Block 25. My heart was pounding. I knew that now they were loading them. We heard nothing. The motors turned again.

A powerful, inhuman cry pierced the air. We all sat up and gazed at each other with wild and terrified eyes. "Aaaaaa!"— The cry came from the trucks again. It started low and grew as the trucks approached and faded like a siren, leaving behind it an echo of torment and dread.

Stefa's desperate eyes looked at me from the other side of the bunk. Mine must have looked the same. We must not go mad. We must look at this as rationally as possible.

They were killing Jews because they said that the Jews were responsible, that they had caused the war. People are dying everywhere—I tried to explain to myself. But my mind could not encompass this horror. They are dying everywhere.

Fine, but they die in battle—from a bullet, a bomb, a grenade. Obviously that kind of death was also senseless... but here, this frightful, incomprehensible helplessness. What could be done? How could it be prevented? Today, they took them, tomorrow they could come drag us into the truck and...

But nothing—we could feel nothing, nothing but boundless hate.

At this moment the hate spread throughout all the bunks. It pervaded the whole camp.

* * *

The *lagerkapo* who had taken part in the selection entered our hut. Together with the *aufseherin* she went from one bunk to another whispering something to them. We squirmed nervously.

This visit could bode no good. The *lagerkapo* spoke loudly:

"Which one of you would like to go to Oswiecim, into the city, to the men's division? Easy work, civilian clothes and good food." She said

Hasidic rabbis after selection at the ramp, on their way to the gas chambers.

this with a cunning, malicious smile.

"Well, volunteers!"

She was showered with questions from all sides, very naive questions as it proved later.

We from Pawiak observed this suspiciously, but we could not guess what new trick was concealed in this invitation to an "easy job."

The block-senior stood at one side and was talking to a prisoner in a low voice. I got through to her. She must know something.

"It's for the *Puff*"[52], I heard. "They're taking them to the *Puff*."

"What are we supposed to do there?"

"Nothing. You must take care of twenty men every day."

"What kind of men?" we stuttered, dumb with fright.

"Those who have been here a long time, those who hold positions. I don't know what kind. Anyway, not SS men, only *häftlings*."

"Is it really voluntary or will they chose?"

"I don't know. Anything's possible. You can't leave the block." I ran to Zosia. She looked very frightened. The *aufseherin* was sizing her up. I decided to act.

When *aufseherin* shifted her glance for a second, I signaled to Zosia. She jumped off the bunk.

"Let's beat it, Zosia, quick."

I ran to the entrance. The *torwache* would not let us pass.

"I've got *durchfall*. I must go to the latrine. She too. Let us go."

"I can't. They're slipping through every second. I'll get a bucket for you."

There was a shout inside the barrack. She turned away.

---

[52] Brothel. In mid-1943 a brothel was established in the main camp, Auschwitz I, where a dozen or so female prisoners, mainly prostitutes, were employed. Visits here (primarily by functionaries and criminal prisoners) were intended as a means of reward for effective work.

We took advantage of that split second and ran for the latrines. Zosia tugged at my stripes.

"They're following us."

I looked around—they really were coming after us. The *lagerkapo* shook her fist at us. Then a game of hide-and-seek started between the huts. We peered from behind a corner— they were coming from two different directions. They seemed to spring up from the ground. Finally, they left us alone.

Exhausted by the chase we returned to the hut. It turned out that there were enough volunteers to fill the requisition. Their numbers were taken down. All eyes were turned to the bunk next to ours. I heard someone say: "You, a Pole, for shame! You should be ashamed of yourself."

"I'm hungry. It's none of your business," a girl answered. "Don't butt in."

We could see that she was struggling with herself.

"We're all hungry, pig!'

The girl began to cry.

We wondered about that *Puff*. Why such privileges and for what kind of prisoners?

We later learned that the prison authorities conceived of the idea because male prisoners had been discovered plotting, conspiring and discussing politics with growing frequency. The authorities decided to create a safety valve. Sexually starved men were to find release in the *Puff*.

The specter of the *Puff* was to be the terror of the block for a long, long time. Every time the *lagerkapo* appeared, we would be afraid that it was starting again, but fortunately the girls changed every few months. No one could stand it longer than that.

The rainy season set in. We were drenched at the roll calls on the *wiese*. There was never anywhere we could dry ourselves. The mud never dried. It was impossible to walk, as our clogs would stick in the mud.

We often wondered which days were easier to bear. Rainy days mixed with hopeless cloudy atmosphere were probably most appropriate. Heavy rain or gloomy leaden skies complemented our camp reality. It was the best backdrop for our gray faces, bare heads, striped uniforms and hungry, numb glances. We were wandering back and forth from the barracks to the latrines, stumbling in the mud, each day more and more resigned and silent. All you could hear everywhere was sighs.

One night, just before roll call, one of the women was caught sitting on a dish used for soup. She was an older woman and she must have been ill. They dragged her off the bunk and the block-senior beat her unconscious. For punishment we all had to kneel in the mud for an hour. Everything ached afterwards our legs, back, head and heart. Almost all of us ran a temperature that evening. The next morning many were sent to the hospital.

For the first time, I also wanted to go. What good would it do for me to freeze and starve? Why should I try to persuade my friends as well as myself that a miracle would occur? I would die here anyway. Why prolong the suffering? There were no roll calls in the hospital. I'd just lie there until I died. I confided these thoughts to Zosia.

"You mustn't, Krysia. You may get a parcel. Things may change."

I decided to wait a few days. A parcel really arrived for me; a parcel packed by my mother's hands. I couldn't open it. My friends waited and I had to cry; I really couldn't refrain from crying. Every sign from the outside destroyed our balance. We were gradually growing more apathetic and forced ourselves not to think. A parcel would shake us out of this state—it would force us to remember, to yearn.

Just about this time, I met Roma. She had been a teacher in Silesia and had come to the camp eight months earlier. She had been released from the hospital after a long and complicated illness. Tall and slim, she appeared to be almost transparent. Only her huge, blue, constantly surprised eyes betrayed her suffering.

Roma told me of her hearings at Auschwitz. Although I had been at Pawiak for a few months, I could not listen. She told me of the torture wheel from which she had been taken off half-alive and unconscious. She spoke of her illness.

I didn't understand how she could live after all that. It's true, however, that she received many parcels—three or four a week. She was quickly returning to health. Roma bribed the block-senior so that she could sit on the bunk without being prodded and pushed around all the time like the rest of us. She was the favorite of the block-senior. After a few weeks Roma told me:

"Well, the worst is over. Now I believe that I'll live. I've gone through everything they could think up to finish us off. I know that I'll live."

That day during the evening roll call, a black car rode through the *lagerstrasse*. A Gestapo man jumped out of it in front of our block and walked up to our block-senior. We were very frightened. After a while Roma's number was called out. Roma left our ranks and went slowly toward the car.

She didn't return. While she had been at the hospital, they examined her case and sentenced her to death because she had taught Polish to schoolchildren. After her death, parcels continued to arrive for her. Those on the outside still believed that she ate them.

* * *

Our quarantine was coming to an end, and we were separated. The overseers selected girls for working squads. Zosia was chosen along with many others. Zosia and I were stunned by this new blow. I didn't know then that you could ask for things in the camp. It didn't occur to us that we should speak up—and try our luck. You could ask people under normal conditions, but here... who cared that we wanted to be together? If we were to betray our desire, they would separate us even more readily.

So we were separated. Zosia went to the "Budy," another section of the camp.

A permanent *Aussenkommando* composed of three hundred women was organized in the Budy. The barracks were not surrounded with wire. The women worked hard in the fields. In addition to the Budy, there were other similar squads in the vicinity. They were named after the villages that had been there before: Rajsko, Babice, Harmenza.[53] Rajsko, as far as conditions were concerned, was the best. Vegetables and flowers were raised there. To get into that squad was the most cherished wish of all prisoners. Another ideal spot in which to survive was Harmenza. This was a farm with an artificial chicken hatchery. We knew least of all about the Budy. Working conditions in these squads depended largely on the *aufseherins* in charge. A small percentage of the fortunate worked in these squads.

Zosia and I made a pact. We planned that she would get sick and they would then send her to our hospital, as there was no hospital in the Budy. Then we could perhaps be together again.

So they went: Stefa, Marysia and Hanka—all to Camp B.[54] I remained behind. It was to be better for me this way.

[53] H. Himmler ordered the establishment of several sub-camps in the camp vicinity between 1940-1944 for purposes relating to agriculture and animals. They were: Gardening in Rajsko, poultry and fish farming in Harmenza and agriculture/animal breeding in Babice, Budy, Plawy and Brzezinka.

[54] Camp BIb sector of the camp in Birkenau. From March 1942 to July 1943 male prisoners of various nationalities were kept there until July 1943 when they were transferred to the newly built BIId sector. This sector then became a camp for able-bodied female prisoners who were employed in outside working units. Female prisoners undergoing the entrance quarantine along with the sick and those who worked inside the camp were kept in Camp BIa.

I was to help in the *Schreibstube*,[55] the office. Wala[56] took care of that. Wala had been in the camp for two years. She had come in one of the first Polish transports. She belonged to the few who, in spite of everything, had not grown insensitive or lost her charm. As she was working in an office, she could wear civilian clothes and her hair had grown again. She looked like a dream against the grayness of the camp. She had liked the verse that I made up during a morning roll call.

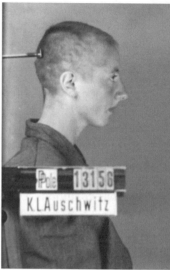

I had never written poetry before but because I could not stand the roll call and the hopeless waiting on the *wiese*, I began to make up verses. There was nothing to write with or on. The simple words I recited came from the bottom of my heart:

> Over Auschwitz the sun rises,
> Pink and bright the light it sheds.
> Young and old we stand in rows,
> Stars die above our heads.

I treated this act of creativity as charade—a charade that at the same time was a blessing because it allowed a break away from reality.

[55] Camp's office.

[56] Wala Konopska (No. 13156) was a Political Department employee who was a notable exception, an example of a *kapo* who did not give into the pressure of the executioners, her superiors and "colleagues", who remained humble and helpful to co-prisoners and who became for K. Zywulska a guardian angel, even.

72

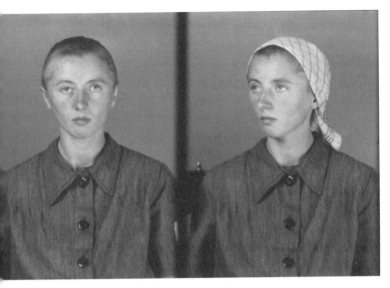

A picture of Wala Konopska, from camp records.

My companions picked up these verses. They learned them from one another and recited them with great sincerity and feeling when sitting on the bunks or in the latrines. This is how the poem "Roll Call" reached Wala. She became interested and asked for the author. She found me—a solemn and bald *musselman*[57] (camp slang for the most haggard and dirty prisoners)—and decided to take me under her protection.

As an old and influential *häftling* she prevailed upon the block-senior to keep me in quarantine. I was to wait for a job allocation. In the morning I walked around the *wiese* unsuccessful in my search for familiar faces. There were only Czech and French women and a few older Polish women. They sat around in groups and talked of old times. Most of them were here because of their children—their sons and husbands.

[57] A prisoner extremely exhausted physically and mentally, passive, with a fatalistic attitude.

Weak and tired, they realized that they could not last long, but they defended themselves from the hospital and bravely stood at the roll calls. I couldn't find a place for myself. The weather was very sultry. I looked into the latrine—it was frightfully crowded. I noticed a few free places.

As I was making my way in that direction, someone called out, "Don't go, watch out." Sitting on the boards in the space between was a masculine looking German woman, a black *winkel*. On her knees sat a very feminine girl with long hair. She gazed at her partner with rapture then she kissed her on the mouth. It was a long kiss. You couldn't imagine anything more revolting—this kind of "love" in these surroundings. I rushed out and ran across the *wiese*, feeling revolted and dirty. The other women were killing lice. I also began to itch—something was crawling all over me. I put my hand inside my belt and found something, the first louse. I didn't know how to kill it. I was nauseated and weak at the thought that this was only the beginning. The louse cracked between my nails. Then I caught the second and the third, so huge and so frightful. In a half hour my nails were red, but just then the dinner gong sounded. In these same hands I held the dish and ravenously ate the turnips out of it.

The next day we were taken to be deloused. First we went to the *sauna*. This meant that we were going to wash—we all repeated this with delight. Today we would be clean and perhaps we would not itch because they would delouse our stripes.

We marched in fives to the *sauna*. They actually took away our uniforms and put us under the shower. The shower lasted three minutes because other blocks also had to be deloused. They did not give us soap or towels. We went out, teeth chattering. Outside, one of the *sauna* workers was dipping a cloth in a dish filled with a fluid disinfectant. Single file we moved up to the dish. Each one was rubbed under the arms and between the legs, a fact that caused the SS men standing on the sides to burst into gales of laughter. We could see that they were fascinated by our clumsy and shy gestures. When a woman would try to escape the dish, they caught her and dragged her to it by force, swearing at her rudely. They were most attentive to older women for whom this naked display in the open air was a terrifying experience.

Some old lady asked, "Will there ever come a time when their mothers will parade in front of us?"

"I think it will come..."

"And will we also laugh at them?"

"I don't think we can do that, but we will cry for the whole world to hear: Those are the mothers of criminals. Those are the mothers who brought them up that way."

The uniforms did not come back from the fumigators. We waited naked for two hours. The time for the roll call was approaching. The *aufseherins* had to count us—the roll call was sacred. We were ordered to go out naked and stand in front of the barracks. We went, dazed.

The other occupants of the huts were also naked.

In front of one of them stood a number of children, "Aryan" children from the district of Zamosc.[58] Children aged six and seven. They had come here with their parents in 1942. This was when they were still gassing Aryans. Their parents had been gassed or were given a phenol injection in the heart. Things, however, changed for the better, as all the "old ones" told us. In 1942, for instance, general roll calls used to be held. On January 31, 1943, the last general roll call had taken place during which the entire camp stood for fourteen hours in the frost. After the roll call all the women had to run toward the camp. Those who ran a little slower or

---

[58] According to the so-called *Generalplan Ost* ("General Eastern Plan")—see note 162 (p. 241). At the end of 1942 approximately 1,300 men women and children from the Zamosc region were sent to Auschwitz. In February and March 1943, several dozen boys from the Zamosc region were murdered with a phenol injection to the heart in the "hospital" of the main camp in Auschwitz I.

who stopped were taken to Block 25, the death block. And those who had survived the roll call suffered horribly because of frozen and swollen hands and feet.

The children who had outlived their parents—serious, experienced children—stood now with their lips set in a tight line. Mothers with grown sons stood naked outside in the open. It was a pleasant September day, but we felt cold at six in the evening and after our bath. The *aufseherins* and SS men arrived finally. They laughed at this sight, counted us and drove away.

The uniforms finally came from the *sauna*—wet, because they supposedly had been disinfected. We put them on and felt colder still. I decided to take mine off. I lay down naked on my bunk. I was dirtier than before the delousing and in the morning lice were again crawling all over me. The uniforms were not dry yet. After the morning roll call, fifty per cent of the women went to the hospital. "I won't go," I repeated stubbornly, although I knew that I was running a temperature. "I won't go until they carry me there." The sun came out at noon. One of the "old ones" spoke to me and gave me a piece of bread. I stopped shivering.

The one that gave me the bread was stout and cheerful and had very long hair and wore civilian dress.

"What are you doing?" I asked. "You are doing well. You look great. How come?"

"You see, I just left the bunker. I was there for eight months."

"Hold on, for what?"

"I don't know myself. One day they came for me and took me away. Apparently there has been some change in my case. They closed me in the bunker... and that's all. I look good because "the boys" organized help for me. The bunker is on the male side. They fed me. They comforted me. I was not moving at all, and that's why I've grown fat. And I'm happy, because finally I can move and I'm on the outside.

You have no idea how great this is here... after the bunker."

I looked at her with admiration. How much she had endured there if here is "great."

"Don't worry," she added. "A person can endure much more than he realizes. You will be here a few months. You'll see.

"A few months? Impossible."

"I thought so too. Everyone thinks that and yet can withstand the worst. If when they arrested you, you had been told what awaited you, you wouldn't believe that you could endure. And it's been nothing yet... this is only the beginning. Winter is coming. Now, however, it's better. Today they care about the hygiene of the camp. I know it seems strange, but when I arrived, it was much worse."

The following day we went out into the fields. This time I was in a group of a hundred women. Ceremoniously we walked out through the gate, left foot first. The day was cool. In front and far behind us stretched the ranks of stripes also marching into the fields. Behind each group marched a *posten* with a dog. Each group had an *anweiserin*. We passed men who were also going into the fields. We were ordered to sing, in German of course. Some did sing, particularly the black *winkels*. They sang in deep voices strained from shouting.

We passed meadows, empty farms and devastated woods. From time to time, a civilian on a bicycle would come by. Not many could get passes for the grounds near the camp. People were not allowed to speak to *häftlings*. They rode by without looking at us so as not to arouse the slightest suspicion. They went by—strange and distant, from another world. A Russian girl, Shura—a student from Kiev—walked beside me. She laughed playfully, wrinkled her nose and taunted our *anweiserin*: "*Hast du Brot* [59], give me *Brot, ekh, durrah*," [60]

[59] Do you have bread?
[60] (Russian) Dumb, stupid.

she added melodiously. "I would give her *brot, s uma soshlah* [61] idiot..."

Suddenly Shura noticed someone in the women's transport that was passing us. She stared hard then she turned pale and broke out of our rank.

"Natasha!"she shouted and rushed to a girl in the passing column.

The girls embraced each other, crying and laughing. This lasted but a moment. Our supervisor dragged Shura away from Natasha and pushed her into our column.

"Los! du blüde Kuh."[62]

"Where's mama?" Shura called, moving back.

"Nye znayu[63]*"* Natasha answered as she moved away. "And Mishka?"

"Nye znayu".

"Ruhe! [64]—Quiet!" the *Anweiserin* shouted again.

Shura grew silent. Then she began to sob. Suddenly she remembered something and ran out of the column.

"Natasha!" she called, *"Gdye rabotayesh, kakoye komado?*[65]*"*

There was no answer. Natasha was too far away.

"Who is she?" I asked Shura who was still sobbing.

"Syestra. Dva goda yeyo nye vidyela. Saytchas nye znayu, gdye ana. Ana nahvierno golodnayah..."[66]

We walked in silence all affected by this meeting. They hadn't seen each other for two years and now couldn't even say hello, not knowing when, or if at all, they would meet again. They hadn't learned anything about their next of kin.

---

[61] (Russian) You are crazy.

[62] Go! You stupid cow.

[63] (Russian) I don't know.

[64] Be quiet!

[65] (Russian) Where do you work, what unit?

[66] (Russian) My sister. I haven't seen her for two years. Now I don't know where she is. She must he hungry.

"Maybe my sister is also here," went through my mind at that moment. "And she is hungry, as we all are, and maybe my mother?"

We marched along past desolate villages and railway tracks. We stopped before a crossing. The gates were down for a passenger train. The frightened passengers leaned out of the windows and pointed at our long, unending columns. They waved their handkerchiefs until the gates were raised. We went on.

A cowherd with his cows was on the road in front of us. He ran into the field when he saw us. The cows blocked the road, mooing loudly. The *anweiserin* began to curse. The *posten* released his dog. Confusion reigned for a few minutes after which we proceeded again.

A few miles further we were stationed along a marked area. Shovels and spades were handed out. We were already very hungry and tired after this unexpected tramp, and the day was just beginning. Each group of five was assigned to a square of ground that had to be dug before noon.

I dug my spade into the hard ground. Observing the others, I began to imitate them. I learned to burrow in the ground and rest with one foot on the spade when the *anweiserin* had passed. It was most difficult for me to throw the soil. I was too weak to lift the spade. Shura perspired copiously as she tossed the earth with unusual speed, with passion. She mumbled under her breath:

"Imagine that you're digging a grave for them, it will immediately become much easier. Just try..."

The *anweiserin* was constantly circling around us and measuring with a terrifying glance those who rested. Or she talked with the guard, smiling at him provocatively. She would let out a howl in our direction from time to time:

"*Arbeiten—Schweine, los!... schneller...*"[67]

---

[67] Work—pigs, go!... faster.

I was exhausted. A woman collapsed near us. We picked her up and placed her in the field nearby. She had fainted. I began to pinch her. There was no other means to save her. Water was beyond our wildest dreams.

"*Lass diese alte Zitrone! Geh arbeiten! Los!*"[68] the *anweiserin* shouted above my head and threw the shovel at me. The shovel gashed my leg; blood began to flow. I dragged myself to the half dug ditch.

"She's pregnant," someone whispered.

"Who?"

"The one who fainted, she told me she's pregnant."

At twelve, there was a high mound of earth as the ditch grew deeper.

They brought our dinner in a barrel. I stood in line about half an hour before I got my nettle soup. It was delicious, only there was too little of it. I ate it in a few minutes—those were the only minutes of rest.

The women were quarreling. The separate groups were competing with one another not to increase the working tempo but to diminish it. As some fives had already finished their work and were assigned to other squares, those who had not dug their sector in that time were prodded and beaten.

"Why are you so eager?" I heard from all directions. "Big aren't you? You'll get a medal from the Nazis."

"Stay out, I am doing my thing."

"Do not stand up if you have more strength. Now we suffer because of you, because that monkey can see that you can dig up much more during that time and screams at us."

But nothing helped. Many were eager. I don't know from where they drew their energy. They didn't pay attention to their coworkers. There were also moments when one helped the other, shielded her from the *anweiserin's* gaze so that the first one could relax. That also happened but rarely, very rarely.

[68] Leave this old lemon! Go to work! Go!

We put our shovels away at five and returned to the camp for the roll call. Hunger twisted our intestines. We suffered from the cold. Our hands and legs ached. All our bones ached, and we felt our hearts growing weaker. I dreamed of resting, but there was still the roll call. The *aussenkommandos* were marching back to the camp from all directions. All were tired; they dragged their feet, resigned and angry. The bread distributed at the roll call could revive us only for awhile. All of us broke the bread ravenously and gulped it down in one swallow.

We went into the fields for weeks, returning in rain and snow, sinking up to our knees in the mud, weakening in the sun. There was nowhere to hide, no one to complain to. In the morning we ran for our lunchtime soup and in the afternoon for bread. We became familiar with the road, with the faces of the *aufseherins* and *postens*, with all the curses and with the marches played by the band, marches sung by hungry girls. We turned the hay with water reaching our waists. We dug potatoes in gooey wet clay. We planted rutabaga, pulled out weeds.

We tied the grain in sheaves in the heat, our throats parched and lips cracked from the heat. We gathered the threshed stalks in the unending dust of the threshing machine. We often worked without a dinner break. The soup would turn sour in the heat, but in the evening we would bolt it down cold.

The next day we would suffer from diarrhea. If any of us, tormented by her stomach, tried to go to a nearby ditch, the *postens* would release their dogs. Humiliated, goaded, the women did not leave their places—they waded in their own excrement.

One day a Ukrainian woman escaped. A roll call was announced at the camp. Two tables were placed together and the woman responsible for the group of ten from which the Ukrainian had escaped, was tied to them. Her feet were fastened to the planks under the table. Her hands were tied to the table. An SS-man measured out "twenty five" strokes with a thick stick. The girl cried and howled with pain. The *lagerführer*[69], he camp-leader came and held her head. She fainted at the twenty-third stroke. They untied her; she was completely black. Her kidneys had been ruptured. Prisoners carried her to the hospital. She died after a few days.

Sometimes we succeeded in concealing a few potatoes in our uniforms and smuggled them through the gate, in spite of the rigid control. Sometimes we got a *zulage* for our work in the fields—four ounces of bread and a slice of sausage. The one topic of conversation was: Will they give us a *zulage* today or not?

We often returned from the fields carrying the corpse of a companion—left foot first to the rhythm of the music. It was impossible to be alone even for a second. I felt that with each day I was growing more animal-like, that I hated people,— that I couldn't listen to quarrels or laughter. Our eyes became expressionless and we learned to hate in silence. After many hours of standing I lay on the bunk half-dead from fatigue and before falling asleep dreamed for a moment that I was an *anweiserin*, and they, those damned Germans, were prisoners. In my dreams I was suffocating them and beating them up— only that thought could "lull me to sleep".

I was getting thinner, getting dirtier and more and more tired and hungry.

[69] Camp commander.

Chapter Five

Working Under a Roof

One Sunday we did not go into the fields; instead we were ordered to dig a sewer canal in front of our block. That day Wala came over and told me to come quickly to the *sauna*. She knew that at this rate I wouldn't last long. I followed her. This became a turning point in my camp life. Working under a roof—any kind of work under a roof—would make all the difference in my fate. However, I knew that at this point I wouldn't make a good impression, but there was no way to improve my appearance. In the *sauna* I was received by Magda, a Slovakian Jew. I remembered her clearly. She was the one who had beaten us when we first arrived. My blood ran cold.

"I was send here from *vorne*[70] to work," I recited, according to Wala's instruction.

"I can't imagine you working. What can you do? You write poetry. You're supposed to be from the intelligentsia. Well, take a cloth and clean that window so that it shines. We'll soon see what you can do."

"Where is the cloth?"

"Look at her! Maybe I'm supposed to put it in your hand? Organize it yourself."

I saw some rags lying on the floor so I took a piece from a torn blouse. Magda slapped my hands.

---

[70] From up front. From the people in charge.

83

"That's filthy with lice. Don't touch it, you idiot. It's easy to see that you write poetry."

I went to look for a clean cloth. One of the blocks was taking showers. There was the smell of human perspiration in the hall.

Shouts from Magda and others filled the room. I moved between the showers, terribly hungry. Suddenly, everything began to whirl and I felt a swift pang near my heart. I swayed and lost consciousness.

When I opened my eyes Wala was standing over me with valerian drops in her hand. I don't know who called her.

"Don't worry," she consoled me, "You'll get used to it. Just think. You might've been working in the *aussen*. For about six months I used to lift large kettles in the kitchen. I cried every day. I always thought I wouldn't be able to lift them. And look at me now."

"I must have a clean cloth for the windows. Magda, I don't know where..." I mumbled.

Someone gave me a cloth. I went to the *sauna* hall. All the women had gathered there after their bath. I began to clean the window. Magda stood not far off and laughed. I looked around and saw that she was laughing at me. I must have looked very amusing. I had absolutely no strength. Rubbing the panes, I held onto the sill so as not to fall again. They were clean but they kept getting steamed up from the inside. Magda started to scream:

"Is that supposed to be clean? I won't budge from here until they shine."

"But Magda, these windows..."

I didn't get to finish; she struck me.

"I'll tell the *aufseherin* that you answer me back and don't know how to do anything. You'll go back into the fields and die in a few days together with your poems."

"Don't say that Magda! I'll try to clean them."

"I wonder how many hours that will take."

Women on their way to the camp after their transport was admitted.

She went. I breathed on the panes and rubbed them, but it didn't help. I didn't know what to do. I went away from the window. "She can kill me," I told myself calmly. But she was already bawling out someone else. I was lucky.

Zugangs came. She had other victims. She was no longer interested in me.

This transport came from Holland. About a thousand women were in it. They said other transports were on the way. I had to hurry; we might work all night.

It began as usual. The women undressed and had their hair was shaved off. They then went to the showers and came out in groups into the hall, where I "held office." Magda placed me there to keep order. I was to show each one who came out of the shower where to go for her dress, for the clogs and for the *streifen* [71] (a red cross painted on their backs). All of them walked out dazed. No one in Holland had heard of this. They did not know what would happen to them, and did not understand what was going on around them. They asked thousands of questions; but I could not understand them. I motioned for them to go where I was pointing. But I did not seem to frighten them, and they would not listen to me. Instead, each one would look for her sister, mother or friend whom she was afraid to lose. I couldn't manage. I begged, shouted, threatened, but they scattered in all directions, answering me in their harsh, guttural language.

Magda walked in at the height of the confusion. It was late in the evening. The 15th group was just entering the hall. I was helplessly lost in the crowd.

"Krysia!" I heard Magda's voice, "What's going on? Why aren't they lined up in fives?"

"They don't want to, and I can't make myself understood."

"Hit them!"

"What?"

"Hit them. Do you hear? If you don't, you'll fly out of here tomorrow. You're here to help, not to get underfoot."

"But... Magda... I won't hit them!"

She came to me with a stick.

"You will... do you hear? You will! We've got the whole night in front of us. If you don't beat them, they'll never line up! Don't be so delicate. How can you survive Auschwitz if you're afraid to strike?"

"I'm not afraid, I just don't want to."

"We'll see!"

I lifted the stick in the air and shouted. "*Zu fünf anstellen, los!*"[72]

"Stand in fives, quick!" It helped—I asked who knew German. One of them stepped forward. I lifted the stick again.

[71] Streak; line.
[72] Set up; fives abreast, go!

86

"*Ruhe!*"

I asked the *dolmetscherin*[73], the translator, to say that I was ordered to beat them but that I didn't want to and that I asked them to line up. She translated. The stick burned my hand. I threw it to the floor and began to cry. A Dutch woman came up to me, gave me her hand and assured me about something. Then together with the *dolmetscherin*, they began to line them up.

Things began to move. I did not sit down all that night. New arrivals kept coming in. Always the same thing—the same senseless gaze, the same language, everyone looking the same after the shave, all tired and exhausted. And always the same questions, "Where are we?" "Where's my mother? They took her in a car." "What are we to do here?" "When will we eat?" "When will we go to bed?"

I was collapsing from exhaustion. I kept answering, my voice growing weaker and hoarser.

"You are in a concentration camp. I don't know where the cars went. You'll work, don't worry"—and so on.

A new transport arrived in the morning—another thousand women, also from Holland. I don't know where I found my strength. I stood this way another day and night. I kept repeating to myself: "I should be happy. I'm working inside, under a roof."

After the Dutch came the Russian women, evacuated with their children. They brought bundles containing all their possessions.

After their arrival, the children were taken away from their mothers and sent to other camps to be brought up in the true German spirit and as possible cannon fodder to defend the *vaterland*.[74]

The mothers lamented, threatened and tore their hair out.

[73] Interprete, translator.
[74] Fatherland.

We all got to know the funny little Volodia. He arrived in October 1943 with a Russian transport from Vitebsk. He was five years old and very amusing. He would make all kinds of funny faces, mimic the elders, be coquettish and bewitching or behave like a brat. When the camp Commandant Hössler was receiving the transport, all the children clutched at their mothers' skirts and cried from the cold and hunger. Little Volodia ran straight up to Hössler, smiled playfully, saluted and called out, "How are you uncle?"

Hössler was flabbergasted. But Volodia got a smile out of him. After that, Hössler often came to the Russian block, asking from the doorstep, "*Wo ist der kleine Volodia?*"[75]

Everybody in the camp was surprised; a human reaction from this monster, who had sent so many children "to the gas" in cold blood. Several times Hussler even brought Kramer to the Russian block. And Volodia, not discouraged by his mother's despair and the unfriendly glances of other mothers, entertained the SS men as well as he could. He sang his beautiful songs for them. And with well-concealed satisfaction, under a seemingly innocent childish smile he would sing, *Yesli zaftra voyna...*[76] Oh, Volodia was a wise child.

But entertaining German authorities did not win Volodia better conditions. He ate the same portion of bread as the others, the grown-ups and the children. That is why he became ill. Volodia"s mother wanted to ask them not to take her child to the hospital, not to separate her from her child. But the Germans stopped coming. They took Volodia and Volodia died. Hössler came to the Russian barrack that day.

"*Wo ist der kleine Volodia?*"

No one answered him. He repeated his question louder, impatient at the silence. The block-senior ran up to him in great terror and in a tone of apology reported Volodia's death,

---

[75] Where's little Volodia?

[76] (Russian) If tomorrow there will be war—the Soviet loyalty song.

that unfortunately today she could not supply him with his plaything.

"Died... hmm... *schnell*,[77] so soon," he commented dryly. "Are there any other pretty children?"

At the request of the block-senior, starved, sick children began to crawl down from the bunks. Hössler marched past but did not seem to find anything.

"Nothing there," he spat and walked out.

The following day an order came from Berlin that all children were to be taken from their mothers and sent to the district of Poznan for denationalization. The children were small. They could still be raised as good Germans.

They stood for the last time with their mothers at the morning roll call. Two-year old Pietia was fretting. He cried and wandered between the ranks of the columns. The SS man receiving the roll call shouted, "*Achtung!*" and a mere baby, a two-year old child, straightened up immediately and stood at attention like a soldier.

After the roll call they took away Pietia and the other children. The mothers tried to hide them under the bunks. They sobbed desperately, threatened, to no avail.

Hössler came and said, "You should be proud and happy. The children are going where they will be better off. Why do you cry, you stupid women?"

The "stupid women" then died mostly from hunger, cold, despair and longing. Some stronger ones were sent to Germany to work. Any trace of the children disappeared.

* * *

An epidemic of typhus broke out in the camp.

When *lager* B came to the *sauna* for delousing, I met my friends from Pawiak, from whom I had been separated.

[77] Quickly.

Passing by naked, they would whisper who was ill. Many of them were already in the hospital. Nata was in the hospital. Janka was ill, but she was still working in the fields. Stefa didn't look well. She stood shivering in front of me. "I won't last long. I'm not fooling myself."

"What do you do in the fields?"

"I work in the potato field."

"And your heart?"

"I faint every day."

"How is your *anweiserin*?"

"Terrible. You're well off, Krysia. You work under a roof. You can wash."

"I haven't washed here yet. I'm well off perhaps, but only in comparison to you."

There were a lot of rumors circling at that time. The men secretly said that in the vicinity of the camp were strong partisans with whom they were in contact, and that we needed to get shoes at any price to get ready to march, because at any moment partisans might rescue us.

We didn't pause to think that the front was far away or what might happen to these tens of thousands of rescued prisoners afterwards. No one attempted logical thought. We feverishly hung onto every possible opportunity and every hope of getting out. A naive rumor circulated that during an international conference between Churchill and Hitler, Churchill had demanded that Hitler abolish the concentration camps, particularly Auschwitz. Hitler had to give an answer within 24 hours otherwise Germany would be razed to the ground. In general we were convinced that the whole world thought and cared primarily about us.

The *schreiberin*[78] informed us that anyone with the number 50,000 and up could write home. Forms were distributed.

---

[78] Block writer, a prisoner.

You could use fifteen lines. What was there to write about? All the letters sounded the same: "I am healthy. I feel good. Send a package." We cried while writing that first letter. For a moment freedom seemed closer. Home and everything we cared about seemed a lot closer.

They told me Zosia was in the hospital. I went there. Although we had planned that she would pretend to be ill, she was not pretending. They took her there, feverish and shivering after she had worked in the rain for two days. She lay on a bunk on the third "floor," waiting for them to bring her some water.

The hospital consisted of twelve huts surrounded by a wire fence. In each ward were thirty-six beds attached to each other and arranged in what we called the first, second and third floor. The lowest bed was the darkest, but it was very difficult to scramble up onto the third bed. Everybody tried to get the middle bed, but that was always a matter of luck. Between the beds were passages where the chamber pots stood. A stove reaching the height of a chair ran through the hut. The stove served for resting and as an operating table. It stood in the lightest spot in the hut as a dim lamp hung over it.

I scrambled up to the third bed where Zosia was lying. Heads lifted from all sides.

"What's new? Any news? Will it be long?"

All of them, regardless of their environment and social class, were interested in "politics." No one here would ever say, "I'm not interested in politics." Politics meant the front, alliances—Poland's role in the world. Politics meant the possibility of an attack, of a retreat. Our fate depended upon these politics. Each one of us felt it. That's why the most frequent question was "What's new in politics?"

"They're very near," I asserted.

"Who told you?"

"Someone from the *schreibstube*. Hold on for another two weeks. There's a new offensive in the East."

I lied through my teeth because, of course, I knew nothing. Everyone in the camp ate up each bit of news. It gave us the strength to live. In the hospital good news was the only medicine. Zosia smiled at me gently. Her eyes expressed understanding. She finally said, "Tell us more, dear. I know you're making it up, but it's good for us."

As the doctor approached, I stretched out next to Zosia so that she would not see me. The healthy ones were not allowed to enter the hospital.

Zosia was hot. Her eyes shone feverishly.

"Krysia, if you can, bring me some hot water. I can't drink these herbs."

"I'll bring you some. I promise."

I didn't know how I'd get the water or how I could carry it hot to the hospital, but I had to promise.

As the doctor walked out of sight, I jumped out of the bed and went out. It was just a few minutes before *lagerruhe*. Just in front of the hut I stepped on something. Terrified, I sprang back. A corpse lay in the mud, and another just beside it. The moon shone on the barrack but there was a shadow where the corpses lay. I stood motionless. Something squeaked and moved near the corpses. Rats. There were several of them. One sat on the eyes of the dead. I picked up a stone and hurled it at them. It hit the corpse in the head with a sickening thud. I began to run from the two huge, fat, squeaking rats behind me. I sped toward the hospital wire like mad, crawled under it, cut across the *lagerstrasse* and leapt into my hut. I stretched out on my bunk drenched with perspiration. One thought persecuted me—if Zosia should die tonight, they would carry her out and rats would gnaw her eyes out. In my dreams that night, I saw rats crawling all over me, tearing, choking me and jumping at my eyes.

A transport from the hospital came to the *sauna* next day. All of them still had *durchfall* and were swooning from weakness. They were released because there was no room for new patients. Any person released from the hospital had to go through the *sauna* same as *zugangs*. I was stitching a number on the striped dress of one of them as she clung to the window as not to fall.

Suddenly Magda called me:

"What is it?"

She pointed to the overturned stool full of feces. Apparently someone from the hospital...

"Wipe that. Take the stool, wash!"

"I'll get a hose. I'll wash it."

"No. Use your hand. Don't be so sensitive!"

"Oh, Magda... "

"Well, now, quickly!"

She was very angry that day. Despite this, I went to get the hose and started to pour water on the stool. Magda began to froth. "Grab the stool by your hand. Don't save your energy."

I grabbed it. For a moment I was ready to throw it at Magda. She must have sensed my intention, because she stepped aside. Everybody parted in front of me. I walked as if in a trance. At that moment memories of freedom loomed in front of me. I was at home at the table in a normal dress. I had long hair and was reading a book. I could not believe what they had turned me into here. And who had done this? None other than a prisoner. Imprisoned like me. And I had to listen and was powerless.

* * *

The next day I kept thinking about how to get hot water for Zosia. In the afternoon a concert was held in the *sauna* hall. The concert was for the *funktionshäftlings*,[79] the administrative staff, all the *kapos*, the *anweiserins*, those who

[79] "Function prisoners". Prisoners who supervise others.

had survived their initial years in the camp and who now worked as guards and those who guarded the camp for the *lagerkapo*, the *lagerälteste*.[80]They were the most likely to beat prisoners and were the most feared. The names "Stenia", "Leo" and "von Pfaffenhofen" evoked the same horror as the names of the worst perpetrators, the SS—perhaps even greater, because contact with them was more likely.

Alma Rose, a Jewish woman, was to conduct the orchestra. Alma had arrived in a transport from Vienna. They initially had chosen her for the experimental block, the "rabbit cage," but pulled her out after two days when it became known who she was. At that time a camp orchestra was being organized. It was said that information had come from Berlin about a proposed visit of an international commission. They had to show how much good was being done for the internees. Besides that, the camp authorities were frightfully bored. At the request of the *lagerführer* Alma Rose was brought from the "rabbit cage" to join the orchestra. The orchestra still had the task of performing during the *häftlings'* morning march into the *aussen*. For that the orchestra's main instrument was the drum. At today's concert the drum was to be replaced by the violin.

As I was assigned to serve in the *sauna*, I could remain in the hall for the concert. Before it began I stood for a moment in front of the *sauna*. Nearby, the whole of block 15 was kneeling for some misdemeanor. Opposite was the *lager* kitchen. Next to it, a pile of garbage. Greek Jewish women were rummaging in the waste, taking out the bones and gnawing them. A few months ago they came from Thessaloniki and were sophisticated, brunette, slender. After a few days all their glow disappeared. They went through selections, and those few who passed, hovered like skeletons,

---

[80] Camp senior, the highest in the hierarchy of the so-called prisoners' self-government.

crawling and rummaging in the garbage now, nothing like the people they once were.

I walked into the room. The concert has already begun.

When Alma lifted her baton, the SS men and the *aufseherins* leaned back comfortably in their chairs. The *Lagerkapo* gazed threateningly at the *sauna* audience—her look alone silenced everyone. The rhythm of a Strauss waltz sounded through the hall. I looked out the window. Block 15 was still kneeling.

Then Alma played a solo on the violin. Her eyes were closed. Perhaps she imagined that she was playing at the Vienna Philharmonic. She played beautifully. There was complete silence in the hall. I also closed my eyes. For a short moment I saw a large ballroom, flowing dresses, dancers, smiles, women gliding on the tips of their toes.

Alma finished. Nervously she lowered her bow and looked around the hall with unseeing eyes.

"*Ruhe!*" shouted *lagerkapo*. It turned out that someone had started to applaud.

I shook off my dream. The orchestra played a polka.

Suddenly, a most unusual figure rose from one of the privileged seats. She had red hair and her face was made up. She was wearing slacks and carrying a cane. She began to sing to the music in a hoarse, drunken voice. She sang in German. I was surprised that they did not stop her, but instead nodded their heads with approval and smiled even though the singer had a number sewed on and was undoubtedly a prisoner.

"Musskeller"[81], someone whispered to me.

"Why are they letting her sing? Why is she dressed up and why are her cheeks made up?"

"She was the *oberaufseherin's*, Oberka's, friend on the outside. They worked together", she added with irony. "Oberka was one of her girls. She's a *puff*-madam. Didn't you

[81] A prisoner—the bath *kapo*.

No. 1 crematorium at Auschwitz I.

know?" she asked in surprise. "Almost all the *aufseherins* are from the brothel."

As Musskeller returned to her chair in a rhythmical dance step, a Polish woman, the elegant Ewa Stojewska, the actress from Warsaw, appeared after her. After that, a young Jewish woman sang jazz refrains with great sensitivity, clearly satisfying the SS audience.

I slipped out of the hall, poured some hot water into a bottle and ran to the hospital. Zosia's feverish eyes were watching the door. I gave her the bottle. She drank and cried, not knowing how to thank me. In the drowsy silence of the hospital one could hear distant sounds of music above the moaning, the delirious mumble of the sick.

* * *

One day a few of us were sent from the block to the *lager*

B to get blankets that had been sent there for delousing. It was after the *Lagerruhe*. It was first time we were going through the camp gate so late. The wires were buzzing. The camp was asleep. We stood next to one of the barracks, waiting for the blankets. Suddenly, a truck drove up to an adjacent building with a huge chimney. One of us whispered:

"It's a crematorium, look!"

At that moment, the chimney began to emit puffs of smoke, sparks and then, finally it burst into flame at the top. Somebody shouted in the car. Someone, apparently the *posten* in the booth, fired a shot. Maybe out of fear. The embers from the chimney were getting bigger. Somebody put blankets on my head. We returned in silence.

That night I couldn't fall sleep and tossed in my bunk. In the end I got up and went outside the hut. I was strangely restless. I moved in the direction of the *wiese* and the wires. Somebody was escaping from the Jewish bloc. This person glided slowly at first then went faster and finally started running. She raised her hands. I understood. She was walking toward the wires.

"Stop!" I shouted, trying to catch up with her.

An unknown force stopped me and I could not find my voice. "Why?" I thought, "Why stop her? Maybe I should do it myself?"

The wires pulled like a magnet. Finish it. Finish it once and for all. Then there will be nothing. it will be silent. And Zosia? Today she we will be waiting for water again and maybe a package. Or maybe there will be a miracle, an offensive. Still, the temptation was quite strong. There will be roll call soon, then Magda, the *sauna*, lice... but maybe... The girl had already approached the wires.

"*Was machst du, stehe?*"[82] the *posten* shouted from somewhere.

---

[82] What are you doing, don't move!

She shuddered and stood for a moment. Then she dropped her hands and lowered her head. Who knows what she recalled at that moment? Suddenly she straightened up and went forward.

One shot was fired, then a second from the *posten's* booth.

She curled up and fell on her back like a wooden puppet. I breathed a sigh of relief. She was well now. Someone tugged at the doors of a nearby barrack.

"*Zählappell!*" shouted the sleepy *lagerkapo* in a hoarse voice. Lamps illuminated the barracks.

There was a head count discrepancy. Taube came onto the *wiese*. He had found the girl lying on the ground. He took her by the legs, touched her and kicked her in the head. He was angry that there was head count discrepancy and swore under his breath. He called somebody and asked to check her number.

* * *

At twelve o'clock a *lagersperre* was announced, a selection again. This time the day was cold and drizzly. Almost all of the Greek Jewish women, some of the Dutch, and the female Polish Jews from Bedzin and Sosnowiec undressed and went naked to block number 25. But neither that day nor the next did cars drive up to pick them up. We steered clear of block 25, simply to avoid hearing those voices getting weaker. "I am thirsty mama. Mama, water." To avoid seeing those eyes, those hands...

After three days something very unusual happened in the camp. During the evening roll call the death block was opened and its occupants were released back to the camp barracks. When the block was opened, Taube and *aufseherin* jumped back. The stench of decaying corpses was impossible. Nearly half of the victims, lacking food, water and air, failed to survive. This was during the time of our evening roll call.

Freed from the block of death they now walked past us to their barracks. They tried to smile. They looked surprised, half conscious. Is it true? Is it possible that they will live? The half-cadavers dragged on, and we did not understand the whole situation.

This extraordinary event has become a source of great revitalization. Optimistic rumors began to circulate: They may no longer gas or kill people; an order came from Himmler that the military would assume authority over the camp.

The next day the selection victims were herded back to Block 25. Although their numbers had been recorded, and they had been taken to the crematorium in the evening, confirmation for the transport did not arrive from Berlin, so they were released to the *lager*. Just then the confirmation arrived.

I got a package again—apples. I was very happy and took them to Zosia. She ate and her face brightened. Immediately she felt better. She just kept on complaining about lice. All day and night, she was taking off her shirt and looking for them. Her neck got wrinkled, and she lost a lot of weight.

The typhoid epidemic took on more serious proportions. No one interfered with the hospital. The SS men were afraid of the plague. The doctors organized help on their own, with no outside resources. There was no room for more sick. They were lying three or four on a narrow bunk. You were admitted to the hospital only if your temperature was higher than a hundred and two degrees. I knew I would get sick. Some of my friends warned me: "Why do you go there? You'll become infected."

These cautions were nonsense. The same lice were everywhere in the camp. On average during this period, a person killed 50 lice a day. I killed a bit fewer, thanks to my work in the *sauna*, where I managed to wash a few times in the shower and to change my clothes.

In the evenings when we returned to the block we held discussions—most of the time on domestic camp topics, sometimes, political ones. The girls working in the *Politische Abteilung*[83] or in the *schreibstube* kept us informed. Somewhere nearby was the radio. The German boss had said something. Somebody came over from the men's side. Someone else has overheard the *aufseherins* conversing.

"Obereka is raging today," said Stasia from the *Politische Abteilung*.

"What made you conclude that she is angry?"

"She was beating girls returning from work. Two were kneeling because she didn't like their facial expressions, another had her number carelessly sewn on, and yet another tied her handkerchief incorrectly."

"After all, you can always find such infractions, so why today?"

"Today was the more important reason. They didn't want to replace Katia's star with the *winkel* at the *Politische Abteilung*. Oberka has already put her reputation on the line by intervening in the matter, so today Katia returned crying. And Broat is a member of the *Politische Abteilung*, so there is no way this will go through.

"I don't understand. Why will this not go through?"

"Because he is Eva's lover, and Eva hates Katia."

"And who is Eva?"

"She is also a Slovakian Jew, the redhead working at *vorne*."

"Why does she hate her?"

"She's jealous of...her influence in the camp...her looks... just like anywhere else."

"So this is the reason for Oberka's rage?"

"Yes, Katia is her favorite. Katia is liked by all the women, and Eva by all the men."

[83] The Political Department worked under the supervision of the local camp Gestapo. This self-sufficient section collected prisoners' data, conducted investigations and interrogations, maintained camp "security" and performed crematory services. It was housed in Block 11.

"And because these two hate each other the girls in the camp are suffering today more than ever. This is the cause of the authorities' ill-humor and their mood is reflected on the poor *häftling*!"

"Well, yes. You have no idea how many intrigues are there. Remember that if Stenia the *lagerkapo* puts a dozen people to death, the cause most certainly lies in these intrigues."

"Who is Stenia?"

"She's a young Polish girl. We are all ashamed of her. Apparently in every country they find people to implement their program. There are many degenerates in the world. Just think: There are more casualties on Stenia's conscience than on those of many German *aufseherins*. But then, Stenia has no conscience."

Chapter Six

The Hospital

That night I dreamed that Katia, Stenia and Oberka had formed a chain that I tried to break. Zosia stood behind them. She was pale. Her hands stretched out toward me. I couldn't get through to her. I woke up wet with perspiration. They were calling us for morning roll call, but I was shivering and couldn't get up. Could it be typhus? I rose with difficulty and went out of the barracks. My shivering grew more intense. I knew I was ill.

I had heard that it was possible to walk it off, so I decided to try. I didn't tell anyone. I stood at roll call like the others. My fever rose. I fainted.

"You've got typhus," Wala decided, taking a close look at me.

"Wala, please do something. I don't want to go to the hospital." I gave the block-senior some onions, and she didn't throw me out of the hut. I was terrified of the hospital. At least here someone would look in on me, while in the hospital I would rot alone.

All that day I was unconscious, delirious. I would fall into an unusually pleasant half dream where I was on a busy Warsaw street, my hands full of packages. I wandered from store to store and smiled at everyone. My step was even and light and I was well. When I woke, I found myself perspiring on the pallet, with lice crawling all over me. I was very thirsty, but I bit my lips, wouldn't open my eyes and tried to return to that pleasant dream state. I succeeded. I saw myself sitting on the terrace of a large house by the sea. The sun was setting and the sea was multicolored. I held a comb in my hand and was combing my long hair. I woke up again and put my hands to my head—nothing there. I opened my eyes. Two block-seniors were quarrelling and fighting over a piece of bread. "Water", I said once, then twice. No one heard me. I fell asleep again. This time I was walking in a big crowd holding a flag. Someone was shouting, "The war is over! Hurrah! Hurrah for liberty." We marched to the grandstand. On it stood Taube holding a scythe. I rushed forward to beat him. I woke up screaming.

"What is it Krysia?"

"Nothing... water... and I want to get down."

I tried to get out of bed. I tried to stand up but my knees buckled under me. They were like cotton. I fell over a bucket.

"What's that?" I heard from the bunks.

"Nothing."

I said it so quietly that no one heard me. I could not speak louder. I lay on the floor in a delirium 'til morning; then they picked me up.

At noon two prisoners from the hospital came for me with a stretcher. Wala had sent for them.

It was a cool frosty day. The sun stood high. They carried me through the camp covered with a blanket. I felt as if I were flying up to the sky. "How good that I'm dying now," I thought. "What a beautiful death! If it would only last."

Suddenly everything became black and I began to stifle. They set me on the ground. Someone was groaning. Someone said clearly, "Look, they've brought Krysia. Look at her." Someone else said, "She won't last long. She's been delirious for the past few days. Her heart is weak."

They placed me on a pallet. Someone was already on it. I straightened my legs with difficulty. The other one's feet were touching my face. I lay unconscious for several days. My head was splitting. I remembered only one thing—waiting for Wala who every evening brought me some hot water. Parcels arrived for me. I did not have the strength to open them, to see what was in them. I did not eat. In the bed next to mine were some Ukrainian women. They were very hungry. At night, I saw them taking things out of my packages. I could not protest. The woman in my bed was also very ill. She was kicking and twisting in bed. I begged her to stop, but she did not hear me.

One evening I heard Wala say, "The 'crisis' will be tomorrow. If she pulls through it, she'll live. I doubt it, though. Her heart is very weak."

I woke after that night so weak that I couldn't lift my hand. I couldn't move or speak, but, unfortunately I was completely conscious. The others clamored for chamber pots. The air was saturated with the stench of *durchfall*. All my bones ached. Naked patients, covered with sores, were struggling out of their beds. I touched my head. It hurt terribly. My hair, which had already grown in a little, was matted and stuck to my scalp. I couldn't tear it apart. The scabies began to itch. Everybody had them. Besides that, we had sores and blisters. They were most painful between our fingers. They were both fluid and festering, the pain cut like a knife. Over these scabby bodies crawled lice and fleas. It was impossible to sleep. One night I sat up in my bed for the first time and began to tear at my body. I was on the verge of madness, incapable of stopping myself. Blood and pus oozed out. Good, I thought, now I'll get blood poisoning and die. But a nurse appeared, one who was not ill. She patched up my wounds with paper. Again, I did not die.

Other patients were taken to the stove in the center of the barrack. Doctor-prisoners punctured their huge pustules. The pain was unbearable and their cries filled the barrack from morning 'til night. I rarely slept after "the crisis." The nights were horrific. At times I thought that it was all a nightmare.

Naked bald figures would sit up on all the three-tiered beds. They were all covered with sores and plasters. They would kill lice or scratch themselves. The cries of the dying were constant: "*Nachtwache*[84]—basin! *Nachtwache*—water!"

In my block there were also a few isolated insane women. There was a young girl, a Soviet parachute jumper, who had been captured in the vicinity of the camp. She was seized by a sudden attack of fury and beat up everyone around her. Finally they tied her and now she howled through the whole night. The cry was terrifying, as if she wanted to shout the pain of all those suffering here. The *postens* were uncomfortable in their booths.

* * *

Normally, there were about three hundred people in each barrack but during the epidemic there were nine hundred. During December and January 1943, there were days when the Polish dead alone amounted to nearly four hundred. When death was ascertained by doctor-prisoners or nurses, a corpse was taken out behind the hut. When more corpses accumulated, the *Leichenkommando* [85], "the corpse-squad" arrived and carted them to the crematory.

When patients began to feel a little better they got out of bed and holding on to the beds, they circled the barrack's stove. I noticed Nata as she passed my bed. With difficulty she recognized me.

"Did you get any news from home?" she asked.

"Yes."

"Parcels?"

"Yes. But look at my scabies and sores."

[84] Night watch.
[85] A unit employed in moving and transporting corpses to the morgue and the crematorium.

"I also have them. Everybody does. Janka is here. Right now she's just before the "crisis". She found out that her husband is here, and she was so happy that she had protected him. Wiesia died yesterday. Remember her?"

"I remember. She had a little daughter in Warsaw. She showed me her picture in Pawiak."

"That's the one. She had been in Pawiak for two years. Today her friend Basia died. She was only twenty. But that's nothing. Everything will be fine."

"You haven't changed, Nata. What do you mean, 'Will be fine?' Will the dead come back to life again? Will we pull through? There's a typhus epidemic, no medicine, the *krätze*[86] and *durchfall*... And you?"

"I'm just recovering from typhus. This is the third time I've been out of bed. I'm very weak but I want to pull through. If we live, just think how interesting life will be after the war.

"Do you think that even if you survive, you'll be similar to normal people?"

"I know the camp will leave its mark, but in spite of that we'll be happy. We'll be happy because of all these silly things we never noticed before or took for granted. You'll be happy that you're clean, you'll be happy because you'll eat. The forest, the tram and city walk will make you happy."

"Don't talk like that Nata. That time will never come. I don't even know if there ever was such a time. I would rather believe that I was born in the barrack, that I always had lice, that I was always a number. That's easier. Actually I've already forgotten how to think. I only want something for these scabies, nothing more. I hope they guess that and sent it in a package... then I can say I am lucky."

Nata moved slowly to her bed. It was the first time I'd spoken so much. I was too weak to lift my hand. There was

[86] Scabies.

a roaring sound in my ears. All voices came to me from a distance, even when someone stood near me.

Someone called my name. I had no strength to speak. They finally came to me with a letter. The others helped lift me up. In the dim light I recognized my mother's writing. "My dearest child, you are my only care, my only thought. Are you well? Remember you must live."

My hands trembled. They helped me lie down again.

"Don't cry Krysia, you may still see your mother," the woman sharing my bed whispered to me.

I didn't believe her, not for a second. That's why I cried. My mother's face grew dim and reappeared with unusual vividness. Every time I glanced at the letter I would burst into another flood of tears. "All your hopes will come to nothing, mother", I thought. "I'll rot here just like Wiesia, just like the others, and who knows when you'll hear about it?"

"Are you Krysia, No. 55908?" someone asked at my bedside.

"I am."

"Here. This is from the men's side. She handed me a bottle.

"What's that?"

"Mitigal."[87]

"Who sent it? I don't understand. I don't know anyone there."

"Someone named Andrzej. He'd been looking for you for a long time. Contact is very difficult."

"But how did he know that this is the very thing?"

"That's easy—the men also have *krätze*. Even if he took a wild guess, he would always hit the mark. Who doesn't need it? He asked for you. They told him you were in the hospital."

I grasped the miraculous bottle that seemed to have fallen from heaven. Andrzej, Andrzej—the friend from the osiers at the Sola River. He remembered my number and name...I was

---

[87] The drug used to treat scabies at that time.

deeply moved. I rubbed my whole body with the liquid and for the first time in many nights I slept for a few hours.

* * *

Marta was a peasant woman from the Kampinoski Forest who had been at Pawiak. She had been arrested in connection with partisan activity in her district, but she didn't know the exact reasons. Her husband had not returned from the war in 1939. She was alone with her three small children when they came for her. At Pawiak she behaved normally the first few days, but at night she'd sit up and swallow what little air there was in the cell in deep short gasps. She never said anything. Her thoughts were with her home—the meadow, the well, the cowshed, the river and the forest. Sitting in the stuffy cell she lived through the ploughing, reaping and the harvest. She didn't know how the children managed without her. She gazed around with surprised and questioning eyes.

No one asked for Marta. No one sent her anything. She grew thinner from day to day and understood less and less of what was said to her. She would doze off for a bit at night and moan in her sleep, "Where's my cow? I must milk her." I don't know why this longing for her cow moved me more that any longing for people. In Pawiak I would sometimes sit beside her and wake her up.

"Marta, don't shout. Somebody will milk your cow and take care of your children."

"What's coming?" she asked. "I'm afraid."

"Nothing worse will happen. They will release you. It's a misunderstanding."

She would smile bitterly and gaze into the distance with unseeing eyes.

Marta was taken with our transport. After our arrival she disappeared from my sight. I had seen her several times when she sat alone on the *wiese*. She would cover her number with her hand and look around suspiciously. She looked strange without her braids.

One day on the *wiese* I spoke to her. "It's better here, Marta. More air."

"Yes, my lady."

She had called me "my lady" in Pawiak where I was the "senior of the cell".

"Why are you covering up your number?" I asked.

"I don't trust them."

"Who?"

"Anyone... everyone... bad people—they're all around."

I realized that she was suffering from some kind of persecution complex. I didn't see her any more after that. Someone once said: "Do you remember that peasant woman in our cell? She's gone insane."

One night they brought someone to the bed next to mine. They dumped her on top of a fourth person. She was naked. She was moaning and had *durchfall*. I did not see her face. Suddenly she moaned, "The cow, where is my cow?"

Now I raised myself and leaned over toward her bed.

"Marta, is that you?"

The woman opened her eyes slowly. She had aged terribly.

Smiling she whispered gently, "My lady."

Those were her last words. I closed her eyes. After an hour they carried her out behind the hut. It felt as if someone very dear to me had died. But those who had shared the bed with her half the night were glad that she went so quickly. They now had more room for themselves.

"I can stretch my legs out at last. She had *durchfall* and stunk like hell. It's good she died."

"Why did you holler about the corpse? We could have got her bread tomorrow."

* * *

Dr. Maria caught typhus. She had passed the "crisis" and her temperature had fallen, but now this serious, reserved, pleasant woman was behaving like a child. Elzunia, our kindest nurse, stopped by her bedside and to please the sick woman recited a children's poem. She stopped and looked down at the doctor. Lifting her head Dr. Maria begged, "Go on, Elzunia, it's so beautiful ...

Elzunia went on reciting in her sweet resonant voice:

> Why is she not pretty at all?
> Why is she not like any doll?
> Why does she live so differently?
> Why does no one think her lovely?

The sick woman began to cry. She couldn't listen calmly to the story about the little rag doll. She lifted herself suddenly and tried to get out of bed. Dr. Maria was naked. Dr. Nulla and Elzunia glanced at each other, surprised at this complete lack of self-consciousness. The sick woman began to speak.

"Elzunia, please throw the cigarettes into the basket. Put everything in order for the inspection."

Elzunia motioned to Dr. Nulla. With difficulty they led the sick woman out of the block for a breath of air. Scarcely had they opened the door when Dr. Maria tore herself away and returned.

I know, you're taking me out to push me on the wires."

Dr. Nulla and Elzunia looked at each other in horror. Dr. Maria became apathetic. She stopped asking for poems or anything else. One day she sat up and asked me calmly, "Do you notice anything strange about me?"

"Me? No, nothing at all."

"That's good. Thank you. Some of them want me to throw myself on the wires. Why? I'm well already. We'll be free soon."

Before roll call she asked Dr. Nulla to take her out. As soon as they were outside the door Dr. Maria began to run

Elzbieta Panczyszyn (Elzunia), 1945.

straight at the wires. She jumped across the ditch as the guard took aim from his box. Dr. Nulla cried out frantically:

"Don't shoot! *Sie ist verrückt!*"[88]

The *Posten* shot twice. He had to shoot because if the sick woman had touched the wires there would have been a short circuit.

Dr. Maria, who survived the famine, roll calls, lice and typhus, died from a *posten's* bullet.

* * *

One morning, Wala entered the hut and called out: "Malinowska, Helena..." Her face radiant, she added, "Your release has come from Warsaw."

Wala was happy that she could bring this good news to the patient. Helena's bed was finally found. Wala called out, "Get up! You're free!"

There was no answer.

"Why are you shouting, you idiot?" Someone from the neighboring bed growled, "Can't you see that Malinowska's dead?"

"When did she die?" Wala stuttered with tears in her eyes. An hour ago I was talking to her. She spoke about her son.

She stood for a long time with the release in her hand.

[88] She's crazy!

111

* * *

Dead people were taken outside the barracks constantly. In addition to typhoid fever, Block 29 was becoming overcome with tuberculosis; Block 24 with *durchfall* and Block 12 with infectious diseases. Pemphigus was also a big problem. Despite cutting the blisters, new ones forming immediately and patients were dying in terrible agony.

Some doctors, like Dr. Nula Tetmajer, Dr. Irka Konieczna, Dr. Kasia Laniewska and many others, worked day and night taking care of patients with extraordinary dedication and sacrifice. They used injections obtained from the men's side and smuggled in the *Scheisskommando* vehicle by a popular, bustling-with-life prisoner named Henry.

Slowly I learned to distinguish between sincere, heartfelt help and assistance offered for the sake of personal gain. I became accustomed to the absence of selflessness. I stopped being indignant. At the same time, I was touched by acts of selflessness and was moved by simple human kindness and the simple words so unexpected here:

"How do you feel today? Did you try to stand up?"

I got used to seeing parcels rot next to hundreds of hungry people. I got used to the stink of *durchfall* stink, to bald, scabies-ravaged, naked, half-people half-animal bodies. I even got used to the rats, which had become so domesticated and so brazen that they climbed up to the third floor bunks and chewed off body pieces off the corpses. At times the sight of a rat sneaking up on you and looking for loot became creepy at. I wanted to scream, "Wait! Hold on! I'm still alive!"

Wala told me that Zosia had typhus. I knew that no one would escape it, but I tried to delude myself that maybe Zosia... Then Wala added quietly, "It's serious."

I wanted to get up that night to go to Zosia. Two other women lifted me up, but I couldn't stand. I hung like a lifeless puppet; my legs would not move.

"No good," they decided and brought me back to bed. I wondered whether I'd walk again. The inertia, the roaring in my ears, dazed me. At times I feared that I was not normal. I would speak to someone and observe her reactions.

Wala brought me tea regularly. I felt that this was my only sustenance. Everybody looked with envy as I drank the tea, as if they could swallow me together with the liquid. Wala would always say something uplifting—that a friend was improving, that the offensive was going to start for sure; that the boys said they had heard it on the radio.

"Krysia, just another two weeks."

"How do you know that it's two weeks?"

"Everybody says so. Don't you believe me?" she said almost in anger.

I knew that she had concocted this tale but I believed her. I wanted to believe.

"Zosia?" I'd ask hesitantly.

"Zosia is feeling much better. She sends you her love."

"Why do you turn your eyes away if she's better? Ask her to write, at least a word."

"Tomorrow."

"Anything else, Wala?"

"Nothing new. Alma Rose died."

"Typhus?"

"No, she got hold of some poison and killed herself. Drexler[89] followed her body to the crematory." She added dramatically, "*Schade, das war ein wertvoller Mensch!*[90]"

In addition to Wala, who also took care of others who were sick, we were sometimes visited by other "good souls." They brought soup or coffee, and if they unable to do that, they brought good news.

---

[89] Margot Drexler (Drechsler) served as a reporting officer (Rapportführerin). She was responsible for order and discipline in the camp and for organizing roll calls.

[90] Too bad this was a valuable person!

We often said to each other that if all the prisoners with access to the kitchen were a bit more interested in the sick, there would be no tragic accidents. But socialization in the camp was a source of uncertainty. Besides, those with access to the kitchen barracks were mostly those who were the most loud and vulgar.

* * *

Christmas was approaching. Large numbers of parcels arrived from friends and acquaintances. Everyone wanted to send us a sign of life and remind us of their presence during Christmas. I received holiday parcels containing cake, Christmas wafer and a sprig of holly.

The woman who shared my bed had a very bad attack of *durchfall*. The basin could not be handed over fast enough. She did it in the bed. It was impossible to move. With devotion and self-sacrifice, some of our companions would help the sick, wiping them. Sometimes they got water and washed them. That was their job in the hospital. Some were untiring, inspired only with one desire—to help. Some, however, attended only the sick who gave them food, such as cake or an apple from their parcels. Those who did not receive parcels could die for all they cared.

The generic camp remedy was a white paste that looked and tasted like powdered chalk. The bedposts were painted with it so that they would look white. It was applied to inflammations caused by skin diseases and other infections. It was prescribed for *durchfall* and very often it helped.

I tried not to think about Christmas, about the world, but I had to. Everybody took sprigs of holly out of their parcels and hung them on the beds. The *pflegerins*,[91] *nachtwaches*, *torwaches*, and some of the stronger patients set up a Christmas

[91] Nurses.

114

table for themselves. They dressed up and powdered their faces. They ran around greatly preoccupied, deaf to the moans of the sick. I wondered where they had gotten those dresses. They were excited and it was obvious that for this one evening they wanted to forget where they were. Is it possible for even a moment to be away from the stench of *durchfall*, to hear no groans and to create a festive mood?

"Look! The Christmas Tree!" I heard from the side. They were actually bringing a tree into the barrack. All the patients sat up in their beds. It was not large but it was a real fir tree from the forest. Someone got it through the mail. Others had received candles in their parcels. These they contributed to the tree.

On the bed next to mine lay four naked, hungry girls. They had no parcels, none for the holiday or any other kind. Two were killing lice. One was dipping her hand in the chamber pot and rubbing her body. Urine was the only cure for scabies and all other sores. It was the remedy used by the majority. As it didn't have to be acquired, it was the only thing accessible to all, regardless of their position in the camp or the packages they received from the outside. The fourth was dying. She was very young.

"Get up Jadwiga, it's Christmas," said the one who was rubbing herself with urine.

"Let her die in peace," protested another. "Why do you bother her?"

"Jadwiga, wait until tomorrow. It's not done on Christmas."

"Leave her alone and put down that pot or you'll spill it all over her. I'll talk to her."

"Jadwiga, listen! Christmas carols."

The muted tones of a carol floated through the barrack.

In the midst of the stillness of the night...

Jadwiga opened her eyes and asked, "Where am I?"

"In heaven," sighed the one who was killing lice, a pious expression on her face.

Jadwiga began to smile gently when the second answer came. "In hell."

"Don't talk while they're singing," someone growled.

"Hasten to Bethlehem."

Jadwiga looked again. This time she was conscious.

"The wafer."

There was a wafer in my parcel. I broke a piece and put it in her mouth.

"May you be free," she said distinctly as her eyes clouded with tears.

"May you have peace," she closed her eyes.

"Sleep my Jesus," swelled the chorus.

"Basin, *nachtwache*, quick!" Someone from the neighboring bed shouted.

Near me lay an older woman from Lodz. She was crying. "Please calm yourself," I begged.

"In awhile, my child. I'm so ashamed, but my daughter is without me and I won't last longer than a few days..."

"My mother is also alone. She doesn't know either. You should be happy that your daughter is free. She'll live."

"You're right my child. Thank you. The best thing is that she's not in my place. Come closer."

I moved closer.

"I wish for you that you will see your mother over there..."

The lights were put out and the candles were lit. The block-senior came and wished us freedom. We were all solemn and concentrated.

I looked at Jadwiga. She was dead. At home at this very moment they're probably praying to God for her safe return.

* * *

Two figures approached my bed. They were Stefa and Marysia, friends from Pawiak.

116

"You're here?"

"Yes, just over typhus. This is our first time out of bed. They told us you were here and we wanted to give you our best wishes."

"Do you know that we get boiled potatoes today?" Stefa told me. "It's too bad you can't get up yet. You could crawl up to us. We're on the third."

"Where did you get potatoes?"

"We got them for a piece of bacon and one of the *pflegerins* will cook them for another piece of bacon."

"Krysia!"

"What is it, Stefa?"

"My son," she sobbed. "My little one... today, Krysia, if he only knew..."

"Let her have a good cry today," Marysia conceded. Stefa leaned her head against my bed and sobbed.

"Let's go," Marysia said. "It's too long for the first visit."

I was waiting for Wala and some sign from Zosia. I sensed that things were very bad for her but tried not to think about it.

Somebody was reciting poetry next to the Christmas tree, a poem about war and peace, about Christmas and again another poem about death:

> Here on the barrack bunk
> a woman dies like a dog.
> Her eyes wander. She cries.
> Death chooses, she is next on the log...
>
> She shouts, she wants to be alive.
> She must... her children... her home.
> Neither fever nor chills subside.
> Death sneaks upon her... alone.
>
> Kids, waiting to say hello,
> longing for her, crying in regret,

it's good they don't know
she lies dead in the mud yet

She did not lie there alone
your mother, your love
With other corpses was thrown
the hut she remained a part of.

Next to her, not far,
another woman dies,
strength gone, fades another star.
Wet tears begin to rise.

She's twenty years old
beyond the barbed wires there,
her embrace once did hold,
someone elsewhere

Her lover is sad, her mom
waiting for her... for a year.
She will never return, she's gone
like others, her corpse a wartime souvenir...

My heart leapt as Wala walked in.

"Wala, I hope you get out of here. You certainly deserve freedom. And please Wala, tell me the truth about Zosia, please..."

"Zosia's unconscious. That's why she couldn't write... It's good that she's unconscious. She doesn't know where she is..."

"Yes, Wala. Thank you... You're very good."

She left. Oh, to lose consciousness, even for a second, to sleep. But it was so difficult

Jadwiga was taken away. At first I didn't want to let them. I thought it was a mistake. I had just spoken to her. Maybe she was still alive.

Auschwitz fence.

The carols were fading away. The door creaked, a cold current of air penetrated into the center of the hut. Jadwiga was placed out on the snow. Christmas was over.

* * *

A few days passed. I managed to sit up in bed. There was still a din in my ears, but I was more conscious. Any news of Zosia came less and less and I was afraid of the truth. One night, when I felt much better, I said to Wala, trying to keep my voice steady, "Wala, I know Zosia's dead..." I succeeded in tricking her.

"How did you know?" she asked, taken aback.

"Then it's true. Tell me how she died."

"She was unconscious. She didn't suffer. She spoke of you and said you must return. Her heart collapsed. Then I got a sheet. They did not take her out like that, Krysia. She was laid out on the stove all night. We lit candles, we were with her for a long time."

So it happened, and I had to face it. Zosia was no longer here. No trace of her remained. She lay beside the hut for hours. They walked over her and then took her in a cart and burned her. I was not even near her, and she must have been thirsty and there was no one to give her water. She must have had scabies...

I kept repeating this. I answered others and ate just as usual, only every once in a while I would feel my heart stop. I would feel as if I'd never breathe again. It passed. Then I felt as if my heart had been taken out and a heavy stone put in its place. Someone said, "It would be better if you cried. Don't act like this." But I couldn't cry.

Again came the long days and endless, sleepless nights. Those who survived typhoid fever had an incredible appetite. Every few minutes they opened their parcels and were eating whatever they could find there. Seeing those naked, bald, ulcerated bodies, those dull, stupefied, half-animals whose main job was to kill lice, created an eery impression. The convalescents' full energy was directed only toward eating a hot meal, toward getting the *nachtwache* to cook something in return for products from the packages. The time didn't matter (and this was possible only at night). You had been waiting for this soup, while searching for fleas, for hours. Finally in the morning she would come with a smoking dirty pot. The dream was granted. The others who were starving and recovering from typhoid fever with enormous appetites always gave you jealous looks. But you became already indifferent to those glances.

I tried again to get off the bed. With the help of friends I took a few steps. In the third floor bunk I saw Zosia's and my friend, Mrs. Maria, who was lovely and full of culture and goodness. She noticed me and barely raised her head.

"Mrs. Maria, do you know that Zosia..." At that exact moment, I finally realized that Zosia was dead. I started to choke. My legs buckled under me. A naked body began to swirl in my eyes. Friends took me to bed. I cried all night.

* * *

On New Year"s Day they brought Hanka to our hut. She had already recuperated from typhus and *durchfall*. Now she had erysipelas and was fully conscious. I managed to walk up to her.

"Hanka!"

She looked at me, her face strangely altered, strangely exhausted by suffering.

"Hanka, this is Krysia."

"I know, Krysia. I can see, don't you worry. I'll return to my child. I must. They will not destroy me. If only I would get a parcel. I don't know why I don't get one. I haven't received even one parcel. Not one."

"You will return... "

But I felt that she wouldn't return—that this was our last conversation. The *pflegerins* were preparing a New Year's Eve celebration. They were singing, laughing. Suddenly silence fell, someone had asked for quiet. Marysia was reciting a poem by Slonski and then one written in the camp:

> Gone is my elation,
> romanticism is gone too.
> I dream of clean sheets...
> That's what I want from you...

Then someone shouted, "Happy New Year! May next year bring us freedom, and them death!"

On New Year's Day we got cabbage and potatoes instead of turnips. I was eating this dish fit for a king with great appetite. Suddenly I heard, "They're taking someone out again." I looked to where Hanka had been lying. I suspected that it was she they were carrying out. She had died on New Year's Eve. A few minutes later the *schreiberin* called out her name. Someone answered: "She's dead. She died last night." A parcel had arrived, her first parcel, a big one. A New Year's parcel from her daughter.

* * *

The hospital's block-senior announced that we were to be deloused. A new menace hung over our heads. Delousing meant they would take the blankets away. That meant we would be cold, God knew for how long, and that they could make us go to the *sauna* naked. We knew that delousing was a pretext. The epidemic must have killed too few of us. Aryans were not gassed any longer. Something had to be done so that there would be a greater harvest, something that could be called humanitarian. There were always more lice after the delousing.

They did not take us to the *sauna* this time. They only took our blankets for a day and a night and opened the doors. Most of the patients who had pulled through the typhus died from pneumonia.

They were dying like flies. Nata died. She had endured everything: tortures, investigations, roll calls, hunger and typhus. Finally she died of *durchfall*. She drank some water. Nata was calling the *nachtwache* who did not come. She did not hear or did not want to hear. I went to Nata.

"How do you feel?" I asked.

"Everything's fine," she answered. "It won't be long, it will be all right... I'm sure."

"Nata!" I cried out, "You can't. You mustn't... you'll get well. Just don't drink any water."

I didn't know what I was saying. I couldn't hold off her death. Nata was sinking noticeably. But I had to speak to her as long as she was conscious, as long as she heard me. I spoke of strange, useless things—that she must not leave me alone. I was sorry that I did not die, that I must witness her death and that of who knows how many others. She understood less and less. She listened less. She whispered something. I leaned over.

"I'll simply rot... that's why..."

I couldn't hear the rest. She didn't complete her sentence. She was dead.

We often recalled Nata, myself probably more frequently than others, how they tortured her, and how she did not talk in spite of everything they did to her. She was always well. She was always smiling. If she had to die then why not immediately there at Pawiak, and not here after so much suffering? We spoke of her in whispers, as of a real heroine.

* * *

They brought infants to our block. Their mothers were already working. There were several of them. One of them had been born somewhere behind a hut, it belonged to a Jewish woman. No one fed the Jewish baby. Mothers did not have food. Why feed the child? It was not registered anywhere, and if it were, the mother would also be punished by death. No one, therefore, approached the child. It cried, whimpered, grew weak and swollen, and finally it died. Everyone breathed with relief.

One day, a Jewish woman gave birth to a child on the stove, in plain view of the whole hut. In the hospital where each moment brought death to someone, a newborn child wailed. It was an exceptionally healthy and pretty baby.

"I won't let it die. I won't strangle it," the mother decided.

"It's my first baby. It must bring me luck. Help me. I'm sure some miracle will save my baby."

123

She spoke with such determination. She entreated everyone with such fervour that they decided to help her. The strangest thing was that the mother could feed the child.

Nurse Elzunia resolved to conceal the child as long as possible. For weeks they reported that the mother had a high fever, and in case of a surprise visit from the Germans, the child was hidden under straw pallets. Contrary to all expectations, the child grew more and more delightful.

One night, when the child was already a month old, the mother woke up with a cry. Elzunia ran to her.

"I dreamt that my baby died," she whispered.

That morning an order was issued that all Jewish patients must be signed out regardless of their condition. The mother had to be notified, but no one could muster courage to do that.

Dr. Fruma, a quiet and gentle woman, somehow procured a sleeping drug and injected it into the child.

The mother, senseless with pain, was dragged out of the hut.

* * *

I began to move around the block. My blisters had burst. I no longer thought of ever getting out of the hospital. I could no longer remember the roll calls and work in the camp. I had grown accustomed to moans, to death and to the effort of obtaining hot water. I learned to exchange apples for bacon, bread for potatoes, and sometimes to secure a place near the stove at night by force. I opened parcels and ate their contents with unusual speed. I learned to lie for hours and think of nothing. Freedom became just an imaginary illusion. I couldn't remember or imagine freedom anymore. I couldn't imagine that there were times when we were in charge, that there were streets on which you could walk without difficulty that you had people who were close to you before whom it was possible to feel sorry for yourself, that there were pharmacies where you got medicine. Probably it wasn't true. At times I felt that my life began when I crossed the gates of the camp, and I knew that it must cease here. It's just a matter of sequence.

At times, during these hopeless hours, the thought would suddenly come to me: "There must be people who at this moment are playing bridge or talking about a broken cup. There must be women skiing. There must be some who are in the forest. They are armed and can act. And we? We must die one after the other. These thoughts were the weak reflex of a powerless revolt. For in general we were all resigned, using up our remaining strength to vegetate.

Only some momentous incident could have pulled us out of this apathy, and that happened to be a visit of a German doctor. This happened very rarely. There was always great excitement when his visit was announced. The news permeated from block to block, from one *torwache* to another and from the *torwaches* to the block-seniors. Those who did not belong in the hospital, that is, those who were well and did not belong to the hospital service, planned to hide or escape back to the camp. The doctor was to be escorted by the head doctor and by a woman prisoner or a German *aufseherin*.

He usually walked slowly and calmly through the hut— slim, tall and bespectacled. Just like any other human being. A doctor, and yet he aroused dread. Sometimes he would stop by a bed and ask something. Immediately after his departure we would ask what it was he had asked. He had simply wanted a piece of paper removed. That seemed to be of the utmost importance.

Although nothing had really happened, we talked for days about such a visit. He just walked through. The master of life and death had simply passed through, one of "them," a doctor, not the kind who cures, but the kind who kills.

That day news was spread in the usual manner. "He is coming! He is approaching!" Those who could move around were not allowed to remain in the hospital. There were no convalescents in the camp.

To clear the way for "him," the *pflegerins* pushed the chamber pots out of sight and they disappeared between the beds. "*Achtung!*" they entered. After a while the *schreiberin* announced that we were to get out of bed naked and march past the doctor. A selection!

We realized that this must be the end because we all had sores. We crawled out of our beds, wild eyed and dazed. Next to me walked Wisia, shaking with fear. She grabbed me by the hand.

"Krysia, look at me!"

I looked. Wisia, who not so long ago still flourished as a strong girl now had no healthy place on her body. She looked terrible. Her skin was covered with scabies, furuncles and blisters. She raised her hands in desperation.

"Krysia, we will not be saved. They will finish us now, after so many torments."

She looked around as though expecting help from somewhere, I followed her gaze. We were getting closer and closer. Wisia's hand tightly clenched around mine.

The closer we drew to the doctor the more distracted we grew. Every second seemed an age. Our hearts leapt into our throats. Fear paralyzed our movements and thoughts.

The doctor looked with indifference and boredom at this procession of rotting women. Almost all of us were motioned to the same side. We stood crowded together. But this time it was for disinfection. A tub filled with a special preparation was placed in one of the barracks. Those who had scabies were to bathe in it. At first we did not believe that it was not death, yet it was true. Again we won life... But what for? At first we sighed with relief. At first it was relaxing.

After an hour I lay exhausted by the selection process, I scratched again and again, and I was terribly thirsty.

I was getting up more often now, and had learned to walk without holding onto the bedposts. I often sat on the beds of my sick friends where we discussed what we had received in our parcels and what they wrote from home. We would try to read significant information into their letters. If someone from the outside wrote, "I believe we will see you soon," that signaled "significant news" in our language. They could not write it plainly, that was clear from the tone of the letter. Then we would brag how our hair had grown and how many lice we killed. We often wondered, "What can they be doing out there?" By "they" we meant people outside the wires. We dreaded the future when in spite of everything we would become well again. We would have to leave the hospital then. Here we simply caught one disease after another. But on the other hand, what were we to expect when they signed us out? Roll calls, work in the fields, cold. This was just the beginning of February. I realized that I had been sick for three months. We tried to count how many of our group had died, but we could never could all of them.

Sometimes we would sit for hours without a word. Dumb and stupefied, we looked for fleas. And each one would try to remember herself as she had once been, her thoughts, gestures, actions and way of life. But it was extremely difficult. We had lost ourselves and forgotten. Sometimes fragments of remembrance would reach our consciousness, some misty, unreal pictures of the previous life.

Very rarely, there were also moments of liveliness, caused by the news of a new offensive. They were picking up corpses around us constantly. Somebody was constantly crying, calling, and groaning. We were daydreaming out loud.

"Imagine, for example, that right now our soldiers suddenly come and say, 'The gate is open, you can go ahead, you're free'." There was always someone wise. "Don't bother, this only happens in books, books for children. We have to die one after another, whoever does not die on their own, they will kill."

The doctor warned us more and more often that she could not keep us much longer. She would have to sign the healthy ones out of the hospital. Space had to be made for the sick. We had to become accustomed to the idea of leaving. We had to get accustomed to walking. We had to reconcile ourselves to the thought of change. I dreaded the move. Very quickly we found out that any change is terrible. After a short stay in the worst conditions I accepted them and I was afraid that when I was told to move on, it would be even worse. After a few days the nastiest place in the cramped, stuffy bunk seemed possible, because I already knew how this place was.

The middle hospital bed on which I had spent so many months was always dark and I had suffered a great deal on it, but what did I care about straw and boards falling on me from the bed above? I had grown accustomed to it.

"Will people ever understand what we are talking about?" wondered Wisia, who sat next to me. "Will anyone ever understand, no matter how long it takes us to explain? What words can describe what you can get used to in such a nightmare—this lousy, mangy bed, these "herbs" we drink and that our only desire is for them to give us peace of mind and that they not move us to a different place.

Anyone who has not experienced it, will not understand it, the same way no one will ever feel our anguish and torment despite our most faithful account of it. Besides, why should we describe these most horrible scenes? They will certainly arouse horror. After all, our suffering lies primarily in the continuity and the hopelessness. We are constantly in a state of mental and physical pain. It's as if someone close to you is constantly dying, as if someone is constantly spitting on you, and as if all of it is happening at the same time. I don't know how to translate it so that free people can understand it"

"Why should we talk about it? If we are able to leave this place, I'm sure we'll stay silent. And why we even talk about this? After all, we won't get out of here. Why deceive ourselves?"

Wanda, a charming and incorrigible optimist who had been with us at Pawiak, came to sit on my bed.

"Don't despair. We'll get out. I heard that this time it has really started."

"Yes, yes, in two weeks, right? If they would only set a different time limit sometimes..."

That instant the lights went out in the barrack and we heard a long frightening whistle.

"The alarm!"

"Lie still, air-raid alarm!" the block-senior announced in the dark.

The first alarm in the camp sounded like the most beautiful music. Wanda stretched out beside me in the dark. We gripped our hands in silence.

"Oh, if only one bomb would drop," she dreamed.

"So what! We're not strong enough to run far."

"That's all right—that's all right," she repeated fervently. "As long as something happens. This helplessness and the perpetual death all around are worse. They have all forgot about us."

My heart pounded as I waited for the first bomb, a flash that would light up the unfathomed shades of our misery. We waited for a miracle.

Nothing happened, nothing but silence and darkness. After an hour the alarm was called off. Disillusioned, Wanda slipped out of my bed.

"Nothing's happening. They think about us as much as last year's snow. They must have flown over. That's all. Good night, Krysia, try to fall asleep, may you dream of freedom."

* * *

The following morning they brought someone to our hut. She was very ill. I drew nearer to see who it was. The blanket slipped off but the sick woman did not move. Her cheekbones protruded from her pale face. She gazed out of frightened, dying eyes. There was something familiar in those eyes. No! It could not be!

"Hanka?" I asked, afraid of the answer.

"Yes, Hanka. Are you surprised? I've changed, haven't I? I've got pneumonia. It's the end. I know. You know how I wanted to live..."And in a weaker voice she added, "And I haven't accomplished anything yet, and my mother's parcels didn't help."

"Hanka, you're so young. You're strong. Look. I recovered from typhus. Look, I'm walking."

"I also recovered from typhus, and I too was walking. And I had *durchfall*, too. I was in bed too long. I won't live through this. Look at my hands."

I looked. Her narrow hands were grey. Her long fingers stretched out lifelessly on the blanket, separated as if they did not belong to her. I took her hand and began to rub it. Hanka looked on, resigned, understanding and ironical.

"That won't help. You can't revive a corpse. I'm all wet and I can't move. I can't move. Do you understand? That's still so strange for me."

She shuddered, "Death is so frightful here. So sticky and so stinking, so slow, and I know so well how they'll throw me behind the hut on the snow or mud. How's the weather? What day... it's February?"

"Yes, Hanka, February."

"That means mud. There's mostly mud here, Krysia. When they carry me out, don't let them drag my head over the stones. It must hurt even after death. Please, don't let them."

"All right, but you won't die. I'm sure," I said, looking around for some illusory help.

There was silence in the hut. Hanka lifted her head. With

a terrifying look in her eyes she said in a loud and clear voice, "Tell me, who will avenge us?"

All heads turned in her direction. Hanka's head fell back. A tear was shining on her cheek.

By morning she was no longer alive. We placed her carefully on the stove. Her friends Stefa, Marysia and Elza crawled out of bed, as did her friend Elzunia, who had not left her for one second during her long illness. There were no more of us from Pawiak.

We stood in silence. One more of our group gone—the youngest, the liveliest. We did not cry. We did not speak. Stefa knelt down and pressed her head against the stove. She did not even see when they took her out. I followed the corpse outside the hut. The light was gloomy. A strong wind was blowing the strands of Hanka's hair, the hair of a corpse, blonde as it had been when I first saw her at Pawiak. It was long again. I stood outside next to the barrack for a long time. In my ears rang her old, distant, melodious and carefree laughter, which they killed.

* * *

A few days after Hanka's death, I was signed out of the hospital. I stood at the entrance to the *sauna*, just where I had waited when I first arrived, swaying on my feet, shivering from cold, anger and bitterness. How could I stand the cold, the roll calls? This was February. At the same time I realized that it was almost spring. I had been sick almost all winter. I was receiving parcels. The war must end sometime. I must have gone through the worst, and if I succeeded, mother and friends were waiting.

But how could I live without Zosia, without so many others? It could not be true that Zosia was no longer here. At that moment I could see her clearly as she had been before the arrest. She was setting the table wearing a white apron and smiling. She took an underground newspaper and two counterfeit identity cards from under the tablecloth and winked at me mischievously:

"We'll fool the Nazis—right Krysia?"

And in the meantime... Someone called from the *sauna*, "You're a real *musselman* if there ever was one. Come in. After all you worked here before you took sick."

Is Magda still here?" I asked.

"Yes. That dirty skunk! Only the decent ones die, you know."

"I know... Unfortunately, I know it well".

I entered the *sauna* and saw my reflection in the windowpane. I looked like a skeleton. I was still covered with abscesses and there were still scars from sores. Bits of hair stuck out all over my head. I touched my scalp.

"Don't be too happy. They'll come out again," an experienced prisoner scoffed at me.

"Again?"

"After the typhus... understand?"

I was really indifferent. The most important thing at the moment was to what sector and what block they would assign me. I waited in complete indifference while everyone who passed bumped against me in anger.

"*Musselman*, where are you standing? Move!"

Finally I was told that I had been assigned to the functional block, where those who worked under a roof slept. It was obvious that Wala had taken care of that. She arrived in time, just as always, when my case was being decided.

"Well, Krysia, chin up. You stayed in bed a little and now we must find work for you—and you'll write poems again."

They pushed us out toward the exit and lined us up in fives, the old routine. Just across the way they were carrying out cauldrons with soup. The *kapo* was shouting at a woman who had stumbled.

"*Du Arschloch! Du traurige Mistbiene! Du...*"[92]

Near us, a husky peasant woman and a few others were lugging a cauldron. We were taken to help. I stumbled and swayed under the weight. They had to set the cauldron on the ground. Looking at me with contempt the peasant woman said, "Yes, yes, there are some people that are made of shit..."

The *lagerkapo* was beating a girl, triumphantly pulling a few potatoes from under her striper. They had been stolen from the kitchen. Just opposite, on the *lagerstrasse*, miserable, grey, frozen figures were pulling a cart and Aunt Clara was brandishing an iron rod... the same, the same. Only now the women and girls were different, from other transports that had arrived in the meantime. The old ones had died. These were not Dutch, but Czech and Italian women. However, they looked just like the others.

I was the only one to return from my transport. With whom was I going to stand at the roll call today? And the block-senior—would she beat us up? I looked around.

High up, the chimney was exuding red flames. Everything was just the same. An SS man rode by on a bicycle. He kicked an old woman in passing. She gave a piercing cry.

Beyond the barrels of soup, through the stripes, the sun suddenly appeared and was reflected in the mud. Far beyond the wire fence appeared the outlines of snow-capped mountains.

[92] You asshole! You sad dung bee! You...

Part Two

BIRKENAU

Chapter One

Between the Crematories

Thanks to Wala, I was assigned to the *Effektenkammer*[93] unit, the property-registry squad that took over and stored the personal effects of people whom the Gestapo had sent to the camp. These *häflings* were called *kartei-mässig*[94], the "card-worthy." They had personal dossiers, and upon admission their names and other particulars were recorded. The prisoners' ultimate fate was also registered on these cards. This last entry would either be death, transfer or release. Death, represented by the letter "v" (*verstorben*[95]) was entered on the majority of the dossiers that the *läufers* brought from the *schreibstube*. The Third Reich then confiscated the deceased's possessions. Only the belongings of the *reichsdeutsch*[96] were sent home.

Discharges were so rare that the letter "e" (*entlassen*[97]) was almost never entered. Of the thousands of women passing through the camp, thus far only a few hundred had been released. Only *erziehungs häftlings*,[98] "education" prisoners, were released, and they were actually only sent to the camp

[93] Stockroom; to store prisoners' personal property.

[94] Index card.

[95] Deceased.

[96] Ethnic German citizens living in Germany.

[97] Released.

[98] The "education," or "reformatory" prisoners were incarcerated in the camp for breach of employment regulations and discipline. They were to be released after 6 or 8 weeks. In fact, the duration of their sentence was often prolonged, or they were left in the camp indefinitely. Many of them died there.

temporarily, on account of petty crimes or misunderstandings.

The Political Department issued a list of those being transferred to another camp (*überstellung*[99].) Along with the date, a tiny "ü" was placed on the card, and the detainee's belongings followed the transferred prisoner to the new camp.

So the *häftling* could be marked by the letters "ü" or "v." If there was no letter, it meant one thing: the person was still alive and still suffering somewhere in the camp.

The *Effektenkammer* was the office that kept these records and where the *namenskartei*[100]), the index of names and chronicle of jewelry, identity card, document and photograph deposits were compiled and stored. The office issued orders to the store-huts where the *häftlings'* possessions were stacked and guarded.

My assignment in this detail was undoubtedly the highest position one could attain in the camp-hierarchy. The work, after all, benefited the *häftlings*. Its purpose was to protect our friends' possessions. Our working conditions were the best in the camp. It was always possible to "organize" something from the confiscated property of the dead. Items could be exchanged for a delicacy sent in a parcel or if one did not get parcels, potatoes.

I received parcels quite regularly to help satisfy the hunger I had developed after my bout of typhus. The roaring in my ears was growing weaker, and I managed to make new friends. Immediately after roll call I went to work. I didn't have to wait around on the *wiese* or die slowly in the hospital.

I felt useful working. Slowly I returned to life. Here, even our boss's attitude was better—he treated us like office workers. My hair was getting longer.

Toward the end of March, the *Effektenkammer* hut was shifted to a meadow just behind the camp gates. I kept the

[99] Transfer.
[100] Name index.

Veteran inmates load the belongings of newly arrived inmates onto trucks. Birkenau functioned not only for mass killing, but also as a state-sanctioned mass plundering facility.

name-card index for the whole camp. Mechanically and without thinking, I stamped *verstorben* on cards as indicated by the *totenliste*[101].

The smoke from the trains passing the Auschwitz station rose on the horizon. I could smell the spring air through the open window of our hut.

"What are you doing now?" Basia asked. She was a funny *musselman* with glasses and swollen legs.

"The December *totenlistes*" I answered.

"Friends?"

"Almost our whole transport."

"And you pulled through? That's strange. And spring's coming, as if nothing has happened."

[101] List of the dead.

At that moment I noticed the name: Drews, Wieslawa; then Czerwinska, Zofia; Sikorska, Zofia; Hiszpanska, Natalia. I took out Czerwinska, Zofia's card. My Zosia—I read it several times. I stamped it and wrote *verstorben*, XII.20.1943".

"What's the matter?" Basia asked. "You've turned pale all of a sudden."

"Nothing, only the whole Pawiak group is in these *totenlistes*."

"I understand," Basia said. "My whole transport went in December and January, even the healthiest and the strongest. I don't know how I, all skin and bones, pulled through."

The train whistled in the distance and again awakened our longing for freedom.

"I would like to follow it on skis," Basia sighed. "Follow it home".

Looking at her I couldn't imagine that not so long ago she had lived in a well-to-do home and savors the luxuries of theatres, concerts and the gay life of the cafés.

"Kraczkiewicz, Zofia—*verstorben*."

"Pioterczyk Hanka—*verstorben*."

"Skapska, Maria—*verstorben*."

I began to stamp the cards again, remembering each person as through a haze. I remembered all of them as they had been when we left Pawiak, later on the *wiese* and during the quarantine—our conversations, discussions—our hopes and our plans. What remained of all this? The *totenliste* and files...

After work I would visit the hospital, making use of the break before the *lagerruhe*. I could not forget the sick women begging for a drop of warm water. Not so long ago, I had been there, without help. One evening, I slipped in for a glass of water. The *kapo*, a woman in trousers wearing a black *winkel*, was coaxing a girl into the empty washroom. "Come here. I'll give you some hot potatoes." The girl did not understand. Someone offering potatoes! Another woman?

What could that mean? She approached with distrust, examining the expression on the other one's face—the moist eyes and licentious movement. And suddenly, the hungry girl understood. She leapt behind the hut with the black *winkel* after her and disappeared in the evening dusk.

I took this chance and hurried into the washroom.

Todzia, a Polish woman who cleaned the faucets and washed the floors, quickly placed a pot on the stove. I washed my hands. Every minute counted. In a short while Todzia handed me the boiling water, smiling in her usual good-humored and sympathetic manner.

"It's for the sick one, right? It worked out today; the bitch went out."

I slid past the *torwache* into the hospital. A large number of corpses were piled beside Hut 24. Something was moving between the wires. At first I wanted to run but something forced me to look. I moved closer. A small, three-year-old child was sitting behind the hut and sucking the finger of a dead hand. As I opened the door the fetid air struck at me so strongly that my head reeled. I took hold of myself and walked in. In the dim hall, I finally found my friend. She had tuberculosis. I knew that she would die. I gave her the water. She clasped the cup in trembling hands. Near her, Marysia from Pawiak lay completely lifeless. Stefa was at her side crying. Dr. Nulla, always so lively and vigorous, was now lying in the doctor's room, paralyzed. Her huge black eyes sadly followed the movements of the busy nurses. The fact that she was needed and could not help, could not get up, hurt her the most.

A truck loaded with corpses stopped in front of the barrack. Two men from the *Leichenkommando* jumped out of the driver's compartment. They called on nurses from the barrack to come out and help. Two girls from the *Leichenkommando* wearing gloves took a corpse at both ends and began to swing it. Then they flung it expertly on the truck.

One of the girls was smiling and the other was humming. Zosia, a seventeen-year-old nurse looked on with wide-eyed horror. These girls from the *Leichenkommando* were very tough.

"I can't touch a corpse," muttered the nurse. "I tried but it's so cold and horrible."

No one paid any attention to her. The men called another nurse to the driver's seat. She climbed up with them. They kissed. At the same time a swinging corpse flew through the air and fell on the truck with a thud.

I ran out of the hospital. Just as I entered our block, the lights went out. Simultaneously I heard whistles and shouts:

"*Lagersperre! Lagersperre!* Do not leave the block!"

We huddled in the corner of our hut whispering in the dark: "Who? Whom will they take today?" We listened in tense silence for an hour or maybe two—no one knew how long.

The sound of motors broke the silence.

"The hospital," someone whispered. "They're going to the hospital." The trucks stopped. We tried to catch each sound but could hear nothing. Frightened of the silence, we were also afraid to speak.

The trucks moved. The hum of the motors became louder. At the same time we heard voices:

Allons, enfants de la Patrie...[102]

What's that? I pressed my ear against the barrack wall. We remained still. These were French women going to their death. The hymn penetrated every corner and filled us with mortal hate. The singing continued nearby, and then it started fading away. It sounded more and more quiet and miserable, finally lost in the darkness.

[102] (French) Opening line of *La Marseillese*—the French Revolution song that became the National Anthem.

During the selection in the hospital horrible scenes were taking place. Women were hiding and scuffling. They didn't want to be taken. One young girl lay naked among the corpses next to the barracks until the next morning.

"And for what?" somebody said. "She will survive a few more days until the next selection."

"My God!" someone else sighed in response. "Why do we want so much to live?"

* * *

One morning, our chief, a tall slim SS man with a long moustache, who was Romanian by birth, walked into the office and said in his cool, dry voice. "*Morgen gehen wir nach Birkenau*[103]." Birkenau[104] was where the crematories were located. A number of huts had been prepared there to store the belongings of the Jewish transports. The chief had obtained a few huts for our squad. *Zugangs* were arriving in increasing numbers, and our premises had become too crowded.

In the beginning of April 1944, we were moved to Birkenau. We were all afraid of this change. There we would

[103] Tomorrow we go to Birkenau.

[104] Birkenau was the name of the camp established on the grounds of the nearby Brzezinka (Birch Forest) village, following Himmler's order in October 1941 and the following forced resettlement of the village's inhabitants. The camp lay about 3km from the main camp, and in time it was extended to include many sectors. Birkenau was the temporary location of the labor force and the site of the mass murder of Jews brought there from all over Europe, "The Final Solution to the Jewish Question," according to the Nazi *Endlösung der Judenfrage*. The author refers to sector BIIg, operational from December 1943, as simply "Birkenau." Here, in so-called *Canada*, the store-houses containing the plundered property of Jews were located and the personal belongings of other prisoners deposited. Crematorium IV was located in the direct vicinity of the area. The new *sauna*, (which functioned as, among other things, a reception building for the new prisoner transports) additional crematoria and the "Little White House" (a make-shift gas chamber made operational in mid-1942) were all located outside of sector BIIg.

have to look at close range at the people going to their death. I tried not to think about it. This work was a chance won on a lottery where only one in a thousand could manage the chance to live. I must not hesitate. I had seen so many die. Nothing could be worse. The most important fact was that I did not have to work in the fields. Some preferred to work in the fields, afraid of the experience and afraid that our squad would be changed into a *Sonderkommando*[105] because we would know too much.

The *Sonderkommando* was decreed to die regardless of the remaining prisoners. They were disposed of at certain intervals because they were the only eyewitnesses to what happened in the crematories. Then they were replaced by new prisoners who knew that they had only a short time to live.

All this information reached us in the form of rumors. We were frightened but we always arrived at the same conclusion: "They will get rid of us in the end, it makes no difference where we are. There are wires all around."

Yet, when I first passed through the gate to Birkenau, I was oppressed by fear. I kept repeating as we marched: "I won't give up now. I have suffered so much. If the typhus didn't kill me, I won't die from a nervous breakdown. Besides I know everything about the gassing. I've even seen it, but I still can't believe it. Perhaps they're not gassing anymore." I tried to reassure myself.

"Why should we bother about the crematories," Basia said as if in answer to my thoughts. "We've got our work and our purpose. I barely escaped with my life. I won't let it worry me."

She walked at my side swaying on her swollen feet, a clumsy "post-typhus" walk.

---

[105] A special unit of Jewish prisoners who worked in the crematorium. Prisoners chosen to remove corpses from the gas chambers and then burn them in the crematoria or in cremation pits.

Auschwitz—inside one of the camp offices.

My legs also hurt very much. They were heavy and didn't feel like mine. I haven't yet learned to walk. I knew I looked just the same, that we all looked similar after typhus.

"Isn't this an exaggeration, Basia? That we won't care about the crematoria? Do you really believe that it can't bother a normal human being?"

"And you think we're normal? Look, we move on with our lives despite the deaths of so many loved ones, without whom it seemed that life had lost its value. And now we apparently find some charm in it, though we look so bad that a dog wouldn't even look at us."

"Every creature, even the ugliest, least needed, wants to live. It's about instinct. What can you do about it? We aren't guilty! To whom do we have to justify that we want to live? We are young, damn it!"

"You see, you are rebelling. If you want to live, don't worry and don't react to what happens in the crematoria.

* * *

We occupied four huts in Birkenau. Three of them were packed with bales of clothes, the fourth served as our office. Now all the *zugangs* were to come to Birkenau and after changing their clothes and washing in the local *sauna*, they were to be quarantined in the camp.

Our huts were separated from the men's barracks by the width of the *lagerstrasse*, just a street. Only instead of houses—barracks; instead of vehicles—carts piled with sacks and pulled by prisoners.

On the next street stood our residential block. The other blocks on the street belonged to "*Canada.*" The name stood for the fabulous wealth and was given by the prisoners to the huts containing Jewish possessions.

A small piece of land stretched on the other side of our residential block. That was where our latrines stood. Just opposite was a crematory. A wire fence separated us from it. From behind this crematory towered the chimney of a second crematory. And from the side of the barrack where our office was located, we could distinctly see a third crematory. The *sauna* stood alone to the left of all the streets. Far behind the *sauna* we could see the shape of the fourth crematory.

All the crematories looked alike from the outside. They were wide, two storey buildings made of red brick with two jutting chimneys. All were surrounded by a wire fence. Branches were woven through the wire to screen the buildings from sight. From afar you could see only the chimneys.

The Birkenau *sauna* had been built with more imagination and more care. Thousands passed through it. It was a solid brick building. Inside there were showers and dressing rooms as well as fumigators for delousing clothes, and hot running water day and night. There were furnaces in the cellar and a *Bekleidungskammer*[106] in the *sauna* so

[106] Cloakroom; clothing chamber literally.

146

Crematorium III at Birkenau seen from the south side.

that the arriving prisoners could dress immediately.

And surrounding everything—wires, wires, live wires.

The landscape around Birkenau was quite diversified. Several birch tree woods were scattered through the district. The Polish name for the village, Brzezinka, must have been taken from the Polish name for this tree *brzoza*—birch, and *brzezina*—birch forest. Outside the gates a road led to the crematory right by the "little white house." On both sides of the road stretched fields of sweet flag and lupines. Potatoes and vegetables grew between our barracks. Closer to the barracks were lawns or flower gardens. The most romantic spot was in the vicinity of the crematory behind the *sauna*. The "little white house" inspired one with carefree joy and confidence. When the sun shone on that part of Birkenau, one was under the impression that the "little white house" was a rural retreat where gentle folk could find peace and rest. But—this "little white house" was where they carried out death sentences. The prisoners were shot and the walls inside the house were spattered with blood. In this manner they could take care of up to a hundred prisoners at a time.

Chapter Two

Zugangs

"Kommando Effektenkammer, antreten! [107]*"*

We lined up in fives. Our chief was facing us. He stated that a transport from Majdanek had just arrived—about a thousand people. We were to *karteimässig*, "card-file" them. That meant taking down all the particulars concerning each one of them. They would not undress, as they were arriving from another camp and already wore camp dresses. These dresses were, of course, to be deloused in the *sauna*. We were to work all night, as we could not register everybody by evening. We were not to speak to the men under threat of being removed to the *Strafenkommando*,[108] the punishment squad.

We went to the *Canada* barracks, which were empty at that time. There the women from the transport were already waiting. It was an evacuation transport from the Majdanek hospital, only sick and old women along with several young girls, their nurses.

We placed tables in the empty hut and started to "receive." I thought of my arrival and my first impressions of the camp. I knew that a person coming to a camp was afraid of everything and everybody, that she was distracted and terrified. The first word was so important. I decided to be patient, to answer all

[107] Property storage unit line up!

[108] Punishment unit (SK), placement in it was one of the worst punishments in the camp.

questions, to calm them and give them courage. My life began to hold meaning. I could do a lot of good in my new job.

The arrivals were already entering the barrack. An elderly, grey-haired woman with gentle eyes came up to the table.

"Your name?" I asked.

"Majewska, Maria."

"Age?"

"Fifty-six."

"From where?"

"Warsaw."

"Profession?"

"Teacher."

I wrote everything on the card. I was thinking: "She will survive no more than a month."

"Why were you taken?" I asked, unofficially.

"For newspapers."

"How long have you been in the camps?"

"Three years. At first Ravensbrück, then Majdanek, now Auschwitz. But I'm sick and I'll finish this excursion here. And I do so want to live. It won't be long now. Our army is not far from Lublin. The best proof of that is our evacuation. My son is waiting. You know why I'm holding on. It's because I'm locked up and he is free."

Her face had brightened. Some hidden force emanated from her.

"Chin up," I said, "You'll live! Next please."

A bent little old woman came up. She gazed around with agitation.

"Here please, and please do not be afraid. Name?"

"Pietraszewska, Jozefa."

"Profession?"

"I used to be a worker but now I can't work. You can see for yourself."

"Why are you here?"

"Because of my daughter, a communist. They were

looking for her, but I would not talk, and I won't talk now, either."

"They won't beat you here," I tried to reassure her.

"Do you really think so?" She looked with distrust at the SS man standing by the wall.

They passed one after the other, still older women, very sick, hardly able to move. They had been penalized for their sons and daughters. Some of them had been trapped in street round-ups or were arrested because they had concealed someone, fed some stranger who later proved to be a dangerous partisan fighter. Tired and ill they had to wait for hours before the SS men assigned them to a hut.

Hours passed and I did not move from my position. My mouth grew dry and my eyes hot. There was no end to this train of constantly new, miserable, lost and trembling old women. Late that evening only a few more remained to be registered. But they could not move at all. They lay on stretchers on the ground near the barrack. SS men jumped over them cursing because they had to stay late on duty.

Holding the cards in my hand I bent over a stretcher on which lay an old woman.

"Name?"

She lifted her head and looked at me with her wide tear-filled eyes. She had a tiny face and a mass of white hair.

"*Comment?*"[109] she asked.

"*Français?*"

"*Oui.*"[110]

"*Votre nom?*"[111]

Her head fell back and her eyes stared in the distance. Through the open door of the barrack the warm April night drifted in. The sick woman took my hand and pulled it toward her heart.

[109] (French) Say what?
[110] (French) Yes.
[111] (French) Your name?

"My name?... But I'm dying... In a short while it will be unimportant who it was who died."

She spoke in a halting hoarse voice. I knew that her last hour had struck.

"I need your name," I mumbled, "to keep order." She grasped my hand tighter in hers.

"Order you say... Yes, order is most important for them." She raised her head. "You remind me of my daughter. Hold my hand a little longer," she begged seeing that I wanted to move away. "I'll imagine that my daughter is with me now."

She closed her eyes and lay quietly for a second. Nearby the sick were moaning. They were also powerless. My colleagues knelt beside them trying to get information out of the dying. An SS man with a whip in his hand suddenly appeared in the hut. He was whistling. He stepped on a woman lying on a stretcher, jumped over the French woman, looked around and shouted:

"*Wie lange wird der Dreck noch dauern? Wie lange noch?*"[112]

His feet were spread apart and under him lay a dying woman. With hands placed on his hips he looked arrogantly at us as if to say, "I can do what I wish with you. Just try not showing me due respect—just try not being afraid of me."

Silence fell in the hut. Suddenly the French woman pointed her finger at the SS man and with a frenzied look in her eyes shouted in a terrible voice:

"*C'est la guerre!*"[113] she cried with a terrible voice.

"The war! The front is here. God, what a terrible war!"

The SS man wheeled around sharply, swung the whip straight at the face of the shouting woman and with one leap was out of the hut. Blood gushed from her mouth and nose. She collapsed on the stretcher.

[112] How long will this shit take? How long?
[113] (French) This is war!

A wave of hate flooded my brain. I began to choke and wanted to run out after him. I felt I was going mad but the sick woman clung to my hand.

"My daughter", she whispered. I embraced the old woman and began to sob.

"Krysia! Control yourself," my friends entreated.

"These are the first *zugangs*. They have come here to live. Nothing will happen to them. Don't carry on so. Think of yourself. Go out for a second, the chief isn't here."

I went out but I could not regain my calm. What is her daughter doing now? All kinds of crazy thoughts passed through my head. Maybe she's dancing at some Paris dance hall with a German, maybe the brother of the one who was here? Or maybe she's dying in some other camp?

I noticed a fire on the ground in front of the *sauna*. The light of the flame was shining on some figures. I drew closer. They were men from Majdanek. Wasted skeletons. In the light of the flame they looked grotesque. I covered my eyes and turned back behind the hut. Something white was shining in the dark. I was trembling all over, but I kept walking, conquering my own fear. My leg was withheld by something hard.

It was a male corpse, a second and third beside it. I remembered my friends mentioning that a large number of men had died in the transport.

The white color was the lime that had been poured over them so that they would not smell, I thought matter-of-factly. I was afraid to move. I preferred corpses to living skeletons and I could not go back to the hut. The shriek of the dying French woman still pursued me. I must not go mad now. "I am well," I said to myself aloud. "I have survived the typhus. My name is Krystyna Zywulska, my number is." I kept repeating over and over again.

"Come on Krysia. Are you mad?" Basia urged.

"Where? We're surrounded, we're surrounded," I repeated.

"With what are we surrounded? What are you saying?"

"With corpses, wires, crematories, fire, Germans. We're surrounded, we're surrounded!"

"Come on, I didn't know you had such weak nerves. This is just the beginning and you're already..."

In a flash I realized that I was behaving like a mad woman. I'm normal. I must pull myself together. Basia sees and feels the same as I do. I returned with Basia.

"*Kommando Effektenkammer, antreten!*"

The voice of our *kapo* rang out. Our work was finished. We were counted and we went to our hut.

* * *

In comparison with the quarantine and hospital barracks, our hut here seemed luxurious. It had three normal windows and opposite the windows stood our three-tiered bunks. Our mattresses were packed tight with straw and each of us slept separately. Basia and I succeeded in occupying two middle bunks right opposite the windows. Zosia and Joanna, two girls from Lodz, slept in the bunks above. I immediately became friendly with Zosia, She reminded me of my dead Zosia and maybe that's why she became close to me. She gave me a nightgown, the first in so many months. Zosia looked proudly at me and at the gown.

"Well, satisfied?" she asked.

"Naturally, only why the excitement?" She seemed to think that I took her gift too much for granted.

"The nightgown, that's why. Just as if you had slept in a night-gown all your life!" Zosia fumed.

"But I really have slept in a nightgown all my life."

"Eh?" She leaned out of the upper bed. "But that was in the other life. That doesn't count. You count from the time you were tattooed. You didn't exist before that. Now they count you every day. Now at last you're a human being, you're someone."

"Birkenau has touched Zosia in the head," Basia stated as she vigorously polished her glasses.

"Where did you get that nightgown?" I asked.

"Organized it in *Canada*," she said with some pride.

"I don't think we ought to wear things which belonged to the gassed."

"Look at her!" Zosia was practically falling out of bed. "Is everything to go to the Nazis? That would be better you think? It's all the same to the dead, and they... if you only knew how much they have sent out of here. The *Canada* barracks were bursting. Trucks were taking that stuff to Germany all the time. So why should we go naked? I'm not so stupid. I've been freezing long enough."

"Zosia's right," Joanna said from her upper bed. "We're not sure of our lives. Let's sleep in nightgowns as long as we're alive."

"Sleep girls. You must be tired after so many *zugangs*."

This was the block-senior. There were about three hundred women in our block, sixty in our room that was separated by a corridor from the three hundred girls from *Canada*. The block-senior could afford to treat us normally, particularly as she belonged to the intelligentsia. Her duty was to count us, report to the *aufseherin* and watch that the room orderlies kept the hut clean. Outside of that she could sit quietly in her room with the *schreiberin*. With a little imagination she could, at times, create the illusion of home.

"We'll manage somehow," Basia said in a drowsy tone. "Don't think about those from Majdanek. Sleep well."

Why should I care that some French woman was dying at this very moment? Why should I care that those hungry men were standing in front of the *sauna*? The important thing was that I had a nightgown, that there were no fleas, the sores were disappearing, my hair was getting longer and that we were supposed to be released from the roll call. I knew I was really lucky to be in this squad.

Jewish boys from a newly arrived transport on the ramp.

I was really lucky to have my own straw mattress, two blankets and a block-senior who did not shout or beat us. At the same time I thought about the dark bearded faces in the glow of the flame and saw the parted legs of SS man and his whip. I heard mad screaming: "*C'est la guerre!*" In the end I fell asleep.

The following morning I was again stamping and filing cards. The weather was beautiful. I opened a window. They were leading a group of people out of the *sauna*. The group was moving toward my window. At the head of the group walked a thirteen-year-old boy. He must have been with his mother. Behind were a slender older man with glasses and a small beard, a very old woman and a lame young man. All were very pale. A young boy with an unusually attractive face was pulling his mother by the hand. She moved unwillingly as if sensing that each step brought her closer toward death. We all stood at the windows. "To the crematory," Basia who was standing behind me whispered. "Did you see that boy? Wasn't he handsome? Krysia, could it be possible that in a few minutes he won't be alive? Krysia, he didn't do anything to them."

"A Jew," I gave the usual answer. That one word was to justify everything.

The same SS man who had struck the French woman on the previous night walked behind the group. He sauntered along slowly waving his whip. He was obviously satisfied with himself. It was clear that he was engrossed in his own personal affairs. From time to time he suddenly remembered his job and he then raised his whip and shouted.

"*Los weiter ab!*"[114]

The group moved away. I had to see how they entered the crematory. The old gentleman glanced in our direction. I leaned out of the window.

"Krysia!" I suddenly heard a warning hiss.

I pulled back and noticed our chief. He was looking at me from under threatening brows:

"*Ja, was schaust du dort, ist was interessantes.*"[115]

"*Nein, ich wollte das Fenster zumachen.*"[116]

"Well, what are you looking at? Something interesting?"

"No, I was just closing the window."

"If I see any of you," he said slowly in his dry voice, "looking out of the window instead of working, I'll dismiss the squad, and the guilty ones will be sent to the punishment-squad."

I knew that my fate was being decided. I thought I would hear that I was to return to the camp, to a lousy hut, to work

[114] Keep moving ahead!

[115] Yes, is there anything interesting out there? What are you looking at?

[116] No, I was about to close the window.

in the fields. But I was so agitated at the thought of the other people that I did not realize the danger that threatened me.

The chief was deliberating, touching objects on the table. He finally turned and walked out.

Deep silence fell in the office. Each one of us pretended to be busy. Each one tried to delude herself.

"They're burning," Basia whispered. She did not even pretend to work, with her chin resting on her hands she stared through her glasses into the distance.

"I'm afraid to look through the window."

"You don't have to look. Can't you smell the smoke?" I noticed a light acrid smell.

"I smell it, but I don't believe it. I still don't believe it!" I cried.

"You'll believe when they do the same to you. Let's go out and see."

We went out. The chimney of the first crematory was smoking. Clouds of flames and soot shot up into the air.

"Now do you believe?" Basia asked. "Look, that handsome boy is burning and that middle-aged gentleman who looked like one of my professors. People are burning there."

" I saw them walking, I saw how they went in, now I see a fire... and yet I do not believe, I can not imagine it. I do not understand a thing..."

* * *

It was time for dinner. In the second hut in which Zosia was working, stood a stove. We weren't allowed to cook, but we did so on the sly. One of us, acting as a *torwache*, would give warning whenever an official approached. We always managed to remove the pots in time. The hut was stacked with long sacks so that it was possible to hide them.

Men from across the way, who belonged to the men's *Effektenkammer*, had already noticed the presence of women in the vicinity. Occasionally, one of them dropped into the

157

women's hut for a second and brought us information: Where the transport had come from, news about the next transport, about the last communiqué (eavesdropped in the chief's room). They would listen in on the radio in their chief's office.

I went to Zosia under the pretext of looking for a lost sack. It was necessary to have an excuse ready in case I should bump into our chief or the *aufseherin*.

Zosia was cooking our meal. She had exchanged bread from her parcel for potatoes. She was very proud that she was preparing us something to eat.

"You know Krysia, that doctor, the one with the glasses, was here asking for you."

"For me?"

"He said he heard that there was someone here who wrote poems. He wanted to read them."

She looked at me from the corner of her eye to see what impression this unusual news made on me.

"Don't you realize that we can interest men? Your hair has grown about two inches."

She was bending over me and measuring my hair with her fingers. She looked at me with surprise because I had not reacted to her mood.

"And we're having a hot dinner—well, aren't you glad? You should be happy!"

Do you know that they're burning people right under our nose... I saw them going there, I saw a boy who was pulling his mother by the hand," I murmured.

"I'll pour off the water from the potatoes. I have some gravy powder and we'll have soup," she said brightly.

"Zosia are you mad? Didn't you hear what I said to you?" I asked in a mood of black despair. She was stirring something in the pot, with her back turned toward me. She did not turn around. "Did you hear what I said?" I repeated.

"I don't want to listen to that. It's a good thing there are no windows in this hut. I can sit and cook, and if anyone

158

comes in I simply pretend to be looking over the sacks. I don't want to know what's going on here. I don't want to know! Understand? I want to return." She whirled around and flourished the spoon.

"Alright, Zosia," I said. "I won't talk about it, but you can't escape it. Everything here is built for one purpose. We can turn our backs. We can try not to remember, but the knowledge that they are burning people a few steps from here must deaden all other impressions. That one thing must remain the strongest."

"But understand, I'm not conscious of that. I don't want to be. I'm normal. That doesn't reach the consciousness of a normal person. A normal person would never believe it.

"And the SS who are in charge of the crematorium, the camp?"

"They are abnormal. They are criminals, degenerates, sadists. They only look like people."

"Yes, but people like that are in every nation."

"Eat your soup! I want you to talk to Wacek, but I don't know how to arrange it. He's got courage, I tell you. All by himself he organized the ambulance. He procured everything himself and he's always smiling though he's been here three years."

"I see that you want to find a boyfriend for me."

"Yes, I must admit I do, because you take too much to heart here. I've observed you from the beginning."

"I promise, I'll be better."

The gong sounded for the end of the dinner. I returned to the office. I could smell valerian drops. Aha, their nerves couldn't stand it.

We went to the *sauna* after work. We each had our own soap and towel. Standing naked under the shower we were reveling in the hot water.

"Life is beautiful!" Basia shouted above the noise of the water. Just an hour ago everything had looked so dark and now shouts of rapture!

"Wash my back," she grimaced playfully. "Do I have many scars?"

"Irene has more," I comforted her. We all had scars from the scabies and sores.

"And will they disappear?"

"They'll disappear with you," Tanya answered from under another shower. She spoke in her musical Russian accent, convincing as always. Tanya had learned to speak Polish in the camp.

Suddenly I felt a cold gust of wind from the door. A man without a jacket but wearing a cap, an SS man, stood in the door and scowled at us. Some of us began to shriek. He let out a wild guffaw and lifted a hose from the floor. He jumped to the faucet and began to spray us with cold water.

Our shrieks increased as we ran to the wall. He came after us with the hose, directing it at the most bashful ones. We fled to the adjoining room where we had left our things. Quickly we pulled our dresses over our wet bodies. We were ready in two minutes.

"See, how beautiful life is," I mimicked Basia. "Beautiful my life. Your life depend on idiots, perverts. Today, he sprayed you with water, tomorrow he will use gas, because he will be in a better mood."

She laughed at me.

"You forget a small detail—that you're in a concentration camp, in *Vernichtungslager*. Perhaps you have really forgotten? You want them to pamper you here?"

"You've washed yourself, so be happy. A little while ago, a cup of water seemed like an unattainable dream."

"You're right, Basia. What can we do? Now when I'm not hungry and don't have lice, some sense of dignity and humanity returns, and yet they humiliate us so much."

"There is good advice for that. When you look at the fascists you do not see people in them. Think of them like animals, because that is the case. We are in the power of wild animals. We must try not to come into contact with them, and if we can not manage that, we must learn to look at them with contempt.

We were lying on the block. Zosia descended to us for small talk before the bedtime. We outlined a plan for lunch for the next day. The three of were running a "household" together. When a package for one of us was delayed, it arrived for the other ones. The rest organized themselves the same way. Among us no one was hungry.

But famine prevailed throughout the camp as usual, and the epidemic of *durchfall* was spreading stronger than ever.

In the evening hubbub someone spoke of the quite unbelievable fact that one of the political prisoners, a Pole, Zofia Kossak-Szczucka, the great Polish novelist, who was in the camp under another name... [117] was leaving for the freedom quarantine... We couldn't believe it. It was too beautiful.

You could hear sighs from several beds, cries of envy, admiration... grief... So it is nevertheless possible... So you can get out of here after all. Maybe they will begin release others. Maybe the situation beyond the barbed wire has suddenly changed...

"I wonder what is happening in the world?" Sighed the typist, a mother of seven children, the oldest of whom was fourteen years old. She was the most in control and the most calm. Despite her age she worked the hardest.

"The boys listen to the radio in the chief's room, and we must try, too," someone suggested.

"Wacek said the arrival of a transport of Italian Jews had been announced," Zosia said, proud that she knows in advance when the transport will happen.

"New emotions await us." Joanna sighed.

---

[117] In later releases of the book (starting with the third, in 1951) Z. Kossak-Szczucka became an anonymous Pole, a political prisoner. The reason was that in 1945 she remained in Britain, whence she came back during the "political thaw" in 1957. In early 50's communist Poland she was a "traitor" and (in Orwell terms) an "unperson". She published a memoir of Auschwitz called *From the Abyss.*

Chapter Three

The Girl with a Skipping-Rope

The following day we were checking the contents of the *zugangs'* sacks. These sacks were to be deloused in the *sauna* and were piled in a small room adjacent to the large *sauna* hall. As I worked I heard someone moving in the hall. I looked and saw groups of people entering—men, women and children—tired, battered and sitting on the cement floor. They spoke in Italian. I noticed a girl of seven with dark olive skin, huge dark eyes and long black hair. I couldn't tear my eyes from her. With graceful movements she glanced around the hall. Then she unwound a skipping-rope and took a few hops with her long slender legs. She didn't notice the depressed and despairing expressions of the waiting crowd. She didn't know the true purpose of the place she had come to. She obviously considered the room suitable for playing. She skipped over the rope with the seriousness of a child for whom the world was still a vast playground.

An SS man entered the hall. He had a protruding lower jaw, small darting eyes—almost invisible behind the rounded cheekbones—jerky nervous movements and a skull on his cap. His appearance evoked a shudder of dread.

The girl with the skipping-rope stopped and turned to follow the gaze of the others.

"Hustek," I heard a low masculine voice.

"What does that mean?"

"That devil that came in is called Hustek. He's making the selection."

It was then that I became conscious of the man standing beside me. It was Wacek. He had been pointed out to me just once, but I immediately recognized his mischievously raffish face in glasses. That face was now displaying an expression of hate.

"Why don't you go away? The chief may come any minute. How did you get in here anyway?"

"I noticed you through the door."

"Look at that little girl," I whispered.

"The one with the skipping-rope?"

"Yes."

Hustek was intoxicated with the opportunity of deciding the fate of all these people. He cast about the room in search of faces distorted with pain and fear. He seized old women by their arms and pushed them to the "death side"—he threw out orders in single words:

"*Hier! Los! Stehen! Gehe!*"[118]

He finally unbuttoned his uniform jacket, breathing heavily after this ecstatic activity. He looked around the hall. The girl with the skipping-rope decided that the time was again suitable for playing. Moreover, it was apparent that she didn't know the feeling of fear. She had probably never come in contact with evil people. She jumped over the rope, her huge innocent eyes turned on Hustek. I could see that he was stupefied for a second. Then he stretched out his hand and pointed. "*Los! Schnell!*"[119]

A smile lit up her pale face and, without the slightest suspicion, she skipped to the "death side."

Wacek was still standing beside me. He suddenly seemed very close. I knew that he had experienced the same feeling of horror at what had happened that I did.

"She doesn't know," he breathed, "She just skipped over."

[118] Here! Go! Stand! Go!
[119] Go! Quick!

A transport being unloaded on the ramp at Auschwitz, prior to selection.

Basia, who had been checking sacks not far from me, warned me with a nudge.

"The chief, Krysia. Watch out!"

Wacek disappeared as swiftly as he had appeared. I bent over a sack and began to read over the list of items on the index card. There was turmoil inside me.

"*Ein Rock... Eine Bluse... Eine Kittelschürze...*"[120]

Everything checked, I took the sack on my back and left. They were just leading out the selected group. I looked for the child. She was buttoning up her coat, just as if she were going for a walk. She was at the same time speaking with animation to an older woman, probably her mother.

[120] One coat... One blouse... One apron.

I caught up with her to have one last look—to remember her always. As she passed me, she pulled a beret out of her pocket and put it on her head.

I stifled a scream. Why the beret? In a short while there would be no trace of her.

There were mostly older women and children in the group. Behind them came the men. It was a small transport, about two hundred people. They were glancing about with agitation. They sensed something evil, something incomprehensible. Some of them, noticing our numbers, realized that we were prisoners. Afraid of the answer, they begged us, "Where are we going?"

A man with the thoughtful face of an intellectual, very distinguished looking, lifted his hat as he passed me.

"*Donna,* where are they taking us?"

It could be my father; the thought flashed through my mind. What could I say?

"Disinfection," I answered calmly with a smile so as not to rouse their suspicion.

The men's faces brightened. Some thanked me, breathing with relief. They were thanking me for a few minutes of illusion. The transport moved away. It was closed by two *postens* carrying rifles. They walked slowly, laughing at something, probably a joke. I dropped the bag in the second barrack. No. I am sure I won't find a solution... You have to live on.

* * *

Zosia ran out to me.

"Krysia, do you remember the *läuferin,* Mala?"

"Yes, I think I do. She was a favorite of *aufseherin* Oberka's."

"She escaped."

"How? I don't understand."

Zosia's cheeks glowed and she spoke with animation.

"It's a very romantic story. Mala came here with a Belgian transport. She's a Polish Jew and she knows languages well. She's pretty and clever, so in the two years that she was a messenger, she succeeded in gaining the confidence of the officials. She met someone from the men's camp and they fell in love. He's a Pole from Warsaw. Everybody in the camp knew about it. He also held a job, so they could meet often."

"But how did they escape?"

"He dressed up as an SS man and she as an *aufseherin*. He got all the necessary passes and papers, but I think someone helped them. Anyway they were successful. Didn't you hear the alarm?"

"No, I was busy. An Italian transport arrived."

"Why did you go there?"

"I had to, I was checking the sacks in the *sauna*."

"Don't think about them Krysia. Be happy that she escaped. You can see for yourself that it's possible to get out of here."

The only topic of conversation was Mala's escape. We worried that they might be caught. Vigilance in the camp was increased. The chief fell into a rage again. She made inspections in the barracks—beating, cursing. She would appear unexpectedly and make the women kneel at the smallest pretext.

And we were happy for the one who had been successful. Before falling asleep, we would imagine Mala walking somewhere—free; Mala without a *streifen* on her back, without a number; Mala in some city arm in arm with her beloved—smiling at people, no wires around them, happy. They walked out of here—unbelievable! No one thought that their freedom was not real freedom; that they were afraid of the Gestapo; that they had financial and many other difficulties. All that was unimportant—the important, the most important, highest fulfillment of our dreams was to get outside the wires, finally to be able to function, and then.... Everything would be all right... for sure better than here...

* * *

Some packages arrived.

"Krysia, you have a huge package from Warsaw!"

I ran to the room at the end of the barrack. Colleagues from the packing department were taking packages out of a big sack. I checked my name in the notebook. Basia had gotten one too. The *aufseherin* checked their contents before giving them out. She sliced bread, opened boxes of marmalade and checked any paper, to see if by chance something was written on it.

I unpacked a sausage carefully wrapped in parchment, along with pastry, bread and lard. Colleagues that hadn't received a package that day and those who had never gotten one surrounded me. Marysia looked out the window sadly, toward the truck with packages. There was nobody outside the barbed wire who would have thought to or could afford to send her packages. She had already spent two years in the camp, and there had not yet been any sign of life from her family. She had been arrested with all her loved ones. I saw her watery dark eyes full of grief and silent reproach.

Beside me Basia and Nella were unwrapping their packages. Nella received the most packages from her son who lived in Rabka. Always sensitive to others' misfortune, she went to Marysia, gave her a delicious piece of cake and said, "Take it. Don't worry. One day, you will also get a package. Try this cake, for sure it was baked by my son and if he did not do it, it was probably made by the woman who is flirting with my husband in my absence..."

Nella winks comically, trying to make Marysia understand that the most important thing of all is her husband's affair...

Marysia started to laugh, took the cake and ate it, though her tears choked her...

167

"Krysia, look..."

Basia leaned over me with a very mysterious look.

I looked at the small piece of paper she showed me.

"Read it..."

"My dearest little daughter, we pray for you every day. Our only wish is to see you. Your sister is engaged, but we are delaying the wedding until your return. Be healthy, dear, Mother."

"Where was it?" I asked, enchanted.

"In the eggs," She answered, as though it was natural to send letters in eggs.

"I envy you really, Basia. In Polish, ah, I hope my family will come up with this idea..."

"You know, you need to send a letter "secretly" and let them know how to do it..."

"Okay, but how."

"Maybe they will release someone. Anyone who returns home must come through our unit. She has to come here, get her stuff, her jewelry and documents, out of the sac. The person who gives the clothes to her can maybe sew in a letter to home. Then when she's free, she can send it..."

"A beautiful plan, but no one is being released..."

"And yet it happens that *erziehungs häftlings* (those who come here for six weeks) tend to be released... We need to have Ada in the dressing section tell us when she gets a list of *abgangs*[121] so we can prepare letters for home."

"Maybe they won't want to endanger themselves by taking letters. Besides, they can be searched."

"We have to try. Maybe we'll find someone brave and noble. I think everyone who has been here understands what exchanging messages means to us and those closest to us. They can't learn anything about us from those formal letters.

[121] Departures; prisoners released from the camp—mostly due to death or relocation.

The sun was peeking through the window. Typewriters were tapping. From the adjoining room of our chief you could hear the lively sounds of the foxtrot.

Taking advantage of the absence of our *capo*, I was working on a new poem. Directly at the table opposite me sat Irene. She looked funny with her hair barely grown back. She sat stiffly, blocking me from view in the event of a sudden intrusion by the chief. Beside me, Nella worked diligently, occasionally glancing at a photograph of her son, which she managed to steal from her own personal file. Her son was already seventeen, but Nella still acted more vigorously than many of the young women. In a recent letter her son wrote that he had monetary problems and probably would stop studying. Nella was constantly thinking bout how to resolve this.

I looked out the window. I already knew well the view of the *sauna* and the men working there. I could distinguish individual SS men and knew their names. I knew that the man who kicked the Frenchwoman from Majdanek was called Wagner. He was the most refined looking, but he was the most rowdy. Bedarf, whom we called "the weakling," was tall, skinny and pale, with fair hair and a long nose. His expression was always bored, blasé. His faded eyes looked cloudy, cold. He constantly wandered with his hands in his pockets, clearly waiting for something to summon more emotion. Apparently just for his own entertainment he now grabbed a Jew and started smiting him with a whip. Groans from the tortured man reached us, even though the radio played louder and louder, even though three typewriters were tapping together. Irene could not sit still.

"I'll take the bucket. I'll go get water, and see why he is beating him."

"Come on," said Nella. "C'mon, you'll put yourself at risk! And you," she turned to me, "Stop this scribbling. How can you write poetry in such conditions?"

"But the conditions are always like this."

Bedarf picked up his victim by grabbing his jacket. Blood oozed from the nose and ears of the Jew, who was barely able to stand. At one point he grabbed Bedarf's hand. Bedarf retreated and punched him in the face with his fist. The Jew fell to the ground. Bedarf rubbed his hands in disgust.

"*Wasser!* [122]", he roared toward the *sauna*.

Just then Irka passed by, carrying a bucket of water. He beckoned to her. She put the bucket down. We watched, terrified that he might do something to her, but he only dipped his hands in the water, shook them and kicked the bucket, cursing loudly all the time.

Irka came running, out of breath.

"What was he saying, why he was beating him?"

"He was only saying, "*Verfluchter Jude...*[123]" He beat him up only because he stood in his way at the *sauna* entrance. The Jew did not notice him.

"Brute!" Nella shuddered.

I looked out the window. Wacek was moving quickly towards the *sauna* with his doctor's suitcase. He looked around. There was no one, and he rushed to the *sauna* door.

"This Wacek has a job. If someone is beaten up, he is already waiting close by with bandages to dress the wounds."

"Dear boy!" Nella got sentimental. "I wish my son was like him..."

* * *

The dinner gong reverberated loudly. We ran to the hut to Zosia. She was standing over a steaming pot.

"I've got something for you. Guess what?" she asked.

"Noodles?"

"No, nothing to eat."

[122] Water!
[123] Damn Jew...

170

"A letter?" I guessed.

"Yes, and from a man. A carpenter from the men's camp brought it."

"He was in the hut?"

"Yes. Don't be afraid, the *torwache* was there. He asked for your number, but there, take this letter."

She gave me the message, a card torn out of a writing pad, folded in four and tied with a string.

"How did he carry it?" I asked.

"In his shoe. He said that's the best hiding place." I unfolded the sheet, and read:

"Krysia! Please don't be angry with me. I don't think this letter will cause you any trouble. I was so happy to find out that you were well again. Did my medicine help? I know you are receiving parcels, but should you need anything, please count on me. Is your hair longer now? Please answer through my friend. He will be coming to you because he is working there for a few weeks. I envy him. Andrzej."

"Krysia has an admirer," Basia squealed with joy.

"Do you think I should answer?" I said doubtfully.

"Of course!" Basia shouted. "This will be very interesting. These surroundings are ideal for romance. And if you do get into trouble, it's worth it!"

"You would think of something like that." Zosia was annoyed. "Krysia, you must read us your letters. We'll partake of your romance because we don't have any ourselves."

I wrote to Andrzej saying that I was touched and that it was very pleasant to know someone cared, and gave the letter to Zosia.

"It's very silly really," I said. "I don't know anything about him."

"And what must you know?" Basia interrupted. "You know that he's been locked up several years and that he has suffered his share. That should be enough. Tomorrow he may leave with a transport. They can send him to the bunker. And you wonder whether 'it's right', just because you don't know him. Maybe you want a formal introduction?"

Someone was running towards us through the hut.

"Krysia, Basia! Didn't you hear the gong? The *kapo* is raving mad. She said she won't let you eat here." It was Nella, breathing heavily and calling us impatiently. "Another transport. Only we don't know whether for the gas or for the *kartei-mässig*. Jewish women from the Majdanek."

We ran into the office and took our places. The *kapo* was not there. Tanya had just returned from the camp where she was in the political office.

"Three hundred young and healthy girls have come from Majdanek," she told us. "They worked in the *Canada* there. Wala from *Politische* said she heard Hustek say that they are to be gassed."

"Didn't they go directly to the crematory?"

"There's been no decision. They still don't know exactly what to do with them. Those girls know everything. They worked near the crematories over there. They can start a riot—maybe they're scared."

An hour later, Tanya and I slipped behind the men's barracks to the *Canada* barracks. On the lawn between the barracks stood a crowd of women dressed colorfully and with red crosses on their backs. All of them were healthy and pretty. They had long hair and fresh complexions. They seemed to have been specially chosen. A slender blond girl, with deep grave eyes and a very arresting face, spoke to us.

"You work here? In what squad?"

"*Effektenkammer*," I answered.

"Aha, so you're going to register us. That's if we go to the camp of course."

"Why, of course you'll go to the camp. Where could you go?"

"You don't have to cheer us up. We're old hands at that."

"At what? What are you saying?"

"The crematories. Too much has happened in front of our very eyes, that's why they must get rid of us. Please," she looked at me. "Tell me the truth. What do you know about our transport? There's no reason why you should be sorry for me. You must tell me—it's your duty. Just imagine yourself in my place. Would you want me to lie to you? We're not afraid of the truth, not even when it's bad. Please, tell me!" She seized my hand.

"I assure you," I tried to convince her, "I don't know anything. I assure you that any transport which comes to the camp and goes through the *sauna* is never gassed; they won't make a selection among you because you all look so well."

"Then why did they bring us here?"

"I don't know, but I think they are simply evacuating Majdanek."

"Yesterday, when they learned about the approaching front, they called a general roll-call over there. All Jews, without exception, there were fifteen thousand, were shot with machine guns—all except our three hundred. We assisted them in this death and in the death of all our friends, of all those who succeeded in remaining alive through the years of hell. Then we had to strip the bloodstained clothes, sort them out and tie them into bundles. That's why they let us live, but only to do that. Why should they let us live now, after we have witnessed that crime? When they wipe us out, there won't be any witnesses, that's their purpose."

"You're young and healthy. If they had wanted to, they could have finished you off at once. There are witnesses of all their crimes here also, and they may still need you. For how long, nobody can tell. We're all living without a future. But in the meantime we're alive."

"Right now, I'm most haunted by the thought that I could have escaped." She spoke slowly and sadly. "We came in a cattle car. We had all the gold. We took it from the other *Canada*, thinking it would be possible to escape. I began to flirt with our *posten*. My friends would jump off the train. Out of our group of ten, I was to jump last. Nine jumped. I was too late. When I decided to do it, the train was already nearing the camp grounds and the guards redoubled their watch.

"Did the others get away?"

"I can't tell you that. I heard a few shots, but it was all the same to us. We knew that we were going to certain death. Promise me that if you find out anything, you'll let me know beforehand. Before I die one of them must..."

She clenched her fist.

"I promise."

We returned to the barrack. I was scolded by the *kapo* who said that I hadn't worked all day and that I interfered in everything.

A few hours later, the girls from Majdanek went to the camp. They had been washed and their hair was shaved off. They were safe. I was relieved. Tanya leaned over and whispered, "They'll live!"

The following morning our *läuferin*[124], squad messenger, went to the camp for the list of the dead and those to be released. When she returned she said, "Those Jewish girls from Majdanek went up the chimney last night."

"Impossible," I exclaimed. "You must be mistaken!"

"Unfortunately, I'm not mistaken. They were loaded on two trucks last night. They kept their machine guns ready because the girls started a riot. An SS man was hit over the head with a clog and today he's walking around with a bandage over his eye."

The girl stood before my eyes as I had seen her yesterday, begging me to warn her. "I could have escaped, it was too late." Everybody was shocked. "Getting rid of them by underhand methods—criminals. First they take them to the *lager* to quiet their suspicions and at night..."

---

[124] A female prisoner serving as a messenger.

Our *kapo* went to our chief, Bedarf, for his signature on some papers. She asked him with an innocent expression on her face, "What happened to the girls from Majdanek? Are we to register them?"

"Nein, Maria, sie sind vergast..."[125]

"What?" Maria showed calm surprise, as if asking about some unimportant detail. *"Warum, Herr Chef, sie waren doch so jung und hübsch?*[126]"

"Yes. But they had a lot of gold inside which they ate. After gassing the gold comes out of the corpses all by itself. You understand, Maria, that we need gold to conduct this war." He answered succinctly, coldly, as if explaining the meaning of an official document. In the same tone of voice he continued, "Any mail?" Maria drew the current correspondence out of the office folder. "Read it, Maria. I judge that you'll be able to answer it yourself." The *kapo* began to read letters from families of prisoners detained in the camp. All were alike. There were two types of letters from the General Government[127] and from Germany. The General Government letters asked for the personal effects of the deceased, for her ashes, and asked why she had died. Ashes of the dead were, in the beginning, sent to their family for a small sum. Later, because of the pressure of "work," these dispatches stopped. They only answered that she had died of a heart attack, strep throat or due to a common cold, or whatever the prisoners in the political office thought up. One prisoner had told us once that he wrote these letters in series of ten. Ten died of a heart

[125] No, Maria, they were gassed...

[126] Why, boss, they were so young and pretty?

[127] General Government (*General Gouvernement*)—Nazi occupied Poland was divided into two parts: one part was fully incorporated into the Third Reich (including the area surrounding Auschwitz), and the second, called the General Government, was controlled by the German authorities.

attack, the next ten of pneumonia etc., so that he did not repeat himself too often.

Maria was reading a letter from a German. He wrote:

To the lagerführer of the Auschwitz camp: I have been notified that my daughter, Loua Schultz, has died in the camp of heart failure. I thank the authorities for the information. I am proud that she died like a true German on the field of glory. Could you please return her watch? It is a family heirloom. Remaining always at the service of the lagerführer and the Fatherland. With a German greeting, Heil Hitler—Franz Schulz.

The chief listened solemnly to the part about her death "on the field of glory." We were pinching each other under the table. The next letter was of a different tenor.

To the lagerkommandant [128] of Auschwitz. Please write to me in detail how my daughter Danuta Wisniewska died. What did she say before her death? Who took care of her? I ask because I know that my child was young and blooming, like peaches and cream. I ask as a mother: What have you done with her? She was twenty years old and I know that if she had been home she would not have died at twenty.

Maria stopped and looked quizzically at the chief.

"Read on Maria. Read what that crazy mother writes," the chief answered lighting his cigarette.

... She was the only joy and support of my old age. I waited for her return, and now I have nothing to wait for so you can lock me up. My daughter was right when she said that you are sadists...

[128] Camp commander.

"Read, read that stupid nonsense," the chief said, leaning back comfortably.

... and criminals. There has never been anything like that since the beginning of the world. God will punish you all for my child.

"No... *lass, Maria, genug...*[129] Give me that letter together with the envelope."

"He's writing down her address," Nella whispered. "The mother will pay for that letter. Still, how these people do write. Don't they know what Auschwitz means? They either inquire naively about what caused her death, how she died, or they ask for the ashes or they threaten... and yet you have to grit your teeth and be silent..."

"Don't say that, Nella! You have a child yourself! I guess no one has to explain to you that the pain of the mother may lead to madness."

Maria read a letter from a German from Berlin who was asking for the ashes of his dear wife.

We looked up the detail in the *namenskartei* and discovered that his wife was Jewish. The chief cursed the "German idiot" who had called his Jewish wife's ashes "dear."

He finally tired of the letters. He closed the door of his office and turned on the radio:

Oberkommando der Wehrmacht gibt bekannt...[130]

I placed my ear to the wall. Ziutka stopped typing. There was silence in the *schreibstube*. Tanya tiptoed out to inform the others, "Quiet, a communiqué from the front."

Our armies retreated, abandoning a city according to plan...

[129] No... leave it, Maria, enough...
[130] The High Command of the Wehrmacht announces...

177

The door leading to our chief's room was jerked open. The *aufseherin* of our squad, Janda, was standing on the threshold. Janda was not pretty but her features were intelligent, her eyes penetrating. Although she was young, one could immediately perceive that she had a strong character. Janda never struck anyone. She tried to maintain order and camp discipline by psychological methods. There was something in her voice and walk that made her quite charming. We were ashamed to admit it, but each one of us had a weakness for Janda. Janda treated us humanely. No one would deny that. I knew that Janda was a Nazi. She worshipped Hitler and his ideology. As I could not find any connection between this and her humane attitude toward the prisoners, I asked her once when no one was in the office, "What do you think of the system used in annihilating Jews."

"I'm sure Hitler does not know about it," she replied. " 'They' are doing it... I'm certain that he would not permit it."

I couldn't get into a long discussions then, but I wanted to ask why if that was the case, she, ever faithful to this ideology, couldn't notify the Führer about what "they" were doing behind his back.

Janda was now silent. She looked at me with her piercing eyes. "Well, aren't you interested in politics? Have you forgotten where you are."

"Politics don't interest me. I'm interested in the battles on the front... It is printed on our letters that we are allowed to get newspapers."

"Please, don't pretend to be so innocent. Don't let this happen again. I don't wish it, that's all! I don't want to threaten that you'll be dismissed from this squad, but I'm warning you in time."

Janda always appeared unexpectedly. She mostly found us gossiping or raising a hubbub, or she would catch someone cooking during working hours. She never uttered a word. She would only look long and significantly at the culprit. I tried to evade that gaze, but I was persecuted by ill luck. My friends warned me.

"Watch out! She's got it in for you."

Knowing the other *aufseherins*, we were greatly pleased with Janda. We could not comprehend why she had become a supervisor in a concentration camp. Oberka, Drexler, and the other witches could not stand her gentle treatment of the *häftlings* and her being senior to them. They could find nothing against her. Janda could not be bribed, although the beautiful things in *Canada* were tremendously tempting. She tried to be just and maintained an appearance of rigor.

Whenever I passionately proclaimed that all the Germans should be annihilated, someone would always object, "And what would you do with Janda?"

"I, personally, nothing," I would answer, "but the same punishment should be meted out to her for the very fact that she is here."

"And you, Tanya?"

Tanya after some deliberation decided:

"I would kill her with the same feeling that I would kill my sister if she had betrayed a great cause. I would know that she cannot live because she is harmful, but I would at the same time be sorry for her as for my sister."

"But Tanya, she doesn't think that she's betraying any cause," cut in Ziutka, the typist who rarely spoke. "She would betray her cause if she were to leave this place."

Tanya lifted her chin and spoke challengingly:

"In that case let her die for serving such criminal ideals. She's mature enough to see the difference between good and bad."

"And are you sure that you see the difference?" Nella asked doubtfully.

"I am sure. That's why I'm here."

These discussions which began in our hut at nightfall, often continued late into the night. Tanya was usually the most excited and it was she who would close the discussions with that proud toss of her head.

* * *

The chief stuck his head out of his office.

"Maria," he called. "*Zwölf Zugänge*"[131]

"*Sofort, Herr Chef...*"[132] "Nella, Krysia, Irka, Tanya—to the *zugangs*! Call Ada from the sewing room. We'll register them in the *sauna* hall. Take your tables, pencils and cards. Irene, go quickly to the second hut for the sacks."

We still had very little experience in registering. It went much smoother later. We took down information and others threw the clothes into sacks. During this period, it was still necessary for everything be explained to us.

We entered the *sauna* hall. Janda was with us. She stood silently as we registered the prisoners.

The *zugangs* were standing in a corner of the hall, the same corner in which the Italian transport had gone through the selection. They were frightened and looked at us with visible suspicion and agitation. I approached them explaining that we were also prisoners, that no harm would come to them, that they were to hand over their personal effects for storage and that these would be returned to them upon their release. The majority of them were *erziehungs häftlings*, reformatory prisoners. They had their own numbered cards from the political division. They were not tattooed. Each one asked whether she would really be released.

"Why certainly. You've come for six weeks—for reformatory purposes. You'll work a little and then you'll leave."

---

[131] Twelve new ones.
[132] Immediately, Herr Chief (Boss)...

"Right, I saw the inscription over the gate *Arbeit macht frei*"[133], one of them said, laughing bitterly.

There were five Polish women from Breslau (Wroclaw) from "Bauer." I asked the one who had laughed why was she sent here.

"Oh, an old guy got mad at me and reported me to the police. He cooked up something—that I said something against the Reich. He got his revenge, the ape. I think what I wish but I don't talk. I'd rather die here than with that old man.

"What did he want from you?" I asked naively.

"He wanted me to go with him. He was always following me to the cows, into the field. At first he was very sweet, then he began to beg, and finally he threatened me. Well, he carried out his threats when he saw that he wasn't cutting any ice with me."

"And the others?"

"Oh, all of them have something like that. They get raving mad when we stand up to them. They always find something."

I sat at the table. Irene was putting things into the sacks. An older, well-dressed woman came up to the table.

"Name."

"Krüger, Marta."

"From where?"

"Breslau."

"*Reichsdeutsch?*"

"Yes."

"Do you have any documents?"

She handed me a bag of photographs, all of them of a young German officer in uniform. I looked at the back of one:

Meiner allerliebsten Mutti, Hans. Kijew 1943 [134].

---

[133] Work makes you free. Given the true significance of the camp, one can not but recall the association with the words crowning the gate of Dante's Inferno: *Abandon all hope, ye who enter here.*

[134] My dearest mom, Hans. Kiev 1943.

"Why were you arrested?"

"Because I had Jewish ancestors."

"And this officer?"

"My son. He's at the front."

"Your husband?"

"Killed on the front. I had one more son, a child—not quite sixteen. He also died from a bullet. May I keep his photograph?"

"No. They'll take it away from you. You must wash and change your clothes."

"Please take your clothes off," Irene said politely.

Mrs. Krüger objected. She said that she was clean, that there were men around. It's true. A few men were working in the *sauna*. I thought of the time I had arrived. How I was prodded and beaten. We were polite and she was still difficult—this German woman whose son was now destroying our cities.

"That's the order, *ein Befehl...*[135] Please, undress immediately!"

It worked. Irene was quickly throwing the things into the sack while I wrote down the items on the label:

"*Ein Rock...*

Ein Büstenhalter... "[136]

She moved toward the shower abashed and dazed like all the other new arrivals.

The next one was also a German woman. Her manner was provocative and she was heavily made-up. "Profession?"

"*Dirne*"[137], she answered with pride.

It was enough to look at her, to recognize her trade. She refused to undress. Irene became impatient.

"Step on it! That's nothing new for you. Don't pretend to be so shy," she shouted.

---

[135] A command.
[136] One skirt... one bra...
[137] Prostitute.

"Irene, stop! Remember how we acted."

"When I first got here, I assure you that I did everything they told me to do," said Irene bitterly. "I knew where I'd come and that there was no way out for me. I was only too happy to escape a beating. These men aren't bothering the woman. Undressing in front of them doesn't mean a damn thing here, does it?"

"But they don't know what things are like here yet," I said. "They're still thinking like outsiders. Give them a chance to learn."

"Then the quicker they learn, the better," Irene said brusquely. "They're better off than we ever were, that's all I know."

Chapter Four

White Powder

Zosia beckoned to me through the window. I ran out to her. "Krysia you must look. It's horrible, but you must see it. You must remember it forever."

Zosia accentuated each word. She pulled me by the hand. Some of our girls were already standing on the road. They were pale and rigid. Their eyes were turned in the direction of the nearest crematory.

A ladder had been placed at the small window of the crematory. An SS man stood on the highest rung. His green uniform was clearly visible in the fading light. He put on his gas mask with a quick, nimble gesture, pulled on his gloves and opened the window. He raised himself to look inside and then swiftly pulled a bag out of his pocket. Holding the window frame with one hand, he thrust his head into the opening and with the other hand spilled the contents of the bag into the building. White powder. Then he shut the window. At that moment we heard a great inhuman cry—a cry like the wail of a siren. It lasted about three minutes and then slowly faded away. The SS man jumped off the ladder and disappeared behind the wall.

At the same moment, Janda appeared outside the SS mess hall. She looked at us in eloquent silence, as always. For a split second our hostile eyes met hers, but only for a second. In a short while we were all at our places trying to convince ourselves that what we had seen was not a nightmare but the truth.

The selection of a transport of Jews on the ramp at Auschwitz.

That same evening we learned from the *sauna* boys that this had been a transport of Jews—foreigners. The whole transport went to the gas without selection. That was the order from Berlin. The Jews realized what was happening when they were in the dressing room, that is, the ante-room to the gas chamber. One of the women, they said, a Polish Jew, attacked the SS man on duty. She snatched his gun and shot him. Then she wounded another guard and the other Jews attacked the remaining SS men[138]. The camp

---

[138] On the 23rd or 24th of October 1943 a transport of Jews—men, women and children—were brought from Bergen Belsen concentration camp. In the dressing room of Crematorium II one of the women grabbed the revolver of SS-Oberscharführer (Senior Squad Leader) Josef Schillinger and fatally wounded him. She also wounded SS-Unterscharführer (Junior Squad Leader) Wilhelm Emmerlich.

185

Likely local Jewish community leaders in the vicinity of the gas chambers.

authorities were quite upset about the affair.

Two days later a funeral was held in the camp. The dead guard had been one of the worst persecutors in the men's camp. He had boasted of the number of people he had murdered with his own hands.

We saw Taube stamping around irritably with his face all bandaged up. He must have got it from that transport.

On Sunday, the day of the funeral, I walked into the second hut. Wacek ran into me. He startled me terribly. Everybody was so upset that day that any little thing made us jump.

"Wacek, please leave this hut immediately. How can you be so careless?" I asked.

Wacek pulled a bottle out of his pocket.

"I'm not careless, but today I had to drink to their death,

to funerals like this one today. May there be one every day, thousands of them. Let's drink, Krysia, to their downfall!"

He tipped the flask and handed it to me. I took a long draught. The vodka was strong. I began to feel dizzy almost instantly.

"To their downfall. May we survive them Wacek!"

"We must! Let's drink to our friendship." I drank and we shook hands.

"*Baracken schliessen!* [139] Somebody's coming!" the *läuferin* on watch shouted. We moved back. After a while Wacek ran out of the hut.

* * *

One day the *läuferin* returned from the camp almost in tears: "Listen Krysia," she said to me, "Something unpleasant has happened. Something very unpleasant for you."

I tried to guess what it could be, but I could not think of anything. Maybe somebody had died? But no one spoke of death with such emotion. What could have happened? Maybe somebody from my family had been arrested and brought to Auschwitz.

"Tell me quickly what has happened."

"Your poem has been discovered," she said tearfully.

"Which one? How?"

"*March out into the field.*"

I had poured all my pent up hate into that poem. I shuddered at the thought of it now being now in their hands. The *läuferin* said that *lagerälteste*, the camp-senior Stenia, had found the poem during an inspection and immediately referred it to the authorities. The chief was raving mad. The poem had been translated and they were resolved to find the author. I realized that the victim of the inspection knew who

[139] Close the barracks!

187

had written the poem. Knowing the methods of investigation at Auschwitz, I recognized fully that my case was lost.

I waited for the Gestapo. My friends were deeply concerned. They tried to reassure me, but I felt that they already looked upon me as dead. Nella destroyed all the remaining poems. With a strange feeling of joy I watched as they quarreled with her. They did not want the poems destroyed. They wanted to bury them, they wanted to hide them come what may, "because this will be the only souvenir of Krysia".

Charming, golden haired Edka Stopczynska, one of the youngest in our squad, had memorized all the poems I had written. She had learned them during the long evenings in the camp. She explained to the others, "You can destroy everything. I will recite them to you from memory... if anything should happen," she added quietly.

Then she came up to me and looked at me as if to memorize my features. I knew that she liked me, but I knew that she was more sorry for my "creative talent." She was always watching me and pestering me with questions. "Have you written anything new?"

Wala sent me a message. The situation was serious. The girl was still under investigation. In connection with the poem, they had already arrested another girl from the FKL[140], who had come from Pawiak. Her name is Alina Obraczkiewicz. There was no use in fooling myself. The Gestapo would come for me.

I returned to the dormitory block convinced that this would be my last night. After a short while the block-senior called out my name. My legs felt weak under me. I turned around to take a last look at my friends. I knew that in a few seconds I would look upon the horrible faces of the Gestapo and then the torture would begin. At that moment, Alinka, the

---

[140] *Frauenkonzentrationslager*—women's concentration camp.

most pleasant block-senior, entered the block with a huge box in her arms.

"For you Krysia, a parcel."

"Is that why you called me?"

"Yes. But why are you so pale?"

I took the parcel, recognizing the writing of someone very dear to me, who was now thousands of miles away. I began to look through the carton and found a photograph of my mother. Her gentle eyes looked at me sadly as if to say, "Live! You must live for me!"

Today... now. Could it be a sign, or was it simply acci-dental? Nella, Basia, Joanna, Edka and the others surrounded me. They looked at my mother's photograph with tears in their eyes.

Something snapped inside me. I burst into tears. Nella patted my head.

"You won't die today because you received a photograph of your mother. You know that parcels never come here at this hour. It must be a good sign. You'll see Krysia, a miracle will happen. No one will betray you."

I did not undress that night. In spite of their reassurances, I did not believe in miracles. I watched the door. My head seemed about to burst. I grasped mother's photograph. I was unhappy that I would have to die, and for so many months I had been convinced that life meant nothing to me.

The hours dragged slowly as I waited. Each sound in the vicinity of the barrack made me jump. But it was only the wind rustling the dry leaves of the hazel shrubs around the crematory. In my thoughts I bade farewell to everything I had grown to love. I thought of the senselessness of my whole life. I had survived typhus, the unending roll calls, the mud, only to die now that freedom was so near.

The night came to an end. The lights were lit in the block and Basia rose to open the window.

"Well, they didn't come, did they?" she asked triumphantly. I couldn't refrain from laughing.

"Yes, they were here but they didn't want to wake you up. They took me quietly and killed me," I said. Basia began to shout:

"Crazy Krysia, crazy Krysia—they won't come, they won't come. You'll live."

After a few days of tension, I regained hope. Finally, I received a message from Wala:

Alinka Obraczkiewicz, the girl from Pawiak, when asked who wrote the poem, said that it was Lucja Harewicz who had died in 1943. She kept obstinately to her story. You're lucky Krysia. Please write something good. And now I'm very happy that the chief and the others read what we think of them. Both women will go to the punishment squad. Who knows, maybe that is best for them now.

* * *

We worked until noon on Sundays. After work we would return to our block and lie on our beds. Several books were circulating in the camp, books we had taken from the newly arrived prisoners. They were the third volume of *Emancipators* by Prus, *The Story of the Yellow Boot* by Domanska, *Escape* by Aldanow and an old French novel by Alfonse Daudet. We knew these books by heart. We hunted for books every time new *zugangs* arrived, but we discovered that people do not bring books to a concentration camp. Sometimes, someone from a street round-up, luckily for us, brought a book. We would read it aloud or tear out a few pages and give them to a friend who was already waiting impatiently.

For the camp bread that was often left over, we could buy all kinds of clothes from the Jewish women in *Canada*. On Sundays we would take off our working aprons and dress in our newest styles. At first, I objected that I would never put those things on. I realized, however, that everyone went through this period of questioning, only to conclude that it was better to use and destroy these things than to let them go to the Germans.

* * *

The Volksdeutsche occupied a separate room, even in the camp. They feared of mixing with us.

Dark haired Ada had a "coloratura" voice. We always asked her to sing. And Ada always sang the same songs: *The Lark Song* and *Ave Maria*. Then she would give us a parody of Kalinowna's monologues. We would always laugh at her Cleopatra in a nightgown belted with string.

We all leaned out of our beds to look at the few girls who were able to fool around a bit. We had to forget for a moment at least what was happening around us. Otherwise it would have been impossible to live.

The Ukrainian women—there were a few in our group—hummed their folksongs. Tanya sang a Russian song and a French Jew from *Canada* sang a few songs at our request. Sometimes Nella leapt into the middle of the room and performed a brigand's dance to the accompaniment of our claps.

"How wonderful it would be," Basia sighed, "If all the world could unite just as we have here, look how well we all feel together. There are no class or social differences. Yes, yes," she sighed again, "Auschwitz unites people—it's a wonderful invention."

"Are you crazy, Basia?"

"But I like it here and when they open the gates one day, it will be difficult to leave this place."

She stretched on the bed languorously like a "Lady in the boudoir," making the appropriate faces.

I lifted my hand to slap her when sudden silence fell in the hut. I looked toward the door. Oberka stood there.

I wanted to disappear, to escape, but there was no way out. I only pulled up the blanket so as to conceal the sheet. One of the girls was smoking a cigarette. She tried to hide it, but the smoke betrayed her. Oberka struck her in the face and took down her number. She would go back to the camp. Oberka passed through the room. I envied those on the upper beds. They could hide from her. She lifted a blanket with the end of the cane she carried so gracefully. There was no linen on that bed because the owner did not have bread to spare for the purchase of a sheet in *Canada*.

"*Blockälteste!*"[141] Oberka called.

The block elder, thoroughly frightened, stood before her at attention.

"You all seem very well off here. They were laughing when I walked in, smoking cigarettes. Do you think you have different rights than the rest of the camp? Remember that even though you are *die Damen von Effektenkammer*,[142] we will put you in your place!

"Yes," the block elder affirmed obsequiously.

"And you, if you permit this conduct, straight to the bunker you'll go, *verstanden?*[143]

"*Jawohl, Frau Oberaufseherin*[144]."

Oberka walked out.

The girl who had been smoking burst into sobs. She knew that she would again be exposed to fleas, beatings, unending roll calls, hard pallets and cold. Basia resumed her former position.

"There you are," she said languidly. "I told you that this place is wonderful. It's never boring because you never know what will happen. If I were home this Sunday evening, Aunt Anyela would come in and start on her troubles—that

---

[141] Block elder.
[142] The ladies of the property store.
[143] Understood?
[144] Yes, Mrs. senior overseer.

Tadeusz, her son, is again carrying on with some actress, that it's frightful... and I would have to sit and listen. I couldn't walk out on mother's only sister, the widow of a late colonel," Basia yawned. "God, how boring that was! And here, international society, unexpected visitors, the newest styles, the whole gamut of emotions, people of integrity and the basest swine, here we struggle, here we live!" I was horrified at what she was saying. "But Basia, there is nothing here but death—death and decay. You're talking nonsense."

"Yet, just consider awhile, Krysia. If you were sure that you would get out of this place, would you be sorry that you had seen all of this? Don't you realize that you've experienced something? Something that other generations had not seen. You've seen the lowest depths."

"I think," I said, after reflecting for a moment, "That I will not regret this time here, although I realize how many illusions I forever lost here. But do you think that our most vivid emotions are from a lack of perspective in fact? I know that this experience, this schooling that Auschwitz gave me, I would not get anywhere else. Nowhere else you can see so well "naked man". In any civilized society, people always have masks, here they must be the way they really are."

Chapter Five

Jumping Jacks

Days passed swiftly from one Sunday to another. Within a week none of us knew what a day it was. It was not important. Until finally one day at noon the *läuferin* whistled the end of the workday. This meant it was Sunday. The *Lager* was filling up. New *zugangs* were arriving from everywhere. They came because of various offenses, for making statements about the regime that were too loud, for underground newspapers, for smuggling, for doubtful ancestry, for sabotage, for failing to appear for work, for an arbitrary extension of leave, from the roundups, from Wroclaw, Hamburg, Berlin. Poles, Russians, Italians, French. Political and "antisocial." *Reichsdeutsch* women were brought, punished for the help they gave to foreigners, for having had romances with Poles. Mothers arrived for having thrown themselves on the rails when their sons went to the front. Pale, extremely emaciated men came— Jews from the ghetto—without faces, without individuality, without expression, without content, burning eye sockets, skin and bones. We had a nickname for them: *musselmen*. Looking at them you had to think about one thing: How to get bread? Where to get as much bread... for many days... how to feed them? You looked long and helplessly in their direction. In the end you had to turn around and say something stupid to calm yourself.

Girls came from different sections of the camp and told us how many people were dying. How they were dying. How every day they were invariably rounded up and forced to work. How every day they continued to march to the rhythm of the drum through the gate into the field. How every day they invariably led naked, sick, half conscious creatures wrapped in blankets to the hospital to finish them out. How invariably every day old and newly arrived prisoners fought for a little soup on the *lagerstrasse*, how they threw themselves on a wild turnip barrel, regardless of anything and anyone. How every other block was kneeling at the gate as a punishment. They knelt because of badly tied handkerchiefs, for confusing the rhythm of the march, for nothing—for making faces, for Oberka's bad mood, or on Taube's caprice. They told how in the hospital some were dying of hunger and exhaustion, and next to them or even on the same beds the "wealthy" ones are dying of infectious diseases while lying on the boxes filled with Canadian bacon, eel, canned food and chocolate.

I knew it all too well. I listened feeling as if I were a hundred years old. Apathy, withdrawal, rebellion and hatred swept over me, and finally, always above all, towering powerlessness.

Spring flooded through the wire. It rushed from the blue sky, swept through the barracks, and cast a green coat on the birches and golden one on the sweet flag. We were looking through the window at the white house situated in this remote area, thinking about the fact that the walls inside were spattered with blood. We had to look at a blue sky disturbed and obscured by smoke from burnt human bones. Somewhere in the world was Warsaw and the Vistula. Our hearts shrunk in desperate, painful longing.

In the evenings after the *lagerruhe*, when the lights were switched off, we began to whisper. It was the hour of memories. We recalled how it was, where we were a year or two ago at this time.

During recent months our hair had grown faster and our scars had disappeared. We washed often and took fresh undergarments from *Canada*. We were in a privileged position. Out of thousands of women in the camp, there were sixty of us in our squad.

One day Zosia ran into our barrack and whispered to me, "A letter from Andrzej."

I went to the latrine. That was the only place where we could do all the things that were forbidden, like smoking a cigarette, reading love letters and speaking our minds about the camp authorities.

Andrzej wrote about himself and his family.

It's strange, I have many acquaintances and friends here, but I want to be friends with you. I need a woman's friendship. I don't know whether you women feel the same but we, after satisfying our hunger, we feel the need for love. It's funny because there is no way to meet and I don't believe that I shall leave this place. I find it difficult to believe after so many years. But the knowledge that I shall receive a letter from a woman makes my camp existence easier. You don't know how much your letter meant to me. I thought of you, how you looked when you were writing it. I imagined someone completely unreal because there in the osiers you were so homely and so funny. You were a bald, flea-bitten striper, and the sun was as hot as it is today. Remember? Unfortunately, I no longer go to the Sola River. I sit in a large, gloomy barrack-room and dream of freedom.
Today they caught a girl who had escaped from the camp—a läuferin, I think. She was taken with my friend. They are in the bunker—and I envied them so.

Could they have captured Mala? That couldn't be. I read that one sentence several times. Everything had been in vain— that wonderfully maneuvered escape and our happiness. It wasn't Mala who was important. Thousands like her died here everyday. It wasn't Mala's cause. It was our cause. It meant that no one could escape from here. It meant that the Gestapo was omnipotent. We had almost forgotten about them, and they sought and found them. So we were in their power to the end. Poor Mala had scarcely tasted freedom and she was already sitting in a cell and they were surely beating her.

News about the capture spread immediately. There was mourning in the camp. Each one felt as if she had been affected personally.

For several days the boys passed on information about the bunker through the grapevine: that they were beating Mala, that they questioned her. "He" was supposed to have taken the whole blame upon himself. Mala did not squeal.

Once there was a report from "trustworthy sources" that no one had been captured, that the authorities released this rumor to scare off potential candidates from escaping. We talked about it for some days. I wrote to Andrzej to find out the truth. Mala and the bunker were our chief concern.

"Look there," Nella said, catching me by the hand, "What are they doing?"

Wagner was standing on the field in front of the *sauna*. The men who had been dismissed after roll call were now bending, jumping, turning, stooping. Wagner was running around the field and snapping his whip like an animal trainer, and the men, young and old, fell, bent and jumped in rhythm to the short orders:

"*Los! Auf! Schnell! Laufen! Los! Auf!*"[145]

If someone was a second late Wagner was beside him in a second and struck him in the face. At the same time he would call another order and run to another victim. Everyone was rushing breathlessly. A few of the older men fainted. Basia, whose father was in the camp, looked at this sport

[145] Go on! Up! Quick! Move! Go on! Up!

with hostility. The men were completely exhausted. Dazed, frenzied, they listened to the orders with all their attention to avoid being hit. Nella covered her eyes with a desperate, hopeless gesture.

"I cannot stand to look at it, I cannot, it is terrible what he's doing with them!'

I couldn't recognize anyone among the stripes. I tried to see Wacek. But all of them were in such a wild rush that it was impossible to see anyone. The striped clothes blended like in a movie with a deliberately accelerated pace. When they came nearer, I saw the sweat pouring down their faces. They were breathing hard. Wacek was not among them. He must have been nearby with his bandages. I noticed him behind a hut with his satchel beside him. I ran to the men's side of the barracks. Wacek was startled:

"Go away. They'll see. What are you doing! Are you mad? Do you want to join the jumping jacks?"

"Why are they doing jumping jacks?"

"They found a message from a woman on one of them, and a bottle of vodka on someone else when they searched the barracks. At the men's camp they uncovered a conspiracy, forty boys are in the bunker. They'll do them in—but go away. Don't stay here any longer, they just sent one of your squad to the camp."

Wacek was very upset. He peered from behind the hut to see whether anyone was coming. Basia came by with a bucket to warn us that our chief was coming. I succeeded in running away just in time. Basia began to scold me.

"They have just shaved one of the Jewish girls for talking to a boy through the wire and then they sent her to the *lager*. You know what that means. Did you suffer only to tumble now? I could never forgive myself or you. I forbid you to speak to him and I won't allow any messages to Andrzej. That's enough of that! You know what they do to us for sending messages!'

* * *

"They brought in a men's transport last night, French partisans," the block-senior told us one Sunday.

We were writing home; the same fifteen lines. We borrowed expressions one from the other. Phrases like: "Spring brings so many pleasant memories." "I know that I shall be with you next spring." "I think of you especially before falling asleep." "I see our home clearly and my longing grows greater."

These sentences seemed rebellious and we wondered whether they would pass the censor. After all why should we long for home? The remainder of the letter had to be optimistically informative. "I am well." "The parcels come regularly," and then we thought out some appropriate ending. "I am sure that the good Lord will not abandon me."

Nothing we wrote in German on those printed cards—nothing was ours. It was not honest or true. Every letter was like the one written by my friends, like the previous letter. It was just a sign of life. And sometimes you wanted so much wanted to write a lot. Together with Basia we decided to prepare letters "secretly."

The next week released prisoners were supposed to go home. So I announced in the official letter, naturally by cipher: "Zosia (my other name) wrote to me, that she will write you a long letter. I'm very curious what is going on with her."

We finished our correspondence and went outside. Irene took a bucket and went to find out about the French partisans. One of the braver girls who knew French went toward the men's barrack where the Frenchmen were grouped. They did not know where they had come. They had not eaten for two days and they were deathly tired. They begged for water.

One of the Frenchmen began to despair when he learned that he had come to Auschwitz.

We stood together in front of our block and wondered why they were bringing everybody here. Suddenly we heard a shout and a shot as someone rushed toward the *sauna*. A few minutes later Bedarf appeared dragging a male body by the leg. The head, covered with blood, humped over the stones. It was one of the partisans, who could not deal with it anymore. He had attempted to throw himself on the wires and was injured.

Czesia, who just a while ago had said, "It's good that they've brought us some men," turned deathly pale and slumped to the ground.

I ran to Wacek. The others poured water on Czesia. As soon as she opened her eyes she whispered:

"He must have been still alive, he must have been warm—that boy."

No one answered her. Czesia looked at each one of us in turn with the huge scared eyes of a seventeen-year-old girl. What could we say to her?

"Is that the first corpse you've seen in your life?" Irene grumbled. "Have you gone soft all of a sudden?"

Czesia wrinkled her brows and with great effort, as if trying to forget a nightmare, she said:

"I can't look at so much blood. He was all smeared with blood. He reminded me of someone I used to know, a boy on the outside. Just think, a partisan fighter dying this way! And that villain dragged him..."

She could not forget this small incident. That night I could hear her moaning in her sleep.

When I entered the *schreibstube* the following morning, a few women in stripes were already waiting there. The *aufseherin*, Grese, was with them. She was called *die schöne Irma* [146] because of her slim figure and golden hair. Her eyes

---

[146] The *beautiful* Irma was the youngest SS *aufseherin*. The embodiment of cruelty, she was known for her sadistic tastes, perversely tormenting prisoners (especially slashing them with her glassy whip and kicking them with her hobnail boots) as well as exploiting them sexually. She paraded

Irma Grese during her trial. She was convicted on August 8th 1945.

were dark and cold. She was now snapping her whip at a police dog whose every movement sent a tremor through the waiting prisoners. This fact obviously entertained the beautiful Irma.

The *aufseherin* had come with the women who were to be released, and this game with the dog was the last "entertainment." I passed through the room so as to get a good look at them. All of them had black *winkels*. I recognized the one who used to beat me and who had taken my bread from me when I was working in the field. She had been my *anweiserin* then. So this kind are going to be free. Yes. "Such" are being released.

I walked fast by the *abgangs* and madly rushed into the office to tell the others about it.

"They're free, the worst! The most horrible! Those who tortured us! They're free. They'll mix with the "great German

around in a specially tailored, close-fitting, bluish uniform, highlighting her physical qualities. After the war, she was sentenced to death and hanged.

people" and no one will ever find them. And I couldn't even say anything to them in farewell because Grese was there playing with her dog." I was ready to weep with exasperation.

"Maybe you want to be freed." Nella mocked me. "Do not be angry, this does not help you! It is better that this kind is leaving here... there will be one less... and over there, she pointed to the wires, "There all are mingled... You cannot distinguish the good from the bad."

The *abgangs*, already in their civilian clothes, walked into our office for their documents. They looked so strange in their hats and high-heeled shoes. They even walked differently. They gazed differently. They had different moves. They were getting ready for freedom.

Basia stared at them steadfastly. "You know, they're going to swim this year, in the ocean," she said to me.

"Don't be silly! The German coast is bombed constantly. They'll miss the camp, I assure you. They're not too anxious to leave this place. They had authority here, they were important. They have not even thought of swimming in the ocean." Behind the wire fence the silhouettes of the mountains stood out clearer than ever before. The *abgangs*, carrying their bags, were passing through the camp gate. One of them glanced back and called out to us, "See you outside!"

Nella had tears in her eyes.

They turned behind the first crematory and disappeared. Grese walked behind them, the police dog jumping at her side.

* * *

At night we were awaken by a rumble of cars and shouting. A well-known, tragic, last scream.

"O God!" Basia woke up. "I just dreamed that I jumped into the water from the high diving board... What happened back there?"

"I think the transport is to be gassed, but I don't know

where they are from. Nobody came during the day. This is probably from the *lager*."

"Transport S.B.!" Said someone in the dark.

"What is it?"

"*Sonder Behandlung*.[147] These are from the *lager* selection. The *lagerführer* chooses them and Berlin approves. Until it is approved, they wait at block No. 25.

We already forgot about block No. 25. It seemed like that when we move away from this section of the camp all these horrors had already stopped there. Meanwhile, selections went on. "They do not rest!" as Basia kept saying. After each transport it seems to us that this might be the last. There at block No. 25, more and more are still waiting for death.

I couldn't sleep. I kept listening. Basia covered her ears and hid under a blanket. She wanted to continue her dream and jump from a trampoline. I walked to the window where Czesia, Zosia and Joanna were already standing in their night shirts. They looked extraordinary, against this background, in the moonlight. The growl of returning empty cars could be clearly heard.

Fiery fire zigzags blasted up, squirmed, writhed. Sometimes they shot out violently, as if stoked by something inside. In the air there was boundless silence. Flames soared in the dark blue starry sky screaming for vengeance with threatening, powerful red color.

Imagine, Krysia—wrote Andrzej—Yesterday for two hours I was outside the camp. We had to bring some beams into the camp. They took several häftlings to load them. What a feeling! I was unconscious with excitement. During those two hours I wanted to gulp some freedom. I never thought that a peasant hut, a

[147] Special Treatment. The code name for the records of prisoners who were to be sentenced to death.

*well, a barn, field paths, ditches and everything would
be so full of charm... You would not believe the trees
in bloom and young, healthy, smiling women with colorful handkerchiefs on their heads, walking through
a field waving to us for a long, long while. One of
them just looked at me sadly, I cannot forget the sight.
She looked like she was gazing at the deceased. And
actually, actually she was right. I imbibed the fresh
morning air, full of the smell of spring. I inhaled the
intoxicating freedom as the greatest of gifts... Ah, Krysia, to walk with you through a field of grain or through a shady forest on a day like today! And imagine.
I had to come back. There was roll call in the camp.
And back to the barracks again. And how about you?
I know the crematoria are smoking.
These forty, of whom I'm sure you've heard, are going
to be shot tonight.
And what else can I write? Be healthy, Krysia. Life is
beautiful. Now, I know, and so what?*

Packages arrived. For the third day already, there was
none for me. I was very anxious. This time Zosia got one. We
didn't have anything to eat, but as usual at the last moment
the situation was saved. Only eggs arrived, most of them
broken, but we were sincerely glad even about that. We gave
girls from the packing department shirts for the hospital. We
gathered a few with Nella. Wala was going to distribute them
among patients.

We already unpacked the package when the chief suddenly
came in. He was in a good mood. He stated that we get the
good stuff, and that we should treat him!

"With poison!" Irene whispered through clenched teeth.

When the chief left the office, I noticed a strange
commotion around the girl from the parcel room. She was
saying something with great excitement.

"She was changed completely. I saw her. Her hair was black. She must have dyed it." The girl was speaking about Mala. I drew closer.

"They brought her to the camp at nine in the morning and took her to the *blockführerstube*. They were to show her to everyone so that no one would doubt them any longer. They wanted to keep her until roll call and then hang her. But Mala had a razor blade and cut her wrists. One *blockführer*[148] rushed up to her and called out, "*Was machst du, Mala?*"[149] Mala hit him in the face and said, "Don't touch me you Nazi animal!" Then Oberka began to make fun of her, laughing because she had been caught. "You thought you might deceive them, the great German Reich... oh no, such a man has not turned up yet!"

"Mala was getting weaker. Blood spurted out of her wrists while Oberka stood over her and abused her. Suddenly Mala leapt up. I don't know where she got her strength—her face brightened with a happy smile and she shouted so loudly that the girls outside the *blockführerstube* could hear her, "I know I'm dying, but that's not important! The important thing is that you are dying with me. Your hours are numbered. You're dying, you hateful viper and thousands of vipers like you. Nothing can help you, nothing can save you."

Those were her last words. Oberka had a fit. The *blockführers* were shaken. One of them was supposed to have had tears in his eyes. It was the one she had struck in the face. He had liked her very much when she was a *läuferin*. He took out his revolver and finished her off and carried her body out of the *blockführerstube*, leaving Oberka there mad with rage and the puddle of blood."

"Mala was placed on a hand-cart. They called some girls from the block. They were the *läuferins*, Mala's closest friends.

---

[148] Block leader.
[149] What are you doing, Mala?

Oberka, pale with rage, walked out of the *blockführerstube's* greenhouse, the one with the pots of flowers in the windows. She pointed to the crematory, "Quick, take that filthy swine there."

"Mala's friends pulled the cart through the whole *lager*. As it creaked past in the sunny morning, her beautiful face and her striper all in blood flashed in front of our eyes last time. We stood at the windows of our huts and said farewell to her."

Chapter Six

The Greek Women

The mail arrived. There was no letter for me. This was not the first time that I was going through a period of anxiety. With sincere admiration I looked at my fellows who had no contact with anyone outside the barbed wire. Still, you were living from package to letter. My concern at that time reached such a state that I started to see my loved ones in all the *zugangs*. I imagined my sister being caught and beaten and that they were finally bringing her here. In every old woman I met in the camp I saw my mother. I'd become more sensitive, silent. My fellows suspected the cause of my mood. "You don't have any messages, but don't worry, it happened once before because of railways congestion." They comforted me as best as they could. I used to say the same to others...

Janda warned us that we could expect *zugangs*, *Transport aus Breslau*.[150] At least once a week, Wroclaw sent us a dozen women. This time, probably by mistake, the newly arrived were delivered to *lager* A, where we went to watch them. Janda went with us and with her admirer, whom we called Brüderlein. He was one of the less harmful SS men. He had changed under the influence of his love for Janda. Until recently he had entered the bath and was clowning by beating our naked backs half-jokingly, half seriously with a whip, and until recently half-jokingly, half seriously he had sent a dog after us. And then

---

[150] Transport from Wroclaw.

suddenly he began to crack jokes with Janda, and he earnestly fell in love. Janda had decided to educate him. She used various psychological tricks and Brüderlein was walking as "on a string." Once he even said to one of us, "*Sie*," which was a sign of a true internal transformation.

Brüderlein held Janda by her arm. We walked by three of fives, evenly, on a road not surrounded by barbed wire, connecting two sections of the camp. The men we met— hungry "musselmen," raised their stubbed out eyes to us. They sat along the road and beat large stones with small hammers. Others leaned, exhausted, on the shovels in freshly dug trenches. Jealous of us, walking in aprons, neatly, briskly, like on a trip. At the sight of these living skeletons shame burned you that you were healthy and not hungry.

"Let's sing," proposed Janda.

We walked further in silence. How could you sing looking at them? Janda could not feel it. She needed a background for her love and her joyous mood. Currently, the background was crematoria and the pale "musselmen," rocks, ditches and a few trees. Our singing was supposed to make it more fulfilled.

"I will sing, when Germans are pounding stones!" Nella growled. "Now, let her sing alone!"

We went by the *blockführerstube*. Hated by us *aufseherin*, Hase came out of the greenhouse with windows full of blooming geraniums.

"*Die Damen von Effektenkammer*? Well? We'll see what you have there."

She approached each of us, pawing our whole bodies. With triumph she removed from behind quiet, paltry Ania's bra a pair of stockings. She struck her.

"Where are these stockings from and for whom? For trade probably. You have too little grub, so you change it for potatoes? *Was? Du dummes Arschloch!*"[151]

[151] What? You stupid asshole!

Ania was silent. A bruise from the strike was visible on her cheek. Janda, with her back turned away was playing with the dog, pretending that she hadn't seen anything. Hase wrote down Ania's number. We went deep into the camp. Somebody from *blockführerstube* caught up with us. We were told to come back and help load some old ladies into the car. They were sitting in the ditch in front of the house with geraniums.

I went to one of the old ladies and gave her a hand. She stood up.

"Hold me carefully, my child, you do not know how tired I am. At my age, such journeys!"

I helped her get into a truck. The old woman kept saying, smiling and shaking her head:

"Such journeys, such strange journeys..."

"She is crazy," I thought. " No wonder."

My fellows also lifted up other old ladies with difficulty and helped them get into the car. The car moved off.

"Where are they going?" Joanna asked Janda with a well-mannered, polite tone.

Janda looked at her pitifully.

"Schönes Wetter haben wir heute. Nicht wahr, Joasia?"[152]

Yes, the weather was very nice indeed. Why did Janda not respond? At that moment I realized a terrible thing. I just put people on a truck going to the crematorium. I helped this nice old lady, who after all could be my mother or grandmother. I loaded her on this death car myself...

"If not me, someone else would have done it," I thought. "After all. we were ordered, we did not know what we're doing."

"Yes," answered another voice inside me. "The SS men are also ordered. They at least have the excuse that they kill enemies. And we? And me? I should have refused, even if they would have killed me. But this is why they can carry out

---

[152] Nice weather we have today. Isn't it true, Joasia?

all their plans, because no one refuses their requests. It's a lie to say that I didn't know. Yet they also say that they don't know. If I had thought about it for a moment..."

I could not put the thought to rest. I couldn't cope with it. On the other hand, the fate that befell the old woman, was it any worse than the camp torture? Wasn't it just easier to die that way?

"So this is even a humane thing," mocked a familiar voice within. "They too, explain their crimes the same way—on the grounds of humanitarian need."

"O my God! O my God!" moaned Nella, walking next to me. If a year ago someone had told me that... "

The *Lager* looked as usual: the gray, sunken faces of half-dead people dragging themselves in stripes and clogs, feeding on the kitchen trash, the happiest ones gnawing on horse bones. Barrack orderlies, *stubendienst* [153] lifting barrels with soup. Sometimes in the middle of the *lagerstrasse* an SS man with a whip gives rise to a panic. Generally it's empty. Who could still move—worked in the field? The sour smell of turnip hovered in the air.

I heard a whistle on the ramp. A train arrived with a new transport from Greece. Janda told us to go to the *zugangs'* barrack and watch the transport.

I went to a huge empty barracks, where for the first time I understood the main meaning of the word "Auschwitz." I realized how accustomed I had gotten, if I managed to come in here without a tremor. How familiar I had become with the *lager* terminology: *zugang, lagerstrasse, aufseherin, blockführerstube*. I didn't say "friend" anymore, only "*häftling*." I didn't ask, "Who are you?" but only "What's your number?" Now I knew how frightened and scared these Greek women would be. I knew how they would look, what they would ask. I knew that after several days here their glow would disappear.

[153] Office services.

The hot Thessaloniki sun would be gone and they would turn into "musselmen." They would become livid after several roll calls. Their bodies would become covered with sores, and they would die of typhus. And the rest would be gassed after the selection. I felt a sudden fear of the questions that would follow, fear of the looks of these healthy, unsuspecting women.

It happened as I predicted: beautiful, dark-eyed, tawny and slim, the Greek women looked at each new person with disquiet. They tried to tell us something by signs. One of them knew German. She was speaking to her friends. It was obvious that she thought the question rather risky. Looking at me suspiciously, she asked, "Where did those trucks take our parents?"

"Trucks?" I asked, wanting to find out how "they" arranged these things. "What happened on the ramp?"

"There were three trucks," she said quickly. "The Germans said that those who were tired might ride. We put the older ones into the trucks and they just drove away somewhere, and then they brought us here. Tell me where they've gone. You must know."

"I think they must have gone to some other place, but I don't know. I really don't know."

"Will we ever see them again?"

"I don't think you will."

The others listened tensely. The Greek girl translated our conversation. They began to sob.

Someone jerked the door open and an SS man rushed in. He looked like a movie star. He was tall and smart and he was smiling.

"*Ruhe!*" he called.

"Who's that?" I whispered to one of crew of the *zugangs'* barrack

"Mengele.[154] Don't you know him from the 'rabbit-cage?'"

[154] From June 1943 onwards, Dr. Josef Mengele was the head SS physician in Camp BIIe, the family camp for Gypsies, and later the main

So he is the one! I couldn't reconcile that face with the atrocities ascribed to him. This man was obviously cultured, decent. His face inspired confidence. Could this be the man who perpetrated those shameful experiments?

I remembered Alma Rose, one of his victims, after a few days stay there she had a nervous breakdown...and the others with grafted glands or with their spinal cords removed or those with injections of infectious disease. I stared at the monster with

Josef Mengele.

the smooth face that looked upon us all as experimental specimens. I looked long and hard so as to remember forever that a man who looked like this could be such a beast.

"Tell me please," he spoke softly and politely as if to an audience in the university auditorium. "Is there a Zenira among you?"

There was no answer.

"Please, is there someone among you who knows German?"

camp physician at Birkenau. He carried out experiments concerning the heredity of features of twins and dwarfs, as well as research into *Noma* ("water cancer"). Several hundred female Jewish prisoners were also kept in Block 10 in the main camp, Auschwitz I, mainly at the disposal of physicians Carl Clauberg and Horst Schumann, whose task was to find the best method of mass sterilization, for certain to be used in the *Endlösung* and *Generalplan Ost* programs.

Carl Clauberg.

A Greek woman, a girl with truly classical beauty approached him. She was very dark and very elegant. She was wearing a white turban on her head.

"I speak German," she said coquettishly, with the assurance of a woman conscious of her beauty speaking to a handsome man.

For a moment I thought he would introduce himself and walk out of the hut with her.

"Please help me find Lidia Zenira," he said.

The Greek girl turned to the group and translated the doctor's question.

Why in the world does he want Zenira? He must want to save her. I had heard that sometimes people were pulled out of the transports. Maybe someone who worked with him asked him for this favor. Maybe Mengele was not such a beast after all if he was so concerned about this woman.

A woman stepped out of the ranks and told him that Lidia Zenira, her friend, had come here with her, but that she got into a truck because she was tired.

"A truck?" Mengele asked with a worried frown. "*Schade!*"[155] he mumbled and ran out.

What did he want? We all wondered.

Wala came in just then.

"Ah, Wala, why didn't you let me die?" I greeted her.

[155] Too bad!

"Why did you rescue me? It was no use, you know best yourself, you still need to survive and to see so much!..."

"Do not say that, Krysia, the situation on the front is very good. 'They' are coming apart, I'm telling you!"

"Was that monster, pretty boy, here?" she asked.

"Yes. What did he want, Wala?"

"He's experimenting with twins. He was expecting the twin sister of one of his patients to arrive in this transport."

"He did not find her here. She went into a truck."

"Poor Mengele!" Wala sighed ironically. "Twins are so rare. Maybe he'll have better luck with the transports from Hungary. They are to burn about a million Hungarian Jews. I do not envy you, Krysia, being here at Birkenau. But don't worry, you have to hold on. Tell the girls that life will be hell from now on. But we are tough. We can stand the worst. A million—should that terrify us? It's so easy to say a million."

"Maybe they will not be able to finish, if you say that the front is getting close." Wala looked at me sadly.

"But in the strategic plans we are not taken into consideration. Well, Auschwitz is a little town and there are so many other camps everywhere. I laugh at these rumors about the troops landing... We think that we are the center of the world. Even if we were able to get out from behind the barbed wire, we would never be able to shake this off. The camp will leave its stigma, I'm sure.

We were coming back to Birkenau. I was thinking about the new transports. I felt an insane fear of the period which was to take place. "Run away!" went through my head. "But how, which way? Mala was caught after all."

The men on the road were still pounding stones. We turned on the path leading to the white house. Tall sweet flag was gilding in the fading daylight. The sunset looked like a big red ball, and our hearts were escaping to the fields, the meadows, the mountains, to the vast, open space. But next to us, jumping, ran a dog-wolf, next to us walked Janda.

214

With slow, tired steps, we again entered the pitfall.

* * *

After our bath, we still had a half-hour before the gates to our hut closed. In addition to the wire fences that surrounded Birkenau, there was a separate wire fence surrounding the crematories. These were not live wires. A wire fence separated the men's dormitory from the women's barracks so that there could be no secret meetings at night. At the request of our chief, they put wire screens on our windows. We were enclosed by several cordons of wire. Someone once said: "Pretty soon they'll put a wire fence around me. They'll give us wire dresses." I went toward the *Canada* barracks. I was, of course, carrying a bucket because there was a well on the *Canada* grounds. Through the open doors of the *Canada* barracks, I could see the night shift girls sorting and tying bundles. "The women's transport from Greece," I thought. "I wonder what they've brought." At the same time I realized that Wala was right, we were all become slow-witted.

In the first row of the barracks were spread out dresses, blouses, sweaters, coats; in another row were traveling bags and knapsacks; in the field under the awning were shoes, piles of shoes, women's and children's—of all sizes and all fashions—high-heeled, galoshes, wooden and leather shoes. Still further back stood baby carriages, good and broken utensils and books in various languages. The road over which the crematory trucks traveled with their booty was strewn with photographs, prayer books, and paper money. The girls in the barracks were ripping dress and coat linings in search for gold dollars and diamonds. They were happy to exchange their finds for a piece of bread.

The scattered photographs and the open prayer books were the most eloquent.

I didn't want to pick up those photographs. Why? Why look at faces that were now burning to ashes? But an unhealthy curiosity prompted me. Automatically I picked up a few of them: A happy child holding a huge watering pot over a row of flowers. A blonde little girl peering from behind a lilac bush; an older man sitting at the lab bench; a photograph of a young interesting man with a dedication written in German: "*Meiner allerliebsten Sophie—ein Erinnerung an die schönen Tage in Saloniki... Sommer 1942.*"[156] There was another of a woman on horseback, the same woman holding a violin; a family picture, someone in a bathing suit, at a ball, with a tennis racket and children, so many different children. You walked between the barracks; you walked on the *lagerstrasse*, trampling remnants of memories of these now extinguished, full of mysterious charm lives. So until recently, this woman was playing the violin, a child was watering flowers, the man worked. So until recently, and now...

The SS man on duty passed with his torch, kicking the prayer books and clothing. He looked into the barracks and trained his light on the darkness between the huts. He was looking to see whether anyone was hiding there. He came up to where the shoes were piled and turned back. I was pumping the water very slowly. Just across the street I could see the light in the men's barracks, the wire fence was glowing.

"Krysia," I heard a deep whisper in the dark.

It was Wacek. After a moment's hesitation, I leapt into the dark area between the barracks.

"I'm sorry to expose you to danger, but... but you understand don't you?"

"I understand, the moon..."

"Yes, and so many stars. And everything is forbidden. I'm getting claustrophobia. There are more transports coming. Do they want to burn the whole world, Krysia?"

Someone was approaching. We clung to the wall flattening

---

[156] My dearest Sophie—a remembrance of the beautiful days in Thessaloniki... Summer 1942.

our arms against the sides of the barracks, as if we were supporting it. The torchlight searched in our direction, and falling beyond us, slipped down and moved on.

"Bedarf is on duty tonight. You must go. Wait 'til he gets a little further," Wacek cautioned. We waited in silence. "Your heart is beating so fast. I'm sorry Krysia."

"I'm a little excited."

"Listen, I must kiss you. I must. I can't stand it any longer!" he pulled me toward him.

For one short moment I seemed to be whirling somewhere among the stars.

"Whose bucket is this?" someone shouted from the well.

"Mine."

I ran and picked up my bucket. In my hurry I spilled half the water. The gates closed behind me. I just made it. I immediately crept into bed. Basia was frightfully nervous.

"Where have you been?"

"She had a date," someone said from the upper berth. "She took the bucket."

"Good Lord, you can't do anything here without everybody knowing it!"

"Of course not," Basia answered seriously. "You should know by now. You'd better tell us everything."

"I was kissing a man."

"No!" Basia jumped up.

"Really? How? Where?"

"Does it matter, Basia? Let's sleep. There will be a transport from Hungary tomorrow. They are also still kissing there today. And tomorrow? Good night, Basia! "

"Good night, Krysia!! Life is very sad.

I lay wide awake for a long time. Through the window grill I could see a square of the starlit sky. I could hear the deep, even breathing of those asleep and the sighs of those who waited for the cover of night to give release to their sorrows. The chimney was still flickering. The Greek Jews were nearly burned.

Chapter Seven

Gypsies

The mother of the little Gypsy was sick with typhoid. They did not want to allow the boy in the barrack. The inexorable *torwache* drove the poor little Gypsy away. Entering the typhoid block was not allowed, but the boy came back every day. He pleaded with the *torwache*, danced, coaxed and whimpered, but nothing helped. On the fifth day he squeezed himself imperceptibly behind the back of the *torwache* who was hunched with cold and slipped unnoticed into the center. Guided by intuition and a strange sense of smell, he immediately found his mother among hundreds of patients. But his mother had just died that night. The little Gypsy began to beat the wall with his little fists and then howled for a long time, jerked by powerless despair. His mother was taken out of the barrack. He followed her. He sat down beside her and held her head so as not to let it lay in the mud. He sat there day and night, and more and more corpses accumulated around him. They were searching for him during roll call, he did not move. In the morning a car came from the crematorium. From the hands of the speechless little Gypsy, they tore away the corpse of his mother.

At a certain period there were as many as 20,000 Gypsies in the camp. They had their designated section behind the fence. Within two years, 14,000 had died of "natural causes," typhus, *durchfall* and other epidemics.

Unloading the next transport on the ramp at Auschwitz.

During the night of May 20th the well known "last cry" from the passing cars woke us. We wondered whom they were taking. From some trucks you could distinguish the cries: "Mama, Mama" and clear children's voices. Was this a Hungarian transport? It's probably impossible. We didn't hear the whistle of an arriving train.

During recent weeks, Jewish women from the *lager* worked on the construction of the train track leading almost to the crematoria entrance. It was obvious that they were getting ready.

Since then trains with shipments were arriving so close that you could clearly hear the voices of those newly arrived. This time, however, we hadn't heard any sound. Where are the children from? After all, there were no Jewish children living in the camp.

A moment after the cars went by we thought that perhaps we hadn't heard children's voices, that perhaps we were hallucinating.

In the morning somebody brought the news that there had been a selection in the "Gypsy *Lager*" and that several thousand went "to the gas" last night.

"They are beginning to eliminate everybody!" said Basia, voicing aloud the secret thought of everyone of us. "If the Gypsies are gassed, how can we be sure that at night they will not come for us?" After all, the authorities treated Gypsies better than us. Their families were not separated. They lived together in the *Familienlager*[157], while we were not even allowed to talk to men. Their children were not taken away like Jewish children, and suddenly...

"Next will be our turn," said Ania, scared.

"Why actually us?" I asked, trying to hide my frustration.

"First of all, because we know too much, and, also because now the *kartei-mässig zugangs* will not arrive here. Everything in the camp is switched to burning. Our role is therefore finished."

"And it seems to me that as long as there is at least one Aryan woman in the camp, whose deposits and clothing we are to protect, our role is not over."

"I am afraid they'll no longer be troubled by these deposits. They can at any time, confiscate all of them for the state. There will be even more need to empty the barracks.

It is not difficult in such circumstances to feel the fear of death. The Gypsies who died were not on our minds anymore. Our thoughts were on the imminent danger to us. What was going through my mind were all the details of the moments when they would come for us at night with machine guns, make us get out of bed, go outside dressed in our nightshirts, load us into the car and take us to the crematorium...

I was afraid to think. My heart was contracting. Desperate

[157] The camp in which whole families resided.

fear paralyzed my imagination. Each of us was looking for solace and hope in the eyes of the other in vain. We were swept up by the psychosis of death. I tried to work. I pulled out cards and checked the filing, but it all seemed meaningless. I had not received a letter or package from home in more than a month. Certainly something had happened. Living in this constant uncertainty, seeing more and more people just before their annihilation, hearing their shrill cries and finally, me— all of us—being gotten rid of in some unknown way. And all of this happening now, when I was finally looking like a human being, to die, let ourselves be led into the gas chamber. I may die today and a letter may come the next day. Tomorrow troops could land or another miracle may happen.

"Listen, Krysia," Mela said with a mysterious face. "If they come for us, we need somehow to defend ourselves!"

"What can we do? If you think so, we should act now. When they come after us, it will be too late."

"If we do something right now, such as throwing a stone at Mohl, the chief of the crematorium, when he passes, we will be annihilated immediately and then it will turn out that they did not have that intention regarding us, at least not for now, not for today!"

"That's what this whole horror is about, that people have hope until the last minute. That is why they go. And we, in spite of such experience, we do the same. Can you be surprised by those people? Everything suggests that these are our last hours. We are afraid to face the truth. We must act now!..."

"First of all Mohl is not passing through here at your request. And it is not worth the risk for just any stupid *posten*."

I decided to listen to what the men thought about that. I left the hut and very carelessly accosted someone from the "men's" to send Wacek. I felt that I was no longer in control of myself.

Wacek appeared immediately.

"What happened?" he asked seeing my unusual nervousness.

"You already know about the Gypsies. They say that they will do the same with us."

"How, who says, what are you talking about?"

"Everyone. My colleagues. The *kapo* is upset. The chief gave us such a strange look, besides that, it doesn't bother me, but I feel it myself..."

"The Gypsies were supposed to be gotten rid of for a long time. The order came from Berlin. They do not have enough food rations to feed them. The war is stalled. Camps fill up. They treat Gypsies like Jews. They have to reckoned with us, because supposedly we "share race" with them. You know, they still expect some kind of international committee, and I assure you that they will not touch us. I am surprised that you give in to such fears. It just takes one of you to utter her feelings aloud, and all of you will succumb to the idea. I beg you. Stop thinking about it.

"But perhaps we should arrange something, some kind of rebellion, maybe with you guys? What happens if they come at night?"

"Shut up!" Wacek flushed with anger. We are going to rebel at the right time. Right now it's stupidity, which would bring misery on many who could survive. We must not do anything. Remember that here there is the principle of collective responsibility. Do not worry. Tonight they will not come... And if they come... we will have enough time to act.

"And if they come for you?"

"We shall decide at the last minute. The decision will impose itself. Revolts are spontaneous. Anyway, here you won't be able to organize anything. You won't get any weapons. And so this is a goose chase. Go back to the office and take it easy. A foretaste of death accompanies us always, but now you feel it more strongly, tomorrow I will, and the Jewish woman in the hospital feels it the most, because they can come to get her any second."

Someone was coming. I ran away. I circled around two

huts and returned to the office. I repeated what Wacek said. They listened with a grain of salt.

At night we went to bathe. Each of us had subconsciously thought, "This is our last bath."

"Oh!" Czesia groaned suddenly. "Gas!"

"Gas, gas!" the others screamed.

Indeed, I felt a suffocating smell. Something creeping, elusive was reaching my throat, I became nauseated and dizzy...

"Gas!" I also screamed and rushed like crazy towards the exit.

All this took a second. To our surprise, the door opened and we were able to run out naked to the next room, and some of us during this incredible escape ran out to the court.

I calmed down. Standing next to me was Basia trembling from fear and cold. Tears flowed down her cheeks, tears of relief, tears of amazement, that the doors had opened.

We all looked at each other, crying and laughing alternately. Nella put her hand on her chest: her heart was pounding.

"What was that?" She asked.

Nobody knew.

"Look, maybe we all imagined it? One screamed, and the rest followed suggestion because of the influence of today's predictions..."

"I don't think it seemed to everyone. Although I myself wouldn't have sworn that I really felt something. Maybe there are "olfactory hallucinations." After all, if any of us would have thought about it she would realize that admitting gas to the *sauna*, where there are three glass windows, is nonsense. It would be simply enough to knock out windows..."

The next day someone from the *sauna* service said that, indeed at one point a window opened in the second crematory and a strong odor of gas appeared briefly everywhere.

That night, we were listening to the quietest sounds in the area. But the dark, silent night mysteriously kept quiet. Somewhere far away dogs were barking.

Part Three

IN FLAMES

Chapter One

Twenty Thousand a Day

First came the black limousine. We waited expectantly. Then came trucks loaded with wood. We knew this was Kramer, the chief of crematories, the same one who had stopped us when returning from the fields.

For some days now we had felt a feverish mood in the air. They were getting ready for something. All the SS-men constantly hurried, very caught up in what they were doing. All functions had been allotted—the camp was being organized for burning. Prisoners were digging ditches around the crematories. The furnaces could not handle such a large number of corpses. So, in addition, holes were being dug. We heard the unbelievable fact that they were to burn people alive.

Berlin had issued an order: Burn eight hundred thousand Hungarian Jews within a month and a half. Wala and the others from the *Politische Abteilung* had told us that immediately after receiving this order, a "devil's council" had been held in the camp. Hustek, Kramer, Mohl and the others took part in it. Putting their heads together above the table they planned how to burn eight hundred thousand human beings. Trembling with emotion, with lust for blood and drunk with the size of their responsibility. The gold and diamonds of Hungarian Jews already sparkled in their eyes. They were already envisioning furs sent in secret to their lovers.

Meanwhile, they soaked up the numbers, 20,000 a day! Words were spoken:

Jews upon arrival at Auschwitz.

"Twenty thousand a day—it's not a child's play." They patted each other on the backs. They grinned. "We will do a good job, won't we? That's not just two transports of hundreds of people a week. Here there will be no time to rest. But it's worth it. So much gold! So much food! So many bottles of real Hungarian wine! It's a night and day job, maybe a little dangerous, but what do those stupid Hungarian Jews know? New coats, dresses, clothes and shoes will again be sent to the devastated fatherland. Wise is the *Führer*, wise is the head of the Gestapo, that they came up with such great ideas. And it's so simple. Posters will be put up. The Jews themselves will register, thinking that they are coming to work... " They patted each other on their backs some more.

"Cool trap, *nicht wahr? Verfluchte Juden!*"[158]

[158] Isn't it true? Damn Jews!

* * *

"They're coming!" Czesia called as she ran swiftly through the *schreibstube*.

I looked through the window. I could see a mob of people milling around on the railway ramp. It was 11 o'clock in the morning. The whole camp was tensely waiting for the transports. Five hundred Jewish women had been brought to *Canada* from FKL (*Frauenkonzentrationslager*). They would soon be very busy. The *Sonderkommando*, composed of men selected from the camp and the SS, waited for wine and food. And the whole great Reich waited for the booty.

And they came, all unsuspectingly. At the cross roads they were separated into two groups. One group went straight toward the "little white house," along the path, past the birch forest. The other group turned right and walked towards us. They had to pass our blocks to crematory No. 3. We could distinguish only women and the children. Women in headscarves or coats, rich, poor, young and old women, peasant women from the Hungarian provinces. They hugged their children closely. Small children were carried by their mothers, older children clung to their mothers' skirts and still older children looked around with suspicion. They passed slowly. So slowly that you could see the expressions on every face. They were tired. Some looked a little uneasy, but none seemed to suspect the truth. It was evident that these people expected inconveniences. They knew they could no longer decide their own destiny, that they were in someone else's evil power. That they had to obey someone's mysterious orders. For this, however, they were prepared ever since the Nazis began to occupy their beautiful country. But what awaited them really, they had not guessed at all. Maybe some, very few people—perceived it.

We pretended to be working. Our *kapo* had warned us that our chief would look in on us when we least expected him.

A selection of Jews on the ramp at Auschwitz.

We were to act as if we did not see or hear anything.

From my seat near the window I saw everything and everybody. I looked at every face, I wanted to read the thoughts and feelings of these people. I realized that they did not know. They did not know where they were, why they came here, how long they would walk and where they would go. Nothing around raised a particular eeriness. Death is nowhere to be seen. People are working in the barracks. Along the way are the inscriptions: "Way to disinfection." Wires exist because people are billeted here. They heard about that. That's hard. After all it is a war.

Chimneys?—Simply, there is probably some factory here.

They walked in a long, unending procession. At intervals, there was a guard carrying a rifle. The women talked to each other; some were even smiling.

The procession had already reached the crematories and there was still no end in sight. Finally it disappeared. The oldest women closed the procession. Some could not walk. They had to lean on their younger companions and stopped at short intervals to rest. The *postens*, irritated at their slow pace, prodded them on with rifles. At the very end, a short distance behind the procession, walked a very old woman, probably around eighty. Her arms were spread out and she leaned heavily against the guard's rifle. She dragged her feet and her dim eyes were turned towards the sky, if asking: "God, you see it, and you are silent?."

The young, eighteen-year-old guard pushed her on impatiently. His face brightened when he noticed us. He snapped back his rifle and straightened up. The old woman sprawled on her back. The guard scratched his head, as if trying to make us laugh. His face took on a worried, clownish expression. Then he quickly seized the woman by the hand and began to drag her toward the crematory.

After a short pause came the men. They seemed more agitated than the women, but they did not suspect the truth either. There had been no selection. Young and old were going to the gas. About an hour later the chimney of the fourth crematory, which was just behind our dormitory barrack, began to gush flames. Simultaneously, smoke began to rise from the hole that had been dug near the crematory. At first a thin grey ribbon appeared then thick billows, growing heavier until they spread like a cloud veiling the sky over that part of the camp. The wind moved the cloud in our direction. The smoke covered the sun and the bright light of the day turned into frightful darkness. The smoke carried the smell of burning flesh. It was something like the smell of a burning goose, only much stronger. It choked and stupefied—my head grew heavy with it.

We sat silently holding our heads in our hands. We closed our eyes.

"Shut that window!" Nella broke the tense silence. "The smoke will kill us."

Jewish women and children after selection, on their way to the gas chambers.

Swaying on my legs, I closed the window. A few minutes of silence followed.

"Open that window," Tanya said. "I can't bear it. The smoke's getting through anyway."

I opened the window. Just then the roar of a thousand voices tore through the clouded air. It lasted from two to three minutes. We listened. It came from the direction of the "little white house."

"The end of the world has come," Ziuta moaned. She began to pray.

"That came from the ditches," Irene explained. "They're burning them alive."

The cries faded away. The orderly-room door flew open. We turned our dazed eyes in that direction. Janda looked at us

A selection of Jewish women and children going to the gas chambers.

with her penetrating, serious eyes as if to say, "I know what you feel, but that's the order and you must be silent!"

* * *

Days and months of unceasing dread followed. For several weeks every Hungarian transport went to the furnace without selection.

Later they began to select the younger women at the railway ramp. After they had been disinfected and their hair had been shaved off, they went to the empty Gypsy *lager* (BIIC[159]) where five hundred persons were packed into one

[159] In fact: BIIe.

hut. Older people and children marched to the crematories. Each day, twelve to thirteen freight trains pulled up the ramp. All the luggage and packages were unloaded there.

Large trucks brought clothing from the crematories to *Canada*. A thousand girls worked tirelessly in *Canada* day and night.

Firewood had been piled along the whole length of the road from Birkenau to the women's camp. Did they want to set all of Europe on fire?

The traffic was heavy on *Canada* Street. Loaded trucks drew up to a barrack and empty trucks returned to the crematories continuously. The girls worked feverishly sorting the still warm clothing under the constant surveillance of the *vorarbeiterins* and the shrill whistle of the *Canada kapos*, who seemed to be everywhere whistling and beating. The segregated goods were loaded on other trucks and taken to the barracks.

The girls worked through the night, in the light of the huge reflector and of the red flames from the chimneys. They worked in the smoke and soot. They moved amid the roar of trucks, the shouts of the drivers and *vorarbeiterins*, the warning gunfire of the SS guards. All through the night we could hear the whistles of the trains bringing new victims.

* * *

Throughout the camp, there was strict *lagersperre*. Frightened women sat for hours in stifling barracks, looking through the tiny windows, clearly seen what passed and the selection on the ramp.

After a long interval I got a letter from home. "My dear child," my mom wrote.

This is the third summer you're not at home, but I believe this is the last one, during which we'll not be together. At our place the acacias bloom so lovely. Basia (my sister) sewed herself a new outfit, in which she looks very nice. We miss you constantly. How are you doing?

"How am I doing? My God, how could you write back to make them even guess a little. If only you could write a single sentence: "Can you understand how a man feels in hell?"

Parcels began to arrive again. There really must have been a bottleneck at the post office because of the increased number of trains. But parcels were not essential now. Bacon was literally lying on the streets. One simply chose the right moment, when the SS guard moved away, and slipped into Barrack 13—*Fressenbaracke*[160], the food-hut. With the help of the Jewish men working there, one could pack one's case with fats, sugar, cereals, noodles, and various spices for soups. It was more difficult to obtain canned foods. You had to know someone well. The boys *organized* canned foods and gave them to their dear ones.

We were not hungry now, and nobody was thinking about food. The camp menu, however, had not changed. Everybody still got the same ration of bread, margarine and turnips.

We could not smuggle anything into the *lager* because the guards had been doubled and we could not find an excuse for going there. The usual *zugangs* came very rarely. We wondered, where they now sent people from the usually overcrowded prisons.

We wondered where the Aryan transports were going from Pawiak or from the Montelupi prison in Cracow or the Brygide prison in Lvov.

* * *

[160] Food barrack (literally: grub barrack), taken from the Jews brought to Auschwitz for extermination.

One day we were called to the *zugangs*. They must have been brought here by mistake. Probably some prison had not been notified that no transports were to be sent to Auschwitz. In spite of the *lagersperre*, we entered the camp by the death trail. A train pulled up as we crossed the camp gates. Our chief pulled at his moustache. We marched smartly in columns of five stepping on strewn objects that had been lost or abandoned by the condemned. We walked over satchels, coats, hats, handkerchiefs, prayer books, paper money, photographs and all kinds of papers.

Logs of wood stacked up along the road presaged more transports. The *Räumungskommando*[161] was bustling along the tracks. Men from the evacuation squad, with large crosses painted on their backs, were clearing the cattle cars. They threw out suitcases, parcels and empty baby carriages.

The transport stood in front of the "little white house." The SS uniforms stood out brightly against the dark silent mass of human beings. All the SS wore white gloves. Hössler was directing the people with his cane. The Jews were divided into two groups. At times I could see the despairing gesture of a hand as a mother was separated from her daughter. Hössler himself was separating the struggling women who did not want to part from each other.

The older people and the children moved toward us. I noticed guards with pointed machine guns standing in the ditches on both sides of the road. We entered the empty *lager*. The only people moving about were the *torwaches* with chamber pots and *stubendiensts* with barrels of soup. A *lagerkapo* suddenly appeared carrying her whip. A block-senior or an *aufseherin* accompanied by a dog patrolled the crowded, rotting huts. The *lager* was not important now. Abandoned to itself, it rotted in the stench of moldy turnips and odorous chamber pots. Lousy *musselmen* sat on their bunks in complete, passive

[161] Cleaning unit.

hopelessness. Sometimes one of them would start at a sound. She would then lift her wretched face and look around with a dazed, uneasy glance. Sometimes one cursed loudly, "Dirty rotten life. Damn it, will it ever end?"

They would become a little livelier whenever one of us from the *Effektenkammer* appeared. They knew we were near a radio and we had more freedom of movement.

"Is it true that they are near? Is it true that there's an offensive not far from here? Is it true that our boys are organized—that they are planning something?"

"Of course it's true," we answered without hesitation. "It won't be long now and the boys are ready. Something may happen any minute now. Just be patient a little longer." Sometimes we managed to get a fleeting smile, a brief serene gaze, a flash of hope in a tortured face.

We went to the *sauna* room. There were a few *zugangs* there. One of the girls was so ragged that she drew everyone's attention. Her dress was torn. In her blue eyes lurked fear, distrust and contempt. Her interesting and intelligent face aroused interest.

"Polish?" I asked.

She shuddered, as if pierced by the shock, looking at me suspiciously.

"Don't worry, I'm also a Pole. Here you don't have to worry. Nothing worse will happen to you. Why did they send you here?

She was silent.

"Don't be stupid, speak up. Maybe I can help you with something. You can't talk?

She shook her head violently, denying her own pertinacious thoughts.

I shrugged and went to the others. But I was strangely shocked by the encounter with that girl. I knew she had to be treated terribly recently, and that now she was experiencing something tragically tormenting.

After a few moments I forgot about her. Suddenly someone touched my shoulder. It was she. She stood still shaking her head. She talked in a low choking voice.

"Nothing will help me right now, nothing will help me right now. People are despicable, so despicable! Why did it bother them that I was alive? I did nothing wrong. I was working at the factory. And someone said... "

She stopped suddenly.

"What did someone say?"

She looked at me suspiciously again.

"Why do I tell you this? What do you care? There are a lot of others like me here..."

"You're wrong. There are not a lot like you. Anyway, I accosted you myself."

"It goes like this. First, they shot my father, mother and brother in Lviv. I was there. I ran away, I don't know how. I boarded the train. I wandered through various cities. Finally, I got a job at the factory. I said that I lost my papers. I was constantly scared. That terrible night always came back. I often cried. They guessed that I was Jewish. And one of the girls reported me. Again, I am not sure why did they not kill me right away. Why have they sent me here?

She did not want to undress. She defended herself. She was running away. Finally she took off her dress. Her whole body was bruised. Distinguished were the dark stripes from the rubber truncheons.

Two *aufseherins* passed through the *sauna*. They began to laugh heartily by pointing out the beaten girl. She was so colorful, like a rainbow. The girl made an impression as if she wanted to throw herself at them. "Don't worry," I explained to her. "If they didn't kill you there, try to live. Do not be so sensitive." I gave her bread. She did not want to take it. She stammered:

"Too late, too late, you're good to me. I will not live any longer. There is enough. And why should I live, for whom?

I have no family. I have no friends. I have no homeland."

"What are you saying? You do not have a homeland? Your homeland is Poland. People like you. Many of you will be needed."

"Oh no! There will always be more of those who will say, "What right did she have to survive? After all, she is a Jew." "

"You are talking nonsense. After the war it won't matter whether you are Jewish. Everybody hates the Nazis. Everybody will curse these racial theories."

"You yourself know that this is not true, you just say so. Ninety percent of the intelligentsia always says, 'A Jew remains a Jew!' "

I remembered one of the prisoners, who the day before, looking at the nightmarish death march, said, "Listen, Krysia, these methods are terrible, but anyhow, the Jewish issue in Poland will be resolved. And it is paradoxical, but the solution to this problem we will owe to Hitler."

After this statement, the same girl had tears in her eyes at the sight of a nice Jewish child, and she was the one endangering her own life by giving water to an older Jewish woman...

"Listen," I say with conviction. "This is how it is today, but it will not be the same in the future. Anti-Semitism is a matter of education. In the future Poland there will be different views, fighting the current nationalism. People are not bad, but they often surrender to false propaganda. And after the war there will be not false propaganda. There is hardly a man who did not suffer, and yet, Hitler is our common enemy...

"If you really think so, you're one in a thousand. But I do not trust anyone. And besides all this talk is ridiculous, and so I do not believe that anyone will get out of here."

After a few days I learned by accident that the Jewish woman from the last transport had gone to the wires.

* * *

Photo of the gas chamber and crematorium II, 1943.

On our way back we heard the last cry from crematory No. 2. Our chief was with us. We marched again over the death trail in even columns of five, with our lips set tight. People who had been selected on the ramp stood on the road. Unsuspecting men waited their turn in the birch wood. They were eating rolls and hard-boiled eggs. The eggshells reminded me of picnics in the country, an excursion from a previous life. With difficulty I restrained myself from calling out to them, "How can you eat your eggs? Can't you hear the cries? Don't you see the fire? Don't you sense the smell of corpses from the gas chambers?"

But they saw only the trees, the sun and the cloudless sky. They did not understand their fault, for which they must die. They did not understand that they were not allowed to be born Jews. They could not understand that this was the sole reason for them to be choking with gas in a moment from now.

The guards showed the muzzles of their machine guns above the ditch. The men in the woods trembled. Their troubled eyes sought an explanation. A man knelt and leaned his head against a tree. He was praying.

We turned to the right toward our gates. The transport went straight to the "little white house." A little blond girl picked a flower. Our chief became furious. How could she destroy flowers! How could she spoil the grass! She had the whole road to walk on. A cultured, civilized German could not stand the sight of such destruction. He ran up to the child who could not have been more than four years old and kicked her. The child tumbled and fell on the grass. She did not cry, she only clutched at the flower stem—the flower was gone. She stared at the SS man with wide-eyed surprise. Her mother lifted the child and went with the others. The child turned her head and continued to look at our chief over her mother's shoulder.

"The eyes of that child condemned the whole German nation," Tanya said hatefully, walking next to me." What a monster, to kick a child who will die in five minutes."

The others were silent. I could not look at the chief. The sight of this *kulturträger*[162] the loathsome amphibian who

[162] *Culture carier*; German doctrinaires, with the mission of bringing culture to the lower races, living on the outskirts of the civilized world, tried to cover (especially for the use in the German domestic propaganda—the world since 1933 pretty much knew about the German "chivalry" and methods of *Kulturkampf* (culture fight) and would learn fully after the war) expansive, possessive, and extermination political plans of Germany, which reached its apogee in the two scientifically precise, outrageous concepts: the first is *Endlösung* (final solution to the "Jewish problem")—having the objective of "Europe liberation from the Jews" by their physical elimination by industrial means (especially in the extermination camps)—as a result of its implementation, about 5 million Jews were killed, the second: *Generalplan Ost* (General Plan East)—meticulously detailed, calculated for decades, and with many stages "behind the Ural Mountains" deportation plan and the gradual destruction of the Slavs. During the war it's initial implementation began—such as mass action displacement and abduction of children with (useful race),

SS Reichsführer Heinrich Himmler's visit to Auschwitz-Birkenau.

walked beside us and was so pleased with himself, who was supposedly a human-being, filled me with horrible disgust.

from the Zamosc region in 1942-43. Here, the term *kulturträger* has meaning for which the Germans worked throughout the war—mercilessly mocking.

Chapter Two

Canada

The summer is too warm and too beautiful. It gives rise to so many memories, so many longings.

Sometimes in the most unexpected moment you suddenly recall a river, a boat, a walk under the moon. Everything is so far away, painful, oddly unreal.

In the evening we would sit on the bench in front of our hut and watch the commotion on the street of *Canada*. Just across from our hut the men sat on their steps and played all kinds of instruments. The *hauptscharführer*[163] had organized this orchestra.

Trucks drove up the *Canada* streets at frequent intervals. We could see the red headscarves of the girls working the night shift as they wandered around, with an SS man scattered here and there whom we already knew so well by sight and stories.

The "Blind Man," an SS man with a glass eye, notorious for his beatings and cruelty to the Jews, could be easily identified. Then there was lame Wensch, a hardened Nazi who unfortunately had fallen in love with a Jewish girl from *Canada*. He became the butt of jokes and jeers, and poor Hindzia, the victim of his love, did not know what to do with the feeling she had aroused in him. The elegant

---

[163] Head/Chief Squad Leader; a non-commissioned officer of the SS, the equivalent of a master sergeant.

Slovakian guard was there. He used to sleep until one in the afternoon and was frightfully bored here. And of course we could immediately spot *"Wiener Schnitzel"*[164], a hopeless idiot from Vienna who secretly accosted all the girls behind the *hauptscharführer's back*. Unless aggravated, he was harmless. Bedarf, "Weakling," and Wagner had just been called up to the front. That is why the boys played such jaunty tunes that night. Finally came the SS *hauptscharführer*, the ruler of Birkenau and chief of *Canada*. Beside him walked the *Canada kapo*, a Slovak Jew, Mancy. They were engaged in a friendly conversation.

The drone of trucks sounded endlessly, pillars of fire streamed into the sky and the men in stripes played melodies from the past to the great satisfaction of the SS men.

"Komm zurück"[165], *"Wiener Schnitzel"* hummed with the orchestra, *"Ich warte auf dich."*[166]

The *kapo*, in her zeal to please the SS *hauptscharführer*, shouted and slapped some innocent girl. We could hear the frightened girl sobbing and see her run between the barracks as the orchestra played on.

> *Tell me that you love me.*
> *My heart leaps at your words.*

Lagerruhe! The gates are closed. Some of the *Canada* girls who worked the day shift came to us with the treasures they had smuggled into our hut that day. Our orders had been met. They sold their loot for an apple, or a cake. There was enough bread for all at this time. Some brought us gifts. "We just couldn't let them take it," they said. After we had received our new things we held a fashion show. The Hungarian Jews had brought beautiful lingerie. Each one of us had a silk nightgown reaching

---

[164] Viennese Schnitzel.
[165] Come back.
[166] I wait for you.

Hungarian Jews undergoing selection at the Auschwitz railroad ramp.

to the ground. I didn't launder anything now. After one or two wears I would either throw the nightgown away or smuggle it to the hospital. We put out the lights after the fashion show.

Silence takes over the barracks. I begin to whisper to Basia about our stupor, about our lack of sensitivity to everything around. Who are we, that we can in the face of these atrocities try on dresses, shirts? We don't know how to feel any more. Often, it seems to me that something in me has died forever. I can not worry nor I can truly enjoy anything...

Natasha would return from the SS kitchen about 11 o'clock at night. She cooked for the rulers of Birkenau. Natasha was Russian and exceptionally beautiful, and in spite of her work she did not allow anyone to fool around with her. The SS men would often laugh at her.

"Well, Natasha! Where is your army? They were supposed to be here a long time ago. What do you say, you little Bolshevik?"

"The soup is excellent today," she would answer with an ironical gleam in her eyes.

They were annoyed. They knew that she hated them, that she was not impressed and that she was proud of her powerful country that was conquering the masters of the world[167]. Natasha did not have to worry about Moscow and the victory of the Soviet Union. And they, though they tried to catch her in corners and touch her, though they laughed at her, they did worry about the Third Reich.

I awoke when Natasha came in that night.

'What did they say?" I asked.

Natasha began to laugh. Her dark eyes shone, her blond hair gleamed in the moonlight.

"Stop laughing Natasha. Tell me what they said."

"I can't! They got drunk and do you know that they have a plan? They planned what each one would do when our army comes. They began to talk when they got drunk. They said that Bedarf will be a valet because he polishes boots so well and our chief, Oh—I can't!" Natasha burst into peels

---

[167] This, as well as a number of subsequent such "inlays," is either post-1945 communist censorship, (added as propaganda to build "eternal friendship" between the Soviet Union and Poland), or the effect of the author's so-called "internal censor," the result of "friendly" suggestions. The author could add inserts for the purpose of "improving" the book (in their eyes) doctrinally. It is significant that 85% of all "interventions" in the book occur in less than 10% of the text. These "added propaganda inserts" were done to obtain the stamp of "ideologically proper." This distinction gave the book the highest editorial priority, generally associated with fast print, high circulation and often with the decision to print it at all. We will never know who decided on the final shape of the "inlays", because the original *I Survived Auschwitz* manuscript has been lost. The nature of the changes and the evolution of the text in the available editions, however, are self explanatory. Due to these interventions, the book has become a double witness—also unintentionally, to the two, most dreadful twentieth-century totalitarianisms.

Canada—sorting things after the admission of a transport.

of laughter. "They said that the old guy would fall out in the first selection because he's so skinny. Then they broke the windows as usual. The Blind Man aimed a bottle at the light and instead hit Wagner. Wagner got a huge bump. This was his farewell supper because he's leaving for the front. He's as mad as a hornet. He said to me. "Well Natasha, I'm going to fight your army," and I answered, 'I wish you well!' then I ran fast."

"Oh, Natasha, you'll get into trouble. You can't joke with them. How did it all end?"

"They called Bolek from the *Effektenkammer* and told him to play for them on the accordion. He's still playing and they're breaking things. They broke all the plates. I must go to *Canada* tomorrow and organize some new ones. Same thing every night."

And Natasha, laughing, went to sleep. Basia mumbled in her sleep: "Give me that flower, girl. I will put it on your grave." In the quiet of the evening the sounds of the accordion and plates being destroyed reached us from the SS men's kitchen.

"I dreamed of my home," said Zosia, awakened by the cry of an orderly. "*Aufstehen!*"

"So what about home?"

"My Stasio was so big. I walked into our garden. He didn't recognize me."

We dressed quickly. The day was already precisely allocated with a specified number of minutes for dressing, for making the bed including, "tucking in the edges." It was very difficult not to hit the person from the bottom "floor" and not to be struck by Joanna making the upper bed. Usually two were waiting, and four were making the bed, because there was no way for all six to fit there at the same time. And every day somebody else told her dream. An interpretation followed. A dream about shoes meant home; long hair—a long journey; teeth—a disease, and thousands of different variations. With blood or without blood, boots or shoes, everything had meaning and there was not a single one who doubted the validity of the explanation.

"And what does it mean when you dream about home?" asked Zosia.

"It means, it's close," responded someone in a confident tone of voice.

"The edge of my bed is best today," said Basia admiring her bed. "And yours," she looked critically at mine. "Lord have mercy. If Oberka comes, you are a goner."

We left the hut. The night shift from *Canada* marched in fives to the block. They sang with a loud sonorous voice:

> *Still higher and higher and higher*
> *we mark our soaring flight.*

"It's true," Basia joked. "They are getting higher and closer... to heaven..."

The girls from the day shift stood in fives at the morning roll call. The *blockälteste* together with the *schreiberin* are counting the rows. The sun rose behind the barbed wire. It was going to be a nice day again.

We got out through the gate and passing *Canada's* living barrack we turned left into the office. Ahead of us, on the way to the white house, the transports were going to the gas. Women and children were picking flowers in a long, never ending line.

* * *

The mail arrived from the city of Oswiecim. A young man in stripes jumped out and an SS man came out of the driver's seat and walked into our chief's office.

"*Effektenkammer Kommando?*" the prisoner asked in a loud voice and added in a whisper. "Please get Krystyna Zywulska. I have a letter for her. I must see her. Only quickly because we are leaving immediately."

"I am Krystyna.'

"You?" He was surprised. "I didn't imagine you just this way. I don't know why. What shall I tell Andrzej?"

"Tell him that I am well, that the scabies have disappeared and that I don't believe I shall see him again. Where do you work?"

"In the parcel room. Look at that truck. That's for gassing people. I hate to get into it. We're using it for distributing parcels. It's constructed like a box with an opening in the roof. There are some strange contraptions underneath—twisted pipes and everything[168]".

[168] Cars adapted for the purposes of gas chambers (*Sonderwagen—Special cars*) were never used in Auschwitz. Elsewhere however, for

Then he gave me the message from Andrzej. Andrzej wrote:

Poor Krysia, I know what is happening at your place. We also smell the corpses. Don't break down. The situation on the front is very good. You can guess that from their communiqués. The offensive in the East is in full swing. I have not written for so long because I did not have a messenger. I asked him to take a good look at you. Please send me one of your poems. We have nothing to read. The evenings are unbearable, and the summer is so beautiful. It is so hard at times. So many thoughts pass through my head. I don't know what to do with the unexpended energy that I have accumulated. Write to me. The only bright moment in my life is when I unfold your little card. I must seem very silly because I scarcely know you. But please do not disillusion me. I must believe that you are what I think you are.

* * *

The *Sonderkommando* was coming.

There seemed to be fewer "death processions" that day, a short break. All day long the men from the *Sonderkommando* hauled logs. Wild-eyed men covered with soot and dust, their faces hidden by scraggy beards, their eyes downcast. They dragged heavy hazel branches whose leaves swept the road and raised clouds of dust. The men seemed to be surrounded by the very shadows of hell. They had to stop under our windows for awhile.

We had made up our minds that the men of the *Sonderkommando* must be monsters. Otherwise they would

example in Kulmhof (Chelmno on the Ner), people were killed by means of exhaust fumes, in cars especially constructed for the purpose.

250

not work there. I felt contempt toward them, particularly for one of them who seemed quite intelligent. I could not understand how he could burn human corpses. The guy from the *Sonderkommando* straightened up under my gaze and looked back with a challenging glance.

"Why are you staring at me? What don't you like about me? Is it my beard or the cut of my hair?"

"Your work," I answered contemptuously.

He came closer and began to explain. He was nervous, excited, speaking as if each word could decide his life or death. I was terrified at this reaction to one glance.

"Do you think that I pushed myself? Don't you know that 'they' give the orders? Even though we are very hungry, we still hide during these hellish roll calls. But they found me and pulled me out. What could I do? I could have gone on the wires—you can always do that. Few did. They couldn't deal with that anymore. I want to survive. What if the miracle we're all waiting for happens? Maybe we'll be liberated today or tomorrow. Then I'll have my revenge. Then I'll tell the world what has been going on here—there... inside."

He looked around to see whether anyone was listening and added bitterly: "And the work—well, if you don't go mad the first day, then you get used to it. Do you think that the people working in ammunition factories are doing honorable work?

"Or those in *Canada* who sort and send out all those things to 'them'? We're all under orders, and we're all working for 'them'. Only our work is more unpleasant. I don't want to live for the sake of living. I have no one. They gassed my whole family. I just want revenge."

"Why don't you rebel against them?" I asked. "Why don't you oppose them?"

"Why don't you? Is it only because you work in an office? There are sixty of you. And those thousands who are rotting in the camp, why aren't they rebelling? You know well enough

Canada—sorting belongings looted after a transport's admission.

that at any sign of a revolt they will shoot all of us. And when you try to organize, some snake will always report you for a piece of bread, to show his zeal or God knows why. There are squealers everywhere. Otherwise you wouldn't be here. What do they know? And do you know how many rebelled and went there?"

He pointed up with his finger.

"You think that the *Sonderkommando* are awful people. I assure you that they are like other people everywhere, only much more unhappy."

He pulled his branch and without looking back joined the long column of men that has already moved forward.

"Well, you see," said Irena. "Never judge without knowing the truth. What are they supposed to do?.. Can you tell him with a clear conscience, 'Kill yourself', or 'Kill them'? He'll tell you the same thing. Why do you sit here and stare quietly, just because they have not came for you yet? And how many of our colleagues were killed and how many have they murdered? How many people live—for instance from your transport? And we do nothing... we are also waiting for a miracle... like those from the *Sonderkommando*. Why, then, do we pretend that we are better?"

"You are always afraid to evaluate yourself," Nella speaks slowly and thoughtfully. "You will mindlessly repeat what is the most comfortable for you. And the most convenient way is to always put yourself in a better light at the expense of others."

I remained silent. I was shocked. So those guys over there in the crematorium—they feel, they reflect, they are emotional?

Branches disappear within the fourth crematorium. They serve to mask, they are weaved

densely into barbed wire surrounding the area of the crematorium.

"Idiots," Nella spat through her teeth, "Building up a screen as if no one knew what is happening there."

* * *

The door opened and Danka, the typist, poked her head into our office.

"Listen, is the chief in? I couldn't keep it until evening. I simply must tell you now." We surrounded her immediately. Her face took on a dour, official expression.

"It may worry you," she announced with dignity, "But no letters are to be written to Lvov, Vilno, Bialystok and Brzesc." What wonderful news! We lifted Danka in the air.

I decided that I would listen to the *Wehrmacht* communiqué, come what may. It was almost 3 o'clock. I peered through the crack into the chief's office. The orderly-room was empty. Janda was not there either. Basia and Nella were posted as *torwaches* to watch for the approach of an enemy. Irene stood on guard at the other door to the hut. The *kapo*, fortunately, was out of the office. I turned the knob. Then I turned the indicator. My heart was beating fast—music, Tyrolean songs, and suddenly:

Vnyimanyie, govoryit Moskva. Pyieryedayom poslyednyie izvyestyia... Nashi voyska atagnalyi Nyemcev. Lvov, stolyitza Zapadnoy Ukrayiny, osvoboshdyien.[169]

"The chief! Be careful."

Basia pulls the door. I turned off the radio. I had hardly taken my seat at my desk when the hut door opened. I ran to Zosia. I wanted to share my news with everyone. Wacek came to Zosia's barrack. I told him what I had just heard from Moscow. He confirmed my news. The boys had also listened. Our happiness filled the gloomy hut with a new brightness.

* * *

Our dormitory was bursting with activity. Buying and selling, a fashion show and distributing the supper rations. The bustle started with our return from work. The empty hut, cleansed every day by two block-seniors who had to sweep out all corners, was filled with the noise of new arrivals. French, Hungarian, Slovakian, Polish, Jewish women arrived with their goods. Well they could not stare at the flaming chimneys the whole time. They had to eat and talk. They had to kill the pain.

[169] (Russian) Attention, Moscow speaks. We give the latest news... Our troops pushed back the Germans. Lviv, the capital of Western Ukraine, is liberated. See footnote 167 (p. 246). The emphasis on the Ukrainian capital city of Lviv in a book addressed to Polish readers who often frequented Lviv, the third largest city of the II Polish Republic and which six years earlier was a throughly Polish city and which had been regained for Poland in 1918 with great sacrifice by the Polish people, has very specific, culturally distinctive connotations.

And there were those who lay on their bunks on the other side of the corridor. They were drawn by memories of their home—memories of their lost, distant childhoods, the short excerpt from a life in which they were human beings. They collected what remained in their memories stubbornly. The colorful, iridescent neons of Warsaw from the days when you could still walk freely on Marszalkowska Street[170], when there was no stinking ghetto behind the walls.

Jewish women from France sang lively street songs. The melodies cut through the gloomy, crowded bunks and for a moment we felt the happy, free smell of Paris. A Hungarian Jewish girl huddled in the darkest corner of her bunk and clung to a rumpled photograph that she had found accidentally when unpacking a suitcase taken from that day's transport. It was a photograph of her mother. She was sobbing and kissing the photograph. The girl was oblivious to everything about her. She caressed the photograph and whispered to it, and her mother was at that moment burning in a nearby crematory.

Sabinka, a Jewish girl from Poland, was showing Irene a sea-green angora sweater. Irene tried the sweater over her nightgown. Sabinka cried, "It's beautiful on you. You should have it. I'd hate to let them get it."

"What do you want for it?" Irene asked.

Sabinka was confused. "You can give me something, something from a parcel. We don't get parcels you know. It must be very pleasant, a parcel from home. We don't have a home, not any of us."

"Good. I'll give you something."

Irene decided to sleep in the angora sweater although the night was very warm. She stretched out like a queen, and closed her eyes in order to cut herself off from reality.

Sabinka did not move. The sweater was just an excuse. She wanted to talk about Warsaw with us. She wanted to get

---

[170] Literally, *Marshall Street*. One of Warsaw's major thoroughfares.

away from the Hungarian wailing and the French jabber. She wanted to hear someone say that trolley No. 9 went through the Avenue. She wanted to hear that she might still return there. She looked pleadingly at Irene.

"Is there any news?"

"Yes. Lviv is liberated. They're very near."

"Really? Please Irene, tell me the truth, do you think they will gas us... before... that they will do it...What do you think?"

"We all have an equal chance," Irene answered with conviction. "I don't think they'll have enough time. They'll run in confusion."

"If I could only believe that!" Sabinka sighed.

* * *

"*Zugangs! Zugangs!* Put your clothes on!" Our *kapo*, still somewhat disheveled, burst in from the *volksdeutsch* quarters. "Quickly! Tend to the *zugangs*."

"Where are they?"

"In the Gypsy *lager*. Put your clothes on."

We were ready in one minute. There had not been any normal *zugangs* for a long time. Maria told us that we must register them immediately because they could not remain in the *sauna*. They must make room for the Jewish women from Hungary.

Our chief joined us at the office. The night was very dark. The Gypsy *lager* was in the same direction as the FKL, the women's camp. We had to take the death trail. The *posten*-boxes, so-called "swallows," which stood high above the fence, were bright with lights. Every step took us deeper into the fiery abyss, full of tongues of fire, ominous hissing, evil whispers.

The burning had reached a peak that night. Every chimney was disgorging flames. They were shooting like a fiery volcano in various directions of the dark blue sky.

The crematoria's furnaces at Birkenau.

Smoke burst from the holes and ditches, swirling, swaying and coiling above our heads. Sparks and cinders blinded us. Through the screened fence of the second crematory we could see figures with pitchforks moving against the backgrounds of flames. They were men from the *Sonderkommando* turning the corpses in the pits and pouring a special liquid so that they would burn better. A rancid smell of scorched flesh choked us. Big trucks passed us trailing a smell of corpses. Somewhere from the direction of the "little white house," we were pursued by moans and cries. Together with the flash of reflectors and flames they rose in a frightful, incomprehensible sorrow.

My head was throbbing. My hair was bristling from fear and tension. I felt, as if at any moment the earth would open and swallow us with this hell. Something shocking has to happen. It is impossible to get through this and then move on. Talk, smile... no, this is nonsense...

"Watch out! A corpse." Basia seized me by the hand.

She jumped over something big and black. I turned around and saw a bloated, partly burnt woman's corpse. It must have fallen out of a truck. A little further on we came across a hand. The trucks were supplying corpses to the crematories. There must have been too many in the fourth crematory and the third one must have notified them that they were out of corpses. Cars were bringing a new load.

Basia looked at me with dazed eyes.

"Krysia, I'm so afraid I'm going mad. Everything is getting all mixed up. I feel as if my brain were floating."

"Control yourself—it won't last long. Come on, you'll forget about it!" I answered although I myself was completely dazed.

A train pulled up the ramp and threw out a new load. Thousands of dogs were barking at the arrivals, the majority of whom most probably had gone insane from the accumulation of new experiences.

We entered the Gypsy camp. Suddenly we heard a powerful voice calling from above as if from heaven, calling in German:

"Listen everybody! You're going to your death! They will kill all of you!"

We were struck dumb. I looked up. Just then a few shots were fired somewhere near us. We fell to the ground.

I realized who had called. It was the *posten* in his sentry box. He had broken down. He had stood alone for many nights and looked down from his loft. Surrounded by smoke, surrounded by this unceasing horror, his mind and his emotions could not encompass these deeds. He could not find a place for himself in all this. He had to shout.

After registering the new arrivals, we returned the same way to Birkenau. There were lights in the SS barrack. Drunken SS guards were breaking plates to the accompaniment of an accordion. "*Wiener Schnitzel*" opened a window. The music floated out on the sleeping barracks. He sighed in a hoarse, drunken, unsteady voice:

"Eine schöne Nacht haben wir heute, nich wahr? Schön ist das Leben!..."[171]

* * *

The nightmare continued. The plan was carried out. It had to be because the Red Army was approaching Hungary. Everybody had to be burned and Budapest had not been touched yet. Thirteen trains unloaded at the ramp during one day. After the selection, twenty thousand went to their death by fire. The death procession passed all day long. They went along all the roads to all the crematories. There was always Kramer in his limousine, the Red Cross car distributing cans of gas, the *Sonderkommando* dragging wood, and they, the victims. They attended their own funeral.

Behind came the lucky who were "to live." Everything moved smoothly, as in a modern factory. Old people and children disappeared in the crematories. Loaded trucks moved from the crematories to *Canada*. The lucky women entered the *sauna* from one side, elegant, sun-tanned, charming, with beautifully curled hair; they went out on the other side, barefoot in colored shapeless dresses with crosses painted on their backs. They set them up in fives and suddenly it turned out that they all had the same face. The lean ones, as if to spite, drowned in the wide, gowns that reached the floor, and the gowns just covered the knees of the stout ones. Through the holes and tears stuck out bare arms or backs. They were standing like this for hours in front of the *sauna* waiting until they would reach the appropriate number in order to move into the designated section.

Their clothes were loaded on handcarts and men from the *sauna* pulled the carts to *Canada* where the clothes were unloaded, sorted, tied into bundles and packed. When the barracks were filled, trucks pulled up and took away the wealth to the unconquered Third Reich.

It was some kind of fantastically organized looting of

[171] Today we have a beautiful night, isn't it true? Life is beautiful!

everything that might be in any way be useful to support a powerful war machine. Plunder of gold, diamonds, clothing, dishes, shoes, furs, suitcases, pillage of human labor to the last breath, pillage of teeth, hair, looting of the entire human body.

Those who are left alive were used to perform unpaid work in the factories of ammunition, for cleaning up debris, building roads and railways. They were given food once a day, just so they could still be useful and to prevent them from dying. They took from them everything they owned, and their property was to be organized and sent to dry the tears of the Reich. The daughters of parents who had been burned, had to clean, wash and iron their belongings and deliver them to the German shops. Furniture, carpets, paintings were robbed on the spot and exported from the ghettos of all the cities in Europe.

Sometime later I had the opportunity to talk with someone from the *Sonderkommando*. They explained exactly how it all happened inside. For example, how after the gassing the barber begins his work. How he shaves the hair off the corpses. How, if you put all of hair together it weighs tons. A dentist from the *Sonderkommando* looks in all of the mouths and pulls out the gold teeth. The hair apparently is used to make marine rope, and the human bodies are used to make soap[172]. Nothing is to be wasted. Nazi[173] Germany is a big, economical, thrifty nation.

---

[172] On the basis of currently available sources, it was not found that soap from human fat was produced in Auschwitz. At the time this book was written, that opinion was universal.

[173] The word *Nazi* was added (probably by censors) in the third edition of this book, during the height of Stalinism in 1951 in connection with the creation of the "new democratic" Germany. The old Germany had to be defined accordingly to avoid embarrassing, "ideologically unfair" mistakes. The effect is opposite to what was intended. Nobody in their right state of mind, in the midst of the hell of Auschwitz, had to take the trouble to specify that it was "Nazi" Germany as opposed to any other Germany. There were no other Germanys at that time. Of course, this immediately begs a question: Could the difference between one and the other be so subtle that you might be misled? How revealing. (See footnotes 167 and 226-229.)

* * *

Quite unexpectedly, some *abgangs* arrived in the dressing room. Only black *winkels*, of course. They stood in the corridor not believing their luck.

I noticed a particularly attractive woman. She had a *winkel* with the letter "*E*" (*erziehungshäftling*)—a Pole. I succeeded in getting her alone and asked her whether she would be willing to take a letter with information about the camp and a few poems. I warned her that should the letter be found, she would die for it.

"I'll take it," she said without hesitation. "I'm in the resistance and I consider this a command."

"Then why are they letting you go?"

She smiled slyly.

"Because I'm here for smuggling. I know what I can expect, but someone must take it. I know that very few decent people leave this place."

I squeezed her hand. We decided that should she succeed, my family would send me three hard-boiled eggs in a parcel. She should try to get the letter to its destination as swiftly as possible. If, however, there was no safe opportunity, then she would wait. The letter would be sewn inside her suspender belt. It seemed very important to me to send out a message now. I was sure that no one would ever leave this place. Swiftly, I set down the number of the victims gassed, details on the construction of the crematories. Little Ada from the sewing room sewed the letter inside the belt.

That evening, when passing the men's barrack, I heard music and a woman's voice rising above the men's voices. I stopped and looked through a crack. Wurm, the chief of the men's *Effektenkammer*—formerly a ticket collector in a Viennese cinema—was looking at something with satisfaction. He was beating time to the music. I slipped quietly to another crack. At first I could only see a woman's foot in a long red boot, then appeared the full figure of the dancer. She could not have been more than seventeen years old. She wore a short, full skirt lined with fur, probably a skating skirt, and a transparent blouse. Her movements were supple. She danced with great charm, lifting her skirt and clicking her heels to the complicated rhythm of the *chardash*. Deeper in the room stood Rolf, a *reichsdeutsch* prisoner. He was looking at Wurm with an understanding smile. I looked through another crack. There I saw Herbert, a prisoner from Italy, and Bedarf. They were talking. A sad and very slim Hungarian Jew was playing on the accordion. The dancer was pirouetting on one foot, the other foot raised high. She was snapping her fingers in imitation of castanets.

A party behind the scenes with select *häftlings*. They were united by the black magic of gold. These prisoners *organized* the gold with the knowledge of the SS men. In return they asked for dancers from the Jewish barracks and absolute discretion. Rolf was Jewish by descent. Everybody knew that. But here he wore a *reichsdeutsch winkel* and so he was covered.

Herbert had spent eight years in all kinds of prisons and camps. He knew what to do and how to please. Death was always imminent. And if it was possible to drown this damned war in alcohol, why not? If they should succeed in getting out whole then gold would buy everything. It would then be possible to start life anew and become a decent person.

A blond strand of hair fell over Bedarf's supercilious face. His drunken, turbid eyes followed the dancer's movements. He smacked his lips.

As I returned, I bumped into a couple—Jurek, a Warsaw Pole who was a fireman here, and a dark-haired Jewish girl from France called Ellen. Everybody knew about their flaming love letters and their cooing in the dark alleys between the barracks.

At this hour the atmosphere was saturated with romance. Just because it was forbidden, just because death

SS-Obersturmbandführer Arthur Liebehen-schel, commander of Auschwitz from November 1943 until May 1944. After the war, he was sentenced to death and executed.

prevailed everywhere, just to contradict everything, against common sense. Couples embraced without forethought, on impulse. They clutched at each other for a brief second to drink in the life-giving force, to live through a moment of pleasure while there was still time, while they were still alive, because in a short while it might be too late. Because not far off the others were decaying or burning.

"Meet me tonight! Don't be afraid!" Whispers in all languages filled the night.

They met everywhere, on the *bindles*[174] of clothes, behind the barracks. There were short, meaningless contacts and there were real, sincere, moving emotions fed constantly by threatening danger, emotions which arose from the need to care for someone and to be cared for. Women looked for consolation, hope, a strong masculine arm—they were hungry for the few words, "Don't be scared my little one. Everything will turn out well. Come closer."

I ran between the wandering pairs as the searchlights of the SS men on guard pursued me. I rushed through the brightly lit, pulsating street of *Canada* and the *Canada* barracks filled with all kinds of junk. I finally reached our hut.

[174] Bundles; packages.

"Phew!" I turned, highly excited, to Basia who was already falling asleep. "I just made it. They were closing the gates. You should see what's going on out there! We're not allowed to speak to men, but..."

"We're not allowed to speak to them, that's all. They didn't say any more," Basia commented. The other girls laughed and Ada was squealing, "You don't have to talk you know."

Chapter Three

They're Bringing More Wood

One day, Piri, a young Jewish girl from *Canada*, saw her mother in a Hungarian transport going "to the furnace." She had expected this because she herself had been taken from another city. She ran to the *lagerstrasse* whenever a transport was passing. Several times she was beaten by the *kapo*, Mancy, for this, and once she was turned back by the SS *hauptscharführer*. She thought then that her mother had been in that transport. She worked on the night shift, but she did not sleep during the day. We all wondered when Piri slept.

One day she rose from her stuffy bunk and went out to wash a dish. Suddenly she looked and with a cry began to run toward the transport calling, "Mama! Mama!" One of the girls caught her and pulled her back:

"Piri, don't shout. Better ask the SS *hauptscharführer*. He'll save your mother. If you run there, you'll go with them. Come back!"

Piri began to struggle. Her mother was already at the entrance to the crematory. Piri must have heard what the other girl had said because she answered:

"The SS *hauptscharführer*? Where? What did you say? Where is he? I must see him quickly."

A few of her friends, who had gathered around Piri, ran to look for the SS *hauptscharführer*. They knew what it meant. Her mother was already inside. They flew from one barrack to another.

"Where is the SS *hauptscharführer*? We must save Piri's mother. Have you seen the SS *hauptscharführer*?"

"He just went by with Mancy."

He had just walked out of Barrack 13. He was smiling to himself and cracking his whip. The job was going well. He felt he might even be promoted. Perhaps they would make him commandant of the camp. They should appreciate his work.

Piri ran up to him and gesticulating wildly began to explain to him in Hungarian.

The SS *hauptscharführer* did not understand a word she said. Just then one of Piri's friends approached them and began to translate to German:

"*Ihre Mutter hat...*"[175]

She did not finish. He understood.

"What can I do my dear? I have no influence there. I'm in charge of *Canada* and not of the crematories."

The road was empty. Piri looked helpless. She lowered her head and quietly returned to her bunk. She sat there for hours without moving. Suddenly she sprang up and stared in the direction of the crematory in which her mother had disappeared. The chimney was burning. Piri raised her arms and with a cry fell to the ground.

From then on she often came to our side of the barracks to look for photographs of her mother. She showed us all kinds of photographs and spoke to us in a mixture of German and Hungarian. Her dark eyes shone sadly. At first we listened and consoled her but we soon stopped paying attention to her. She grew silent and did not eat. Her eyes were like those of a beaten dog. We grew accustomed to the sight of the unhappy Piri and did not even notice when, under the influence of some memory, she began to dance the *czardas*. She smiled oddly while doing it.

[175] Her mother has...

266

"She's completely mad," someone said. "She's far better off now." Piri was happy now. She began to eat ravenously and constantly bothered us with her mad dances. A pleasant, sensitive child had been transformed into a raving maniac.

One day, as Piri was performing one of her dances, a Hungarian Jew entered our hut. She was a doctor by profession. The doctor began to tell us that she had been taken for a hearing to the city of Oswiecim. She had been summoned just before noon that day. They checked her number and took her away. She thought they were taking her to the gas and wondered why they had singled her out. But they took her into a room and asked her a number of curious questions. A very smartly attired SS man asked her to sit down and addressing her as asked her whether she had a good journey. She looked at him with wonder. She expected that this farce would soon end and that they would begin to beat her. They explained politely that they only wanted to straighten out a few details. They would, therefore, appreciate it if she could supply them with information. Did they beat her? Was she hungry? Was there anything she wished to complain about?

She sat in crushed silence. They then told her to sign a paper giving her number, the place she had come from and her exact previous address. They thanked her and brought her back.

"They are preparing an alibi," Ada concluded.

"But why? For whom? After all they've done here!"

"Who knows? After the war, they will probably produce documents proving that they did not gas people. They began their careers by staging the process in the Reichstag, and God knows who they'll make now responsible for these crimes."

We could not sleep that night for want of an answer to this puzzle. Would they deny these facts in the event of a defeat? Would they succeed in eradicating the proof? But how? Even if they liquidate all of us, I thought, there is that woman who took my letter. She is free. Only then did I fall asleep.

Suddenly something hard crashed through the grated window. We sat up in our beds startled by the noise.

Nella climbed down from her top bunk and stooped over the object. We waited in tense expectation.

"A teddy bear," she called as she came toward us carrying something in her hands.

Just then we heard men yodeling under our window. "*Ola ri alo...* "

Wiener Schnitzel! Yes it was him!

"That drunken fool." Nella was angry. "Waking us up at this hour. Doesn't he know his

place?'

Wiener Schnitzel and another SS man were standing under our window.

"Well, *Mädels...*[176] are you asleep? You can sleep when you're dead. Have fun while you're still alive, *nicht wahr?*"[177]

"We want to sleep, so please go away," Nella answered bravely in her amusing German accent.

She knew that should the SS *hauptscharführer* or anyone from the camp administrators find out about this little escapade, they could send the culprit to the front as "a reward."

"Oh, you *dumme Mädels*"[178] *Wiener Schnitzel* could not be put off so easily. "You're as stupid as your chief."

We were struck dumb. He must have been very drunk to speak of an SS man in this manner in front of the *häftlings*.

"Just like your chief," he repeated. "He knows nothing about love. How could he?" Then followed a long string of lewd comparisons.

The other SS man began to giggle and some of the girls joined in. This base monologue of a drunken SS man delivered under our window was not a common occurrence.

[176] Girls.
[177] Isn't it true?
[178] Stupid girls.

"You are Aryans," *Wiener Schnitzel* continued. "The same blood flows in our veins, the blood of noble people who know how to love, *nicht wahr*? Who can stop me from making love with you? You're different from those *verfluchten Jüdinnen* [179] on the other side."

"Throw a shoe at him," Basia whispered.

He continued his monologue for a long time calling some of the girls by their names. Nella finally got off her bunk and closed the window. He became very angry. We heard him pulling out his revolver. We hid under the blankets and waited for the shots. He fired but, fortunately, into the air. His companion, who must have been less drunk, pulled him away.

"I can't sleep," Czesia complained.

We went out to the latrines that stood right under the crematory.

The warm July night had wrought a magic charm, despite the odor from the uncovered pits and the two flaming chimneys. Czesia stood in front of the crematory. Her slim, shapely figure was revealed advantageously in the pale blue nightgown she had inherited from a cremated Hungarian. She glided toward the wire fence surrounding the crematory. Moved by an uncontrollable desire, we began to hum a waltz. Czesia curtsied graciously and announced, "Ladies and Gentlemen, in a short while you will see a modern dance, the dance of a dying *häftling*. The dance is called *Beneath the Flaming Chimneys*."

She began a wild pirouette. Her figure, like a golden fury, mingled with the glow of the fire and the light of the moon. Her movements were entreating, threatening, brusque and delicate, soft and vindictive. She expressed suppressed longing, revolt, despair, hope, helplessness and death. She ended with a pirouette. Then she shrank and burst into wild sobs.

[179] Damn Jewish woman.

"I shall never, never be able to dance again! Even if I don't die, there will always be cries of the dying in my dance and in my smile. I shall always remember the stench of corpses even in the most beautiful garden."

* * *

Day followed day in an unending procession. Days filled with smoke and scorching heat. Days of the eternal nervous tension and constant anticipation. Days black from smoke, nights red from fire, and in all this, very short flashes of hope, short moments of joy. A parcel or a letter that came from home, someone smiled, a word of encouragement. Rumor which inspired pity and thrill. They shaved a girl's her hair for talking to a man. Did a search and found gold. The beloved guy of some woman was suddenly sent with a transport.

Natasha reported from the SS kitchen, "They know that they've been beaten, but they're talking about a new weapon which will save them. Someone who was attracted to the wires and stood too close, now lies in the hospital."

She told us of an SS man who was deeply in love with a Jewish girl from *Canada*. He used to come just to look at her and to explain that he was not to blame. Another SS man had kicked a French girl. One of our girls had received a large bottle of goose fat. Someone from the 8th barrack had found a very valuable diamond in a coat lining. She wanted to exchange it for an apple because her sister was sick and could eat nothing but apples.

In the meantime, the "plan" was being executed. Twenty-thousand a day. Mohl telephoned, rushed about on his motorcycle and disbursed the raw material. The trucks passed with charred corpses. Long lines of people waited their turn at the crematories. The Red Cross ambulance was delivering *Zyclon*.

New improvements were made as the gassing progressed. At the beginning people were told to undress in the large

270

SS-Hauptscharführer Otto Moll, director of the crematoria at Auschwitz. After the war he was sentenced to death and executed.

dressing room adjoining the "bath," the gas chamber. Thousands of pairs of shoes were thrown hurriedly on the truck and it was then difficult to match the pairs. They later ordered people to tie their shoes together "so that they would not get mixed up." And people were carefully tying their boots together. In the "locker room" they were given numbers. Some came back before entering the chamber door, asking for another number, since they lost the first one in the crowd. After the gas was released, they finally understood. They then ran madly to the exit, but instead of a door there was a "blank wall." Whoever was further away from the gas grid, suffered the longest. Usually suffocation lasted five to eight minutes. Bodies extracted from the chambers were twisted and intertwined with each other, testifying to the incredible suffering: bitten off parts of the body, eyes coming out of the orbits, broken, knocked out fingers...

Some transports, which knew more about the camp, struggled against entering the gas chamber. Someone would shout something, or someone would suddenly understand and the whole transport would fall into panic. In such cases, which occurred more frequently, they released specially trained police dogs. The biting dogs, spreading panic, drove the crushed mass of human beings into the gas chamber.

A group of Jewish women and children on the ramp.

One day after opening the gas chambers, the men of the *Sonderkommando* heard the quiet whimper of a living baby. Although they had already witnessed the worst scenes you can imagine, this time they were numb with terror.

It turned out that the child was still alive because during the gassing it continuously sucked its mother's breast, resulting in gas not having access to the lungs. Moll, who was on duty, was called. Enraged, he threw the child into a burning furnace alive.

One day an elderly Jewish woman arrived in the transport from Hungary. Her son worked in the *Sonderkommando*. Within the crematorium, the mother noticed her son arranging wood. She ran up to him, delighted. The son, who had long sought his mother among the gassed, was numbed, terrified.

His mother asked him what they would do with them. He replied that they would rest here.

"And where is such a strange smell coming from?"

"From burned rags..."

"And why did we come here?"

"Just to bathe."

The son gave his mother a towel and soap and went with her inside. They disappeared in the depths of the chimney. There were thousands of similar gruesome accidents, tragic encounters and horrible scenes. There was never a day in which information failed to come to us from a direct witness, either in the form of a smuggled message or from an overheard conversation. You could no longer surprise or frighten us with anything.

Everything was possible... except one thing... freedom. Freedom was moving away with every passing day. The good news from the front had not been able to make us optimistic for a longer period of time. Still, there was only one thought: there is no way to get out of hell. The sentence "And when I will home," was meeting a pitiful look.

* * *

Three hundred men from the *Sonderkommando* were notified that they were to leave with a transport.[180] So this was the end. They had expected this moment. They had waited for it in unrelenting fear. But they could not be fooled so easily, not they. They would start a riot as soon as they got to the next camp, or even here on the ramp. They decided to strike as soon as the right people got in their way. They sent out messages to the camp saying that they were to leave at

[180] In September 1944 approximately 200 *Sonderkommando* prisoners were taken under the pretext of transfer to the Gleiwitz (Gliwice) sub-camp, to the Auschwitz unloading platform. They were murdered by means of *Zyklon B* in the disinfection chamber located in the grounds of *Canada* I.

night, but that they would not be killed or burned. We were to get ready. The news was whispered from hut to hut. They were ordered to go to the *Bekleidungskammer*[181], the clothing chamber in Auschwitz to change their clothes. We saw them as they passed our windows. They were singing with heads raised high. The uncertainty and the waiting had come to an end. They knew that they must die, but they were ready to act. They entered Auschwitz and, still joking, went in for their clothes. The door was then bolted and the hut, constructed just like the others, was filled with gas.

This time too, they got the better of the experienced *Sonderkommando*.

* * *

I carefully, meticulously opened my parcel. I looked at every single piece of paper under the light. One was in an egg. I could not understand how it had happened, that it had not broken. I showed it to Basia with pride:

"You see, how mine know how to pack!"

Basia looked at the egg, jumped, kissed me and whispered:

"A hard-boiled egg! Search further, can you remember the secret signal?'

Indeed, I found two more hard-boiled eggs. The letter had been delivered. They had received the letter, so they knew.

"Krysia, do you know what that means?" Basia said, delighted. "This means that even if we all die, the world will find out!"

Just about this time, I learned that a squad of carpenters was working in Birkenau—the boys from Auschwitz. I wrote to Andrzej that I'd had my first hopeful day because the outside knew what was happening here. I felt I was writing to a person created by my imagination. Just then Tanya walked into the *Schreibstube* and winked at me. I walked out.

[181] Prisoner clothing storage.

"Who?" I asked as I passed her.

"An unfamiliar man is waiting for you behind the third hut. Be careful, they're running around the whole place today." Behind the third hut stood Andrzej. He began to explain when he saw my astonishment.

"You see; a year has passed since the river. I had to see you. I got through as a carpenter. It's quite risky because they know me in the camp. But I must tell you something important," he hesitated, "Because I may not have the opportunity to see you again. I..."

He stopped. I suddenly understood. He was going to make a break. He did not have to explain.

"Is it safe?" I asked stupidly.

"I don't know. But I can't stand it any longer. I have an exceptional chance now. I'll try. If I succeed, I'll try to get to your people, if not..."

"And if not?"

"Then you must avenge my death. Maybe you'll succeed."

"Could you take me with you? I don't know how, but I'm ready. I can get a civilian dress, my hair is long..."

"No. You can't come. I'm going with a friend, today. Goodbye Krysia! I'll see you in free Poland, or never."

He looked around alertly, showed his white teeth and went toward the camp gates. There he joined the squad of carpenters that was returning to the men's camp. He looked back once. I stood behind the hut and watched the stripes disappear. That night, after the roll call, the alarm went off. I grasped Basia by the hand. She looked at me with surprise.

"Why are you so worried about the alarm? It's good that someone made a break."

The carpenters came again the following day. They were under a stronger guard. In spite of that, one of them got a message to our barracks. It read:

My friend Andrzej was caught at the last sentry-box. Tell Krysia. His companion got through. No further information about him. Andrzej was hit five times. His body will be burned today.

The train-whistle sounded on the ramp. Tearing the card to shreds, I turned slowly to the hut. So the radiant Andrzej will be no more. There will be no meeting in a free Poland. He died literally a step away from freedom, pampered in the dreams of over four years.

A black streak of smoke spread over the camp. It had devoured him together with millions of other victims.

* * *

The Hungarian transports stopped for a few days.

A group of Gypsy children was playing in the mud in front of the barracks. They were wrestling with the smallest one. They tripped him in the mud and, in imitation of the SS man, called "*los*," "*ab*." Their victim tried to free himself. He wriggled and yelled at the top of his lungs.

We were in the Gypsy camp registering new *zugangs*, a dazed group of German Gypsies.

I approached the boys.

"What are you doing?"

"We're playing."

"What are you playing?"

"We're burning Jews."

I was taken aback. I could not believe my own ears.

That night, August 1, 1944, they burned all the remaining Gypsies from the districts of Bialystok[182] and from Germany. The small Gypsy boys who had been playing at burning Jews and the slim, olive-skinned Gypsy girls, dark-eyed, agile and lively—they were also strangled with gas.

[182] Approximately 1,700 Gypsies from Bialystok, not registered in the camp, were suspected of being infected with typhus and were thus murdered in a gas chamber on the 23rd of March 1943.

Because the Gypsies had been registered and had been given numbers, the *Politische Abteilung* instructed that all their deaths should be registered with the date of August 1st.

This example of idiotic order aroused distaste and indignation. Nobody in the world would believe that five thousand Gypsies died a natural death in one evening. But *an ordnung*[183] was a sacred word. However, the authorities realized that the lie was too obvious. They therefore, concocted an alibi that was even more impudent. Twenty doctors, Poles and Jews, were selected haphazardly out of the list of doctors working in the Gypsy *lager*.

They were charged with spreading a mysterious virus among the Gypsies. The virus was supposed to have produced symptoms similar to those of the bubonic plague. We had heard of several cases of this strange disease[184]. The doctors, who were supposed to be responsible for spreading this disease, were sentenced to hard labor (*Strafenkommando)* and immediate transport. These innocent doctors were forced to sign declarations giving their personal data and then were sent off.

Then again there was a lull. We got news that the Red Army was moving up to Warsaw, that it was occupying Hungary[185]. This last was confirmed by the fact that transports from Hungary had stopped suddenly. We began to feel a little more hopeful. Several days of rain, which washed away the smell of the corpses, were followed by a heat wave. Our nostalgia, slumbering deep under the cover of apathy, was roused again. We began to dream of open spaces, of swift running brooks, of sloping hills. Due to the few days of calm, the rain and the good news, we began to think that the gassing had come to an end. We thought that they had to stop their program because they had no one to burn.

[183] Order.

[184] The disease *Noma* (water cancer, or cheek gangrene), which did not appear in other parts of Auschwitz, was spread among Gypsy prisoners.

[185] See footnote 164.

Ragged Hungarian women were being transported to clear ruins. They came for their last delousing to the Birkenau *sauna*. They begged for something to wear. They were isolated from the camp and could not "organize" anything. Some of them were practically naked.

They peered dazedly at us through our window. Some cried in shame, some cried in envy. They scratched their naked heads and their elegant lingerie, flowered satins, silks and georgettes rode away from the barracks of *Canada* on wagons bound to comfort suffering "Gretchens"[186].

In the still August heat we suddenly heard the rumble of trucks loaded with lumber and behind the trucks we saw the *Sonderkommando* carrying wood, which we had not seen for a long time. We entered the FKL, the women's camp. Again we saw wood stacked high along the whole length of the road. "That must be for us," we all thought.

My tongue became dry, my head throbbed, my heart pounded, my legs grew weak. Again I sensed that well-known feeling of imminent death. We stopped talking and thinking. Again everything became turbid, chaotic—everything seemed to lose meaning. The pulsating rhythm of accelerated blood flow drew a distinction between two concepts: wood and death... death because of wood... wood, so the death...

Maryla, a Jewish girl from Poland, entered our hut and in the tense silence began to read a poem by Wygodzki[187]. It had been thrown out through the wire fence of the men's hospital.

"They're bringing wood, they're bringing..."

I could not understand the words. The words were like an ill boding melody of an approaching, inescapable death. Wygodzki's wife and daughter had been burned and he was now lying in a hut and writing a poem that would die with him and with us.

[186] Popular German name (Maggies), here in the sense of German women.
[187] Stanislaw (Szyja [*Shiyah*]) Wygodzki (1907-1992) a well-known poet, novelist, essayist and translator of Jewish origin.

"They're bringing wood, they're bringing..." Maryla reads, confirming our premonition.

"Stop that!" Czesia, the most nervous one cried out. "I can see all that! Why write poems about that? He must be mad. I wonder whether he'll write poetry in the gas chamber?"

"But Czesia," I tried to calm her.

"I know. You love that. You damn poet! I don't want to listen to poetry. I want to live... I'll read poetry when I'm free. There is such terrible prose here! When I will be free, I'll read about love, listen to music. Here I do not want Bolek's accordion, sentimental tangos under the chimneys or poetry about wood in which people are burning. In here, there can be no poetry."

Chapter Four

Warsaw on the Ramp

Our sleeping and waking hours were filled with tense expectation. We no longer thought of swimming in the ocean, of tramps in the mountains. That's how it had to be.

We stopped dreaming. Wires and fear.

Wacek sent me a message on a small piece of paper.

Krysia! On August 1st an uprising started in Warsaw. In the West our Allies are advancing deep into Germany. The Red Army is taking Hungary. Mein Liebchen, was willst du noch mehr?[188]

Just then Basia burst in with a shout, "Warsaw is on the ramp." We did not understand. We could not believe. Warsaw? Who? The insurgents? Civilians? To a concentration camp? Why? We had long ago accepted the fact that we were criminals. We came here after a trial, or at least as suspects. But how could they bring civilians here? It couldn't be true. They must have brought Hungarians again.

Basia, whose sister and mother were in Warsaw, as well as the others who came from Warsaw, moved around restlessly and looked out on the *lagerstrasse*. I scolded Basia for repeating silly, unfounded gossip. They were fighting in Warsaw. Wacek had just written to me. We had hardly absorbed that news.

[188] My darling, what more do you want?

How could they be here already? "Some people think that the whole world must come here. Everybody's mad!"

"They're coming," Nella insisted.

We ran out. A transport was moving toward us. We strained our eyes to see. They approached. At first came the women carrying bundles on their backs.

Alas! It was Warsaw! We knew without asking. They cast frightened glances and asked. "Where are we? What is this place?"

"Auschwitz."

"Jesus and Mary," a woman shouted, wringing her hands, "They've brought me where my Johnny died!"

"Is this really Auschwitz?" the others asked doubtfully.

"Where in Warsaw are you from?" we ask.

"Narutowicza Square, Grojecka Street."

"What about the Uprising?" we asked.

"What a question!" a woman walked out of the ranks. "Don't you know that there is no Warsaw any longer?"

"There is no Warsaw?" What was she saying stupid, exaggerating hag!? That's just what they had said in 1939 and look how it turned out later?!

But all the others repeated the same words: "There is no Warsaw. There is no Warsaw. Only a mountain of ruins, nothing more!"

Basia is staring at the crowd, keeps track of every face, looking for her kin.

"I felt that something wrong would happen," she whispers, not taking her eyes off the women passing by us. "I was worried that they were fighting there, and were sitting here idly... and now look... they are already here. How did this happen?"

"What do we know, Basia? For two years we've been separated from everything..."

"I know one thing," says Basia stubbornly. "Here you are not allowed for even a moment to have hope, to enjoy, to believe in the possibility of some improvement, to have the illusion of freedom! Hardly any hope, and you hit a wall right away. After so many months of dreaming of Warsaw, Warsaw has came here to you. Expelled, run-down, doomed people. You waited, you sighed, you yearned... So here it is, Narutowicza Square came to you, our mothers, sisters will come next, and they will also go to the lousy barracks. We wanted Warsaw—we have it now."

"But, Basia, it may not be so bad! This is one of the districts. The rest of Warsaw is fighting. These people probably fled."

The men were passing now. I looked for my father. He had been in Warsaw recently. If he is here, I must get him a muffler from *Canada*, I thought. I knew it was silly but I could think only of that muffler. I began to think of other things. "This is August. He won't stand this more than a month, why the muffler? What could it help? Someone who looks like my father is passing by, gray hair, I get closer... No, that's not he." But this was only the first transport from Warsaw.

"Will they burn us?" a man asked me politely.

He must have heard and read a great deal about Auschwitz. "What an idea!" We were filled with indignation. "They only burn Jews. Don't worry."

Four thousand persons came in this transport and among them fifteen hundred women. They were taken to the empty *Canada* barracks. They lay there and look with distrust at each strange person who entered the hut.

We arranged our tables in the *sauna* and began to register Warsaw.

Exhausted and distrustful, the women approached our tables and gave us their data. The line extended far into the grounds in front of the *sauna*. Evening and late night found us at work. Our throats parched, our heads bursting. We repeated the same questions and listened to the same complaints: "What a misfortune has fallen upon us! Why must we suffer? What have we done?"

"You haven't done anything," I tried to explain to some of them. "You suffer because you are Poles."

I tried to extract a few concrete facts about the Uprising. I learned that at 5 p.m. on August 1st the alarm went off. Nobody had known, no one had suspected.

One of the women said, "Do you know what a *szafa* [189] is? How can you know? My son was killed by a *szafa*. I said, 'Go into the cellar!' he laughed. He said, 'Mother if it's to come, I can't escape it'. And my husband was killed. Only my daughter remains. She's a liaison... I was in Okecie and I couldn't get through. Then they came and led us through the dead city. The houses were on fire. Corpses everywhere... What can you know?"

"We know corpses. Next. Your name please."

"Maybe you know," I asked, "The house on Narbutta Street 25? That's where..."

"I do. The house is destroyed."

"Maybe you noticed Filtrowa Street 68? A Mrs. Wojcie-chowska lives there on the second floor."

"Why are you asking and asking? Don't you understand that there is no Warsaw anymore?"

"No, I don't understand."

And Leszno?" Basia asked the woman.

"Leszno is all in flames."

"Let's not ask any more," I said to Basia. "Don't start any conversations. Just make believe that it's an Italian transport. I can't listen to what they're saying."

"Next please! Please answer quickly so we can finish sooner. Then you can go to your barracks. Name?"

[189] (Polish [*shafa*]) Literally—*wardrobe*—the name given to big rockets used by the Nazis during the Warsaw Uprising, the popular name of the mortar projectile *Nebelwerfer* which, sent salvos of rockets. By using *szafas*, Germans created panic among the population of Warsaw. Salvos of rockets destroyed whole houses, and particularly high pressure spikes during the explosion, was causing death by asphyxiation.

"I have plenty of time. I'm in no hurry." A large woman shrugged her shoulders.

"Why that attitude? I am a prisoner just like you."

"I'm no prisoner. You are!" she answered provokingly. "They'll free us because we are innocent and you are guilty. They'll set me free. My brother's a *Volksdeutsch*. To hell with the Uprising." I winked at Basia. We must give her the works.

"You should have told us immediately that your brother is a *Volksdeutsch*. That changes everything."

The woman smiled with satisfaction.

"My fiancé is also a *Volksdeutsch* in the German army."

"Well, well," I hissed, "Undress immediately. Take everything off! Do you understand Polish? Or do you want me to say it in German?"

The woman began to protest, casting about with her eyes in search of a German. I stood up and said, "In the name of the German Reich I command you to undress immediately!" The woman was stilled.

"Where do they come from?" Basia asked.

Nella explained that many of the women who had come in this transport had hung out a white flag. She pulled out a German proclamation to the people:

"Ultimatum to the people of Warsaw! The civilian population is requested to leave Warsaw by the roads leading west. They must display white handkerchiefs in their hands."

One of the women noticed the ultimatum in our hands. She hastened to explain.

"I did not display a flag. They took me by force, dragged me out of the house..."

Some were crying, others were cursing. It was difficult to guess whom they cursed, the Germans or the insurgents. They were confused. Ideas of heroism and cowardice were hopelessly disordered. And above all, they were tired and resigned.

We can not understand a thing. What is happening there, why? We are overwhelmed by the immensity of the tragedy...

after so many years of dreaming, longing, we are forced to see Warsaw in this state!"

Naked "civil" women from Warsaw crowd upon the return of their belongings before entering the bath. I gave old ladies a professional, Auschwitz "estimate.". Maybe they will live a few weeks. It depends on which barracks they will be allocated to, how long they will stand at roll calls. The young will probably be sent further to work.

An old woman was crying because she had left her false teeth with her clothes. How was she to eat? We looked through the sacks. We found her teeth in her sack and handed them to the woman. She thanked me warmly for this insignificant service. I tried to convince myself that I had done something, that I had helped someone in this misfortune.

There is no Warsaw, no family. Everybody was lost. Everybody was behind these wire fences. Everybody was trapped and we were scrupulously writing. The same questions arose constantly: Why? For whom? And the wood outside? What will they do with all these people?

Everything became more confused. The Warsaw exiles moved in front of us in an unhappy kaleidoscope. Outside, the light was turning grey. Only a few miserable figures waited under the wall. Only a few more times would I have to repeat: "Name? Please undress."

In the glaucous dawn of the rising day stand women from Warsaw in groups of fives in anticipation of the morning roll call. There are no more *szafa* bombs or missiles. Gone are the barricades and the battle for Warsaw. New struggles began: with hunger, lice, cold and a ceaseless longing for freedom...

Words of ultimatum to the people of Warsaw sound like ridicule: "All men and women able to work will get jobs and bread, all sick and elderly women and children will receive accommodation and medical care."

"Poor Warsaw!" says someone.

The ramp at Auschwitz awaiting prisoners' transport unloading.

"They will get witless, they will get used to it, like us," someone else adds.

* * *

The Warsaw transport brought books. They had carried away all that was most valuable, not realizing that they were coming to KZ[190]. In the chaotic weariness, in the hum of hundreds of voices, amidst all kinds of touching objects destined for the paper bags, we extracted books. The books belonged to the *zugang* just like a sweater or a coat, but we considered books common property. We felt that after so many months of terror, we needed nourishment for the spirit.

[190] Letters KZ, common name of a concentration camp (abbreviation from KonZentrationslager).

"I have a copy of *Nightmares*[191]," Ziutka, one of the most charming girls in our squad, leaned over to whisper to me. "We'll read it in the evenings."

I looked at her sadly.

"Who will have time to read, if Warsaw has just begun to arrive? We will work at night and I constantly hear that "there is no Warsaw." Our loved ones will come."

"Do not caw. You know that everything passes. We'll read books and laugh, despite Warsaw's burning. You know well enough. How can you forget? Bad and terrible things pass away. Later, in our memories we just look for the nice, cheerful reflections.

Apart from the books, Warsaw also brought money. The following day, after admitting *zugangs*, we moved the tables and sat on the floor to count the money. Hundreds of thousands in Polish paper money. Basia was throwing the bills into the air, embittered and exhausted by the stories about Warsaw.

"Trash!" she said with contempt. "Trash, that's all. And before, oh God, the things you could buy with it. How much you would have to work and suffer to get one bill, and now I have to count them and send them back. All the assets of exiled Warsaw lies here... as well as the money of the Hungarian Jews."

I look at her, terrified.

She jumped up suddenly and furiously kicked over a pile of counted banknotes. I was amazed.

"I won't count it. They can count it themselves."

Staggering she trampled the bills under her feet. Then she opened the door and began to breathe deeply. I ran up to her. Basia swayed and leaned against me.

"I can't. There is no Warsaw. I can't Krysia! Help me!"

We carried her to the hut. Words of the ultimatum flashed through my head: "The population of Poland knows that the German Army is fighting only against Bolshevism."

---

[191] Known (published 1935), a novel by Emil Zegadlowicz, inspired enormous controversy before the war because of its boldness.

287

Basia was sobbing. She was having a nervous breakdown. We could hear a few broken sentences: "The end of the world. There will be nothing, Warsaw... ruins... mother... end... the end..."

There were a million and a half zlotys in the loot. We had counted the money for several days. Our chief was satisfied. We began to work on the jewellery. Wanda wrote down each piece of jewellery taken from the women of Warsaw. Pins, rings, necklaces, chains tumbled out on the table. Wanda was too busy to look at them. When she noticed something unusual, she would call out, "What a beautiful stone. Look how it shines! Look at the color! Why am I writing this down? They will never see this again."

We carried the heavy boxes of jewelry into the *schmuck* [192] room.

We joked with Wanda about her health. Wanda complained that she even dreamed at night that she was counting the jewelry: *Eine Halskette, eine Armbanduhr gelb, ein Ringweiss* [193].

Our barracks became like a museum during that period of the evacuation of Warsaw. I went to the "personals" division. Photographs, albums, diaries, letters were piled neatly. I picked up a photograph—Andrzejewska, sixty years. A photograph lying near her personal effects represented a young man in glasses signed: Jerzy Andrzejewski. Could that be, why it must be, the author of the novel "*Order in the heart.*" I had enjoyed so much. This must be his mother. I showed Nella the picture. Nella understood.

"We must help," she smiled at me. "The mother of the writer, isn't she, Krysia?" And in a moment there was a sweater and stockings for her.

"I'll take them to her," Nella volunteered.

I opened a diary and began to read the fine, cramped letters. I made out the pale pencil marks with difficulty:

[192] Jewelry.
[193] One necklace; one yellow wristwatch; one white ring.

August 20, 1916, we're going to the front. I found fleas again. The canons do not bother me as much as the fleas, and to think that Antos is so close. I feel this must be my last hour... our train is under fire. Mother, I am not afraid. Please tell Antos if he returns...

The diary broke off here. There were a few clean pages and then in the same handwriting:

I am writing again after so many years. This is 1944. I am doing first-aid work in Mokotow. All the houses around are on fire. We shall have to move out in a short while.

And further:

They dragged us out of the houses. We're traveling to an unknown destination.

I looked at the photographs of the diarist. An old worn out photograph of an Amazon on horseback, then a photograph of a nurse with a group of soldiers, a picture of a child and another of a handsome young man with a dedication: "To my dearest one. Antos." Where had I seen the same thing not so long ago? I tried to remember.

Oh, it was on the *lagerstrasse*. I had picked up a photograph of a Hungarian Jew with the same dedication only in German.

I was sentimental about photographs in Auschwitz. What nonsense, this attachment to souvenirs.

* * *

We collected bread for the Warsaw transport because they had not yet received their ration of food. We give them our supper, we treated them like our guests, and we tried to make those first days easier for them. In the evening we endangered ourselves by venturing out to the men with containers of coffee.

The Warsaw boys had lost much of their famous bravado in the camp. They looked at the wire fence and shook their heads: "Can't make a break; high-voltage electricity, the devils work," a bright youngster observed.

"Madame," he stopped me, "Is it true that these wires can pull us in; that you can't climb over them?"

"Don't even try. They'll catch you even if you do get out. The camp grounds stretch over a large distance. No one can escape from here."

The boy dried a tear surreptitiously and turned to his mother: "Don't worry, Mother. There are people here too." He tried a crooked smile. "It will be all right. You'll see. We'll get those Nazis yet."

After the delousing, Warsaw went to the barracks. We had scarcely counted the money when another transport arrived. And again, we began to look for relatives, friends, to wander between the people lying in the barracks. The second transport brought more underground "newspapers." We became more informed and began to feel the tragedy and the senselessness of the Uprising. The people in the second transport were more obstinate. Some of them were happy that they had come here. They could rest a little from the shooting. "Any place is better than over there. Everything is lost anyway."

And again we worked through the night and counted the money the following day. One of the girls had found her parents. We all cried watching that meeting.

We began to look through the documents. I found a letter from a father begging for the return of his child. I found many diaries. All these personal tragedies seemed unimportant and naïve. They died and dissipated in the barracks.

Chapter Five

The Vienna Transport

We returned to "normal life". Italian *zugangs* arrived during the day. Slowly, they lost all individuality.

They arrived drunk with Italian wine and air, giggling as they undressed, not realizing where they were. They resisted, protested. They thought that they had something to say. No one was moved by their humor.

Then a few women, partisans, arrived from Yugoslavia. They were dressed like men. They were proud, dignified and brave. They impressed everyone with their deportment. They knew where they had come and why they had been sent here.

Other women came from a special prison in Myslowice with sentences from the *Sondergericht*[194]. Fortunately, they had not been sentenced to death. There were still experiencing memories of the terrible interrogation, grim imprisonment and loss of their companions.

In comparison with the suntanned, wine-saturated Italian transport, they looked pale and wretched. Their shining eyes looked with disbelief. "Is it possible that we are still alive? That we shall live?"

A seventy-year-old Jewish woman, who had arrived with

[194] The special court was part of Nazi "justice." The courts, operating from February 1933, were the instrument of the horrific Nazi fight against its political opponents and the "race enemy." During the occupation they also took place in Poland.

the Viennese transports, was at the last moment pulled out of the ranks lined up for the gas by our chief.

Wurm, formerly the chief of the men's *Effektenkammer*, was our chief at that time. Wurm took the surprised old woman to his office and told her to sit down.

The old woman did not know where she was to go. She did not know that she had miraculously escaped death.

"I know you," Wurm explained. "You are a Social Democrat."

"Yes, I have been a member of the party for the past forty years. How do you know me?"

"I've been at your lectures."

"Oh, so you... but what are you doing in this uniform?"

Wurm smiled diffidently and spoke in justification:

"You are from Vienna and you know that in every other Austrian family each person belonged to a different party. One of my brothers was a Social Democrat, my father[195] was a Communist and I was most convinced by National Socialism." The others had long ago gone to the furnace, and in the office a Jewish woman was conducting a polite discussion with an SS man.

The old woman tried to enlighten Wurm and said with a gentle smile:

"There are very few families today in which you would find really convinced National Socialists. I am sorry for you. You are serving a limited ideology. But since you have not been disgusted by the system and are taking an active part in it, then you will be convinced by the results of the war and they will be just. Then you'll understand."

"You are militant in spite of your age," Wurm smiled back condescendingly. "Is Vienna destroyed? I have not been there for a long time."

---

[195] After the book's second edition, only Wurm's brother was said to be a communist. (After all, a communist father should never have raised a Nazi son.)

The woman began a lively and interesting narration about the bombing and the life in Vienna. They spoke of mutual friends. It turned out that they had lived in the same district for many years.

Suddenly, without saying a word, Wurm rose and walked out. We were ordered to return her clothing. A button was missing from the coat in which she was to return to Vienna. She requested that we sew on a button because it "looked slovenly." I began to laugh hysterically. The old woman could not understand why we were laughing. Was it so strange that she should want to look neat? Basia laughed out loud. Tanya spoke angrily to the woman.

"Do you know what was going to happen to you if our chief had not seen you? Do you know what happened to the others?"

"No I don't. They must have gone to the showers."

Tanya lowered her voice:

"Have you heard about crematories and about gas chambers for people?"

"I have. But that can't be true."

"But it is true and you as an active and valuable member of the Social Democratic Party should know that it is true," Tanya said with indignation.

"Then why are you laughing?"

"Because you are asking for a button. When they open the gate of the camp you should run fast without looking back."

We watched for the impression Tanya's words had made on her. The woman remained cool. After a few moments, she said, "It may be as you say, but as I am alive, I should like to have this button. I see nothing funny in that."

Tanya handed the woman a large button with a flourish and said. "To the Austrian Social Democrat from a Soviet Communist."

To our surprise, the old woman walked out through the gates under the escort of a *posten*. Wurm shook hands with her and wished her luck. Basia nudged me:

"Do you understand anything? I don't. Where is she going and why? Does the fact that he recognized her, change her Jewish blood, her race?"

Other small transports began to arrive. *Erziehungs häftlings* from Germany, French partisans, small-starved boys from Dachau—all were brought here, no one knew why.

A mysterious group of high-ranking Soviet officers arrived. We noticed in particular a soldier with a beard and a very intelligent face. They proudly marched past our windows without their belts or insignia as if in a military parade.

They—prisoners of war—had, contrary to international law, been brought to a concentration camp.

The Russian girls looked after them with great agitation, as our eyes had followed the *zugangs* from Warsaw. "What will become of them? Will they be sent to the gas? Or will they be shot?"

Natasha and Tanya followed them at a safe distance. The group approached the *sauna*, would they turn or go straight? If they did not turn then they would die. They did turn and entered the *sauna.* We heaved a sigh of relief.

An event unheard of in the history of the camp took place in the *sauna.* One of the soldiers did not permit them to shave his beard. An SS man had ordered the beard to be shaved off immediately and behaved in his usual insulting manner.

"Over my dead body!" the Russian declared. "And how dare you address me that way! Stand at attention when you speak to a Soviet general, you stupid Nazi puppet[196]."

The SS man saluted as if hypnotized and ran out of the *sauna.* No one intervened. The general and the others kept their beards and their hair.

We knew quite well the fate of thousands of Russian prisoners who had starved to death. This incident caused a stir

[196] See footnote 167 (p. 246).

in the camp. "The front is approaching. They are afraid," was how everyone saw it.

Why wood was being accumulated still remained unclear. The *Canada* barracks were still busy. The wealth of the Hungarian Jews was indescribable. Girls from *Canada* were constantly sorting, stacking, tying and sending everything to the Reich. Every day they ripped out some treasures skillfully hidden in various parts of the garments. Apparently some of them scrimp gold in the event a miraculous rescue.

Mancy and Erna were constantly beating someone. The men had to do jumping jacks for any small offence. Prisoner Bolek's accordion accompanied *Ich brauche keine Millionen*[197] every evening.

Still more newly arrived half-naked Hungarian women arrived for delousing, ultimately victimized by desperate hunger and hopelessness. Piri had more and more colleagues. Many women fell into madness.

After work, we read the book retrieved from the Warsaw transport. And when they put out the lights, we listened to the jumbled sounds of the hot August night. Vulgar *aufseherin* Hopman, who was in charge of our building during this period, with her hoarse voice called someone to the accompaniment of a barking dog. The vulgar insults and the commanding cries of the *kapo* of *Canada*, "*Baracken schliessen! Schneller, du Dumme Gans, du blüde Kuh!*"[198] came into the silence of the hut through the wired window. *The* muffled sounds of music were proof of the SS-men's backroom orgies with Jewish dancers.

A deep sigh ends one of a thousand days in the camp.

---

[197] I do not need millions.
[198] Close the barracks! Faster, you fool, you stupid cow!

Chapter Six

Ghetto *Litzmannstadt* [199]

I received a message in a parcel from my sister who was in Vienna with my mother. The message was well concealed in the rim of a box. She wrote about the offensive in the West and of the approaching liberation:

"Hold on just a little longer." I memorized the message and rushed to Zosia's barrack to meet Wacek. We laughed at the stacks of wood. It was too late now.

Wacek rubbed his palms because he had heard the latest communiqué.

"I tell you, we shall burn their corpses with this wood."

Zosia, who was *torwache* at the moment, called to us, "A mass of people are coming from the ramp."

Our happiness burst like a bubble. Was it Warsaw again?

It was the Lodz ghetto. We looked at the moving skeletons that had been walled off for years to starve and work. They looked at the birch trees without knowing that this was their last journey.

In clouds of dust rising from under the branches of the hazel tree marched the bearded and wild-eyed *Sonderkommando*. Behind them came trucks loaded with wood and more men carrying wood. Before them the Red Cross ambulance.

An hour later, the first flames rose from the crematory

---

[199] The Lodz Ghetto was the second-largest ghetto in German-occupied Poland. Situated in the town of Lodz. Germans renamed Lodz *Litzmannstadt*.

chimney. Two hours later, a black, biting smoke curled up from the holes and ditches, and then the overpowering smell of corpses and singed flesh.

There was no way to escape it even for a moment.

I bowed my heavy head on the diary of a young Jewish girl from the Lodz ghetto. The diary was fresh, "still warm," as Maryla who found it said. The final sentences were written hours before in a crowded train going to Auschwitz. The diary's writer just now as I read it, was burning in a nearby crematorium. Her last words were:

And now we're going to an unfamiliar country. How is it going to be? Whatever happens, everything is better than it was there, behind the walls. I curse every memory of this hell. I curse all those who served the criminals, my eternally dark, cold, bare little room on Brzezinska Street, this wretched wall separating us from the rest of the world, our unspeakable misery, the steady patter of clogs in the morning, tuberculosis and the terrible Kriminalpolizei[200]. Damn this place without a bit of greenery, where I lost my best years, where my closest died, where I gave all of my strength to my mortal enemy—in exchange for a food voucher. I write in a tight corner in the bright streak of light flowing through a gap in the car. For two days I have had nothing to eat or drink. Next to me are a few corpses. But it's nothing, the most important thing is that after so many years, we are traveling by train again, and through the gap the golden sheaves of grain can be seen.

[200] Called *Kripo*, criminal police; they, together with the Gestapo and the SD (part of the SS) formed part of the RSHA, or Reichssicherheitshauptamt (Reich Main Security Office). They terrorized the occupied population by searching for hidden Jews and in the camps they co-organized inhumane medical experiments. They wore SS uniforms.

A limo pulled up in font of the *sauna*. Beautiful Dr. Mengele and Kramer disembarked.

Basia and Nella went to reconnoiter. What could be the purpose of this extraordinary visit?

But I didn't hide the diary and looked inside another notebook belonging to the same girl. There I found poems: sad poems about the lives of lepers; poems about hunger, persecution, triumph, crime, and haughtiness; vindictive poems about the rulers of money and weapons factories, the gods of the ghetto.

I found a wonderful piece blessing the yellow lamplight shining behind the wall. This lamplight, lamplight from another world, penetrates into the dark corner of the poet from the ghetto and allows her to create.

Finally, I read the last poem, written under the influence of posters announcing a trip into the unknown... It is the only joyful, hopeful poem, a reprieve. A constantly recurring theme strikes me and sounds at that moment, gruesomely and sarcastically:

> Bumpety-bump, bumpety-bump
> We'll ride to a happy land!...

Basia, who had just returned from the reconnaissance, leaned over to me: "It's the selection again. It makes you afraid just looking!"

I went out. Behind the *sauna* women from the ghetto were undressing. Dr. Mengele, accompanied by Kramer and the SS *hauptscharführer* Hahn, was carrying out a selection. A tiny group of women of average weight stayed on the side of "life." Mengele pulled them from the passing line. The vast remainder, hundreds of emaciated women, had nothing to offer the Greater Reich. It was a waste to serve them food, so they moved on to the site of the crematorium. They walked in single file, ashamed, half-conscious. An extremely skinny girl, whom we could see extremely well passed by. She gazed around like a tormented animal, not seeing anyone, crying:

"People! Where are the people?"

There was no answer. The girl's screams continued:

"Hey! The whole world has gone mad! The whole world has gone mad!"

She stood and listened. We cowered behind the barracks. Suddenly she began to run fast, faster and faster. I leaned out and saw how she forced herself through a group of naked women, how she paved her entrance into the gas chamber...

Bumpety-bump, bumpety-bump
We'll ride to a happy land!...

Part Four

THE FRONT IS GETTING CLOSER

Chapter One

Air Raid

My sister was right, the signs in the sky and on the earth indicated that the Third Reich was crumbling, that it was cracking, and it was evident that soon it would be crushed under the victorious foot of the Allies.

Although the shadows of what had once been people were still going to the gas, and although every day trucks loaded with the "living dead" still rumbled over the camp-street, we hoped that each truckload would be the last. They were hurrying but they would not burn all of them. They were trapped. This was not a rumor, not the first or second year of the war, but the last. Those who had just arrived and those who had just entered would not see it. We also would die an hour before the liberation, but what of it? Our inexpressible happiness at the thought that retaliation had come, that "they are dying," outweighed our personal fears. They had no new weapon. That was just propaganda. The truth was that the Allies had moved forward in the West to Akwizgran and that in the East the Soviet Army had reached the Vistula.

We knew the truth from the communiqués we listened to and from the newspapers smuggled out of our chief's office. We drew our conclusions from the changed behavior of the gentlemen of the *Herrenvolk*,[201] from their vague facial expressions and the sudden transition from sadistic cruelty to

[201] The "Master Race."

the greatest of leniency toward the prisoners. The despised prisoners remained cool and hostile in spite of the beatings and exercises. We winked at each other:

"They're cracking. We must stand this too."

All transports ceased at the beginning of September[202]. We waited a few days. Nothing. No trains on the ramp. Only one crematory was working. The radio went dead. The parcels did not come. The only signs of life were the loaded *Canada* trucks. They were moving at a swifter tempo.

We listened to this silence.

We should organize a strong pair of shoes, Nella advised. "I'm going to *Canada*. Good shoes are important. We may have a long march."

Suddenly at noon one day, the roar of plane engines burst upon us. The alarm began to blare almost simultaneously. We were transported with joy. The sound of the motors came to us like the most beautiful music. The winged squadron boomed in a leaden rhythm and a joyous hope trembled in the air.

"I wish they'd drop a few bombs," Basia sighed as she looked up into the sky.

Irene turned her eyes to where the planes were flying.

"I wish they'd drop a few bombs just to clear the way for us. All we want is an hour of chaos and a partisan unit nearby." Nella, with her head also upturned, laughed at Irene.

"Is that all? I wish for a boyfriend with a car or a gold watch, and a star from heaven."

What was that? Boom—boom—we ran into the hut. The gentlemen of the SS, the rulers of Birkenau, shot out of the SS kitchen and headed for the gates where, we discovered now, a shelter had been built. We could not deny ourselves the pleasure of watching them. Bedarf, our local monster, headed the rout. The others followed close behind. Only Janda stood

[202] Killing by means of *Zyklon B* gas was halted in Auschwitz only in the first days of November 1944.

quietly under the barrack with both hands in her pockets. The bombs were falling close by[203]. Our hut shook from the impact. We stood in silence praying that it would go on.

Czesia broke the silence with childlike statement.

"And I used to be so afraid of bombs!"

The air raid lasted half an hour. Camp C was on fire.

The barracks are burning," someone noticed. "Maybe the wind will turn in our direction."

"What good would it do, silly?" someone explained. "We'll be forced to sleep in the open. They'll release the dogs and you'll have to sit still."

Unfortunately, the "roaring poem" ended, and after dropping their load, the machines flew away.

After the air raid Bedarf and the other SS men scrambled out of the shelter and their faces again assumed a domineering expression. They tried to laugh the whole thing off.

In the afternoon, apparently to mark the occasion of today's events, they arranged a frantic binge for themselves. They drank like people on a sinking ship. They broke everything that could be broken. They sang, shouted, became muddled and then dangerously boisterous. We closed all our doors against unwanted visitors. But they walked in, *Wiener Schnitzel* and the Blind Man. We did not know what to do. We pretended to be very busy. The Blind Man glared at us with his one eye:

"*Na, was, dumme Schweine, lustig, nicht wahr?*"[204]

No one answered. He drew out his revolver and aimed it at Irene.

The door flew open. Wurm, drunk as a skunk, was sitting in a baby carriage squealing at the top of his lungs. He was

---

[203] KL Auschwitz was never directly targeted by the Allies. On the 13th September 1944, however, the American Air Force launched an air raid on the chemical plant at Auschwitz III-Monowitz, during which several clusters of bombs were dropped in error on Auschwitz I and Birkenau.

[204] Well, what, stupid pig, funny, isn't it?

pushed by Hahn. At the same time the orderly-room door opened. Janda stood in the doorway. Her perceptive eyes took in the whole scene at one glance. The noise ceased abruptly. The Blind Man hid his revolver. Wurm cease to howl.

Hahn left the baby carriage and approached Janda. Janda slammed the door in his face. His fury was roused. He found another door to the orderly-room. Then we heard a scream, the sounds of broken glass and a struggle.

We sat rigid, hoping that they would not notice us—that they would not want to "play with us." I felt sorry for Janda. The drunken orgy ended without any unpleasant consequences for us.

Wurm fell asleep in the baby carriage. *Wiener Schnitzel* began to yodel. An hour later Janda appeared, pale as a ghost and told us to clear the broken glass.

The next day we learned that the hospital barracks of the SS men had been bombed. Among the SS were a lot of dead and wounded. Bomb shards also wounded several *häftlings*.

One day Wala from the *Politische Abteilung*, whom we had not seen for a long time, appeared in Birkenau and told us that there was to be no more gassing. An order had come from Berlin. Reliable sources, that meant "the boys," presumed that this was contingent upon the occupation of German territory. It was said that the Allies threatened retaliation if this was not stopped. Although we knew that Wala had access to official information, we were inclined not to believe her. How many times did we think that this was the end but the transports kept on coming? I asked Wala about the girls from my transport. Wala knew everything. She knew who had died, who worked on the *aussen* who worked under a roof, who was in the hospital. I realized that only a very few from my transport had survived. I remember how after my arrival I was frightened by the death statistics. Anyone whom I met then, at the beginning first said, "And so what if I'm alive? Forty of us arrived, and now only four are living..."

Wala had brought the first transport list from Auschwitz to Ravensbrück. She said that this was an evacuation transport. Others were to follow.

We took out *karteikarten*[205] and began to write letter "ü" (*überstellt*)[206], next to the names of the evacuees. I knew many of the women on the list. I came across Stefa's name. Other evacuation lists arrived and still there were no transports to the ramp.

Outside our windows, members of the French Resistance were repairing the trail of death. A cool September drizzle seeped through their thin cotton uniforms. Their eyes were apathetic and hollow. It was difficult to imagine that these men had fought, that they had ever carried arms. Now cold and resigned, they dug the *lagerstrasse*.

Nella wanted to give one of them a pair of socks, but how? When the *posten* moved away she motioned to one of them, opened the window and threw out a piece of bread and a pair of socks. The *posten* wheeled about. We realized that he had noticed. Nella saved the situation. Smiling disarmingly she called to the young *posten*:

"Let it be. I could be your mother, I didn't do anything wrong."

It worked. The guard turned away and pretended not to have noticed anything. The French boy devoured the bread. His friends looked at him with envy and glanced toward our window in dumb expectation. We had no more bread and we were afraid of the *posten*. We turned to our work. What could we do? Thousands of *häftlings* were now working in the fields. There were thousands of hungry people from Warsaw, from the Lodz ghetto, from Hungary. It was impossible to help all of them.

---

[205] Index cards.
[206] Transferred.

A freshly arrived transport of prisoners on the ramp, prior to selection.

Single *zugangs* arrived. Three pregnant women were being led from the ramp. I took a bucket and went out for water. I approached the women. Hungarian Jews. They had been here before. They were selected for clearing rubble—their pregnancy had not been noticed then. They knew why they had been brought here. One of them, with a calm and thoughtful face, pointed toward the crematory:

"I know what that is. My mother died there, and now I. That will be better." She smiled bitterly.

I did not try to deny or comfort them. They knew everything. I felt, however, that I must say something. I felt something very much like shame because I was to live while they...

"And I wanted so much to have a child," another woman said. Then she looked around impatiently:

"When will they come for us?"

"Does it last long?" asked the youngest, who was the most upset.

"No," I said quickly and fled.

A strange woman stopped me at the entrance to our barrack. She had a thick layer of make-up on her face, a watch on her wrist, high-heeled shoes, a tight skirt and—a number. "*Kommando Effektenkammer?*" she asked.

"Here. Are you a *häftling?*"

"*Ich bin ein Sonderhäftling*"[207], she answered provokingly.

"What does that mean? Have you come without a *posten?*"

"That's none of your business. I want to see the *kapo.*"

We entered the office. The appearance of the *sonderhäftling* caused some surprise.

The girl spoke to the *kapo* Maria in a low voice and then walked out coquettishly.

"Don't you know who she is?" Maria laughed. "She's the *sonderhäftling* from the *puff.* She came from the men's camp for her valuables. She's released." She had scarcely departed when I noticed a *posten* leading an older woman.

"Another *zugang.* They're straggling in one by one today," Maria grumbled. When the woman walked into our office, I recognized the Social Democrat from Vienna.

"You're back again?" we asked in surprise. "Where were you all this time?"

"In Auschwitz. In the bunker. They were investigating. They tortured me. They wanted to find out the names of our party members who are working against Hitler. I said nothing. I didn't betray anyone."

Ada took off the woman's coat, with that memorable button still sewed on. We were sorry for her. A few minutes later she stood in front of us with her hair shaved off, wearing a short narrow dress with a red cross painted on the back.

[207] I am a special prisoner.

She shivered in the rain. Just then Wurm walked by bundled up in a rain cape. The woman hesitated for a second then she moved toward him and reached out her hand.

But he was in a different mood today. The old Jew did not entertain him any longer. He stopped for a second and then moved on. Her hand fell limply at her side.

"They lived in the same district," Tanya said with contempt. "He behaved very badly, right my little old lady? He comes from Vienna and you came from Vienna. How sad. You thought that he'd send you home but he sent you to the bunker. You shouldn't have been taken in by his smooth face. You should have looked at the skeleton head he wears. He does not wear it by accident... none of them do. This is their real face."

Chapter Two

A Breath of Freedom

One memorable day, Janda instructed Nella, Ada and me to "find a few jugs."

I ran to *Canada* to look for them not understanding what she meant.

"We're going for a walk," Janda said smiling, "to pick mushrooms."

We shouted with joy. We could not believe our luck. Janda put on her cap and brought out her police dog. We took jugs and walked out. Coming out of the gate, we turn right, towards the white house.

The earth was damp, the sky a pale blue. We entered a crystal clear atmosphere. The nauseating, musty smell of corpses disappeared, the shouts from *Canada* died away. Our step was light and free. Our feet caressed this free plot of land. We entered the woods. No one disturbed the quiet. Janda motioned for us to sit down. I sat on a log. Nella leaned against a tree. Tears dropped from beneath her lowered eyelids.

Is it possible that sometime in the past you could have simply walked through the woods and fields and regarded it as a normal thing to do? Had I ever seen such beauty and harmony in every branch, in every shade of green in every blade of grass? Had I absorbed the scent of the world with such delight? I don't know, I can't remember how it used to be.

I did not want this moment to end. I took some earth between my fingers—clean earth unstained by human blood. The sand flowed through my fingers.

Janda was observing me. My enemy was looking at me. I suddenly thought, "If I could only get hold of her revolver. I could shoot her and the dog and take that road through the forest and across the field and then? It would not matter. That one moment would be worth it."

My eyes must have betrayed me because Janda came up to me and placed her hand on my shoulder. A shudder ran through me at that touch.

"Na, Krysia, gehen wir weiter, nicht wahr?"[208]

I grew depressed. I knew that I would not harm her and I knew that I would return. I was sorry that I had consented to come. Now it would be worse. And tomorrow they might march us in columns of five to the crematory. The magic burst and disappeared. I was afraid to look around. I wanted to return to the camp immediately. I wanted to forget.

And if ever... even if I manage to have real freedom again, can I not associate the most beautiful landscapes, the most charming places with the black smoke, with blood-red flames, with the desperate last cry of the roasted people? I guess I will never be able to do it, never. People will have their own affairs, and I will always be here with my thoughts. My heart will be here. Others will be in the woods, and I will continue to be next to the burning trenches, belching with fire chimneys. Nothing can overcome that. Nothing can cross out those memories.

"It's probably a disability," I said aloud.

Nella looked at me with surprise.

"What?"

"We are crippled."

Nella was thinking. I saw that she could understand me.

[208] Well, Krysia, we move on, right?

The sun shone brightly on the copse. We began to look for mushrooms. We did not find many. Nella spoke hesitatingly to Janda.

"There aren't many mushrooms today *Frau Aufseherin*[209]. Maybe we should come again another time?"

"You will probably pick mushrooms often."

And you?'

"I shall also...[210]" her voice broke. "Let's go back."

The sun rose higher. I remembered my first expedition to the *aussen* of a year ago. Everything had changed now. I was no longer hungry. My hair was long again. I was wearing an apron and stockings. I looked like a human being again. I had known so little then. Zosia was still alive. I had met Andrzej.

Only the sun shone the same and the earth smelled the same. It was so difficult to go back. One thing was common then and today and every other day behind the barbed wire— the eternal, tormenting uncertainty as to what they will do with us tomorrow. We went back the same way. We tried to extend the tour, but besides walking slower we, couldn't think of anything else.

The wire fences loomed in front of us. "I could turn and run," I thought. The dog trotted at my side. My feet stepped automatically across the entrance. We heard shouts from the *sauna.* Basia ran out to me:

"A Jew is getting twenty-five strokes. But, how did it go? I envy you. Did you find many mushrooms?'

"Freedom is very nice, Basia. But it's good that I came back. You know, I've probably gotten used to it. Are there any new evacuation lists?"

I could not wait for the end of the day. I kept looking up at the clock above the table. I wanted to be in bed to dream about that walk. At four o'clock I began to clear my desk. Ziuta, still

[209] Mrs. Warden.
[210] The text was supposed to mean: *My body will feed the mushrooms.*

pounding on her typewriter, smiled at me with satisfaction. Suddenly Zosia burst into the office.

"The third crematory is on fire!'

Just then we heard shots. We ran out. The third crematory was in flames.

SS men, with their rifles pointed, poured from all sides and sped toward the burning crematory. The attack had begun. We heard firing from the direction of the crematory as the fire grew more intense.

The boys from the *Effektenkammer* rushed by Wacek explained the situation. He spoke quickly:

"The *Sonderkommando* rebelled[211]. They reduced their numbers because the transports have been held up. They were to leave today. They did not want to die like the others. This may be a signal for a total uprising."

The flame was already reaching the roof. And was coming out from the window of the gas chamber. Only the chimneys were erect. I felt great excitement. A wave of strange emotion flooded my heart. I gazed hypnotically at the chimneys and waited for them to collapse...

The symbolic meaning of this event was so great that it overshadowed everything else. It was no longer important that the other crematories were still standing and that there were still machine guns and other deadly devices.

The battle itself became important. It was important that on the eve of the Nazis' final defeat, the place of their most heinous, most sophisticated crimes, a place that they would like to hide from the world and from their own conscience, burned in a fire of rebellion, hatred and revenge. The blaze no longer meant the death of asphyxiated millions in closed traps with blind walls. This glow was no longer passive submission to the treacherous, criminal methods of a seemingly invincible enemy.

[211] During the revolt by prisoners of the *Sonderkommando*, crematorium IV was set ablaze in an uneven fight against the SS. 451 prisoners were killed.

Crematorium IV at Birkenau, 1943.

This flame was a part of the approaching front. What a delight to see the lords of life and death, those of "lofty" positions hiding from that front, running scared with their rifles around the burning building. They looked cowardly and small against the handful of characters, a handful of those whom they despised, Jews.

"*Alle Juden Zählappell!*" the infuriated master of Birkenau, the SS *hauptscharführer* Hahn shouted. "*Alle verfluchten Juden Zählappell!* "[212]

All the Jews who worked in the *sauna* and *Canada* ran in great terror and lined up in fives in front of the *sauna*. Hahn stood in the center snapping his whip.

These "damn Jews" had to be watched otherwise they would start trouble. At any rate, he felt safer here than under gunfire.

---

[212] All damn Jews, roll call!

Reinforcements arrived, SS men on motorcycles and bicycles. Scarcely had they dismounted when firing was heard from the second crematory. They stopped and swiftly sped in the opposite direction. At that moment, one of the crematory chimneys crashed.

"It's getting hot," Basia whispered.

Wacek appeared again.

"The situation is improving. Get ready. We may have to run. Let's stay together."

A fire brigade composed of *häftlings* arrived from Auschwitz. Billows of smoke escaped from all sides of the building. The abominable structure crumbled like a house of cards. The second chimney began to sway. It fell with a crash. We could clearly hear clearly of shooting from the third crematory. At that point we could still hear single shots from the second crematory. The fire burned weakly. Then it flickered out. The SS men began to return from "the battlefields."

I shuddered like from a nightmare. The wires were still intact. The sun hid behind Birkenau. Above us the uninterrupted blue sky stretched out.

November brought a fine drizzle and resignation. What about the blitz offensive? The end of the year was approaching and apart from the evacuation of transports there were no other changes. Even single *zugangs* stopped arriving. By order of the commander all the men had to go through the empty *sauna* before leaving the camp. They were unbelievably thin and hungry. They lived on only a *lager's* food portions. Soup distribution instituted fights.

In their hurry they spilled some of the frozen turnips and cereal. A few *häftlings* fell on the ground and lapped it up.

Basia commented sadly, "I wouldn't have believed it if I had not seen it myself. I couldn't imagine myself falling so low." We swiftly collected some bread. It could not be handed out through the window because they would have mobbed us. We had to maneuver it so that the others would not notice.

Our contribution was like a drop in the ocean. The shivering, exhausted *musselmen* shuffled in their large clogs.

When the bread was exhausted we began to distribute mufflers, gloves and socks. Irene had brought a whole bundle of mufflers from *Canada*. No one had noticed. Our typist had been knitting gloves and earmuffs in her free time, sobbing quietly.

A bitter cold penetrated the whole camp. The world looked damp and dismal. The sight of the stumbling, hungry stripes depressed us. Only the mountains seemed to stand out more clearly and closer to us. Hours were stretching hopelessly. The work in *Canada* had been slowed down with the secret consent of the SS men and the *kapo*. The SS men did this in their own interest. The *Canada* barracks could have been cleared within one day, and their jobs would have come to an end and they might have been sent to the scary eastern front. They skillfully divided the work to last for several weeks. Undeniable, however, was the fact that transports no longer arrived.

One day they began to raze the fourth crematory.

We could not believe our own eyes. The women who worked there described in detail the design of the furnaces, the changing room, gas chambers, and vestibule. We stopped dreaming about the illusions of freedom, again, we think differently:

"They're destroying the last traces of their crimes. They will destroy us also. The world will never know. And if someone should escape, no one will believe him—no one will listen."

We held a "family council" that evening. We decided to remain here as long as possible. We knew how it was here. If something bad were to happen it would find us wherever we might be. If we were going to be free, we would be saved here. Anyway, the moods were changing with every hour.

I decided not to think about it any longer. "Let it come— only fast," as the Hungarian Jews had said before they died.

We had waited for this moment for so many years. Why should we worry now? We said that we only wanted to see their defeat that was all. Why be ungrateful now? Why should we want to live?

We became very depressed. The one topic of conversation was, "What will they do with us? How will they get rid of us? Do they know, or are they waiting for an order from Berlin? They won't gas us because they are removing the crematories. They can only shoot us."

The most widespread rumor was that they would drop a bomb on the camp. They would then announce that the Allies had bombed it. No one would bother to verify this insignificant fact.

We wondered whether it would not be better to be transferred to another camp. We would be far worse off but would we not save our lives? Maybe a *lager* deep in German territory would survive until the end of the war and they would be not able to finish. On the other hand we would probably perish in another camp and no one would learn what we had seen here.

* * *

Parcels which had been sent out to the Reich began to return. We could not hide our joy even in the presence of our chief and other SS men. The girls would rush out to the truck to verify the addresses and in this way learn which cities had been occupied by the Allied armies.

Czesia asked the chief innocently "*Herr Chef* [213], why did they return?'

"There must be a bottleneck on the railways." He rolled off the ready-made formula. Czesia then turned to us and winked. That afternoon the *kapo* told us that there was to be a

[213] Mr. Chief.

short meeting with the chief immediately after work. We lined up in the corridor. We expected the worst—the disbanding of the squad, evacuation, gassing. Even the *kapo* did not know what it could be. Our chief walked in. Basia trembled. I knew that this time nothing would save us. This was the end.

"We have appreciated your work. I am satisfied and that is why..."

Basia clenched her fists convulsively. The *kapo*, pale as a sheet, listened tensely. The chief turned to her, "Well, Maria, choose five *brave Mädels*".[214]

"This will be the first extermination," I thought feverishly. Confused, Maria called out five random names. The girls stepped forward. The chief drew some paper money out of his pocket and began to hand it out.

"The Great German Reich has decided to grant you this premium for your work...'

The tension broke. I wanted to laugh. We had won our life again. We could buy some mustard in the canteen for the two marks. That was the only thing sold there. This sudden change in the treatment of the despised *häftlings* amused us. Rewards for good work... What did they expect in return for that? Maybe they thought we would forget? And if they wanted us to forget it meant that they would not kill us. "Too late, my little flower. This won't help you now. You shouldn't have killed millions of innocent people[215]," Ziuta grumbled. After the reward ceremony followed a command, which this time made even the biggest pessimists believe "that they were coming to an end."

The chief ordered that we should remove all the cards of the dead and of the transferred from the card index within the following two days. We were then to make typewritten

[214] Brave girls.

[215] In Auschwitz they killed at least 1.1 million (among them approximately a million Jews) of at least 1.3 million people brought there.

lists of the removed cards. These lists together with the list of *zugangs* and dead *(totenliste)* were to be sent to Buchenwald.

The typists were to work all night. In the office, usually empty at this time, machines were tapping the number, the name and a small letter "v" *(verstorben)* at breathtaking speed, beginning with the first transport. In front of me I had significant, terrible statistics. There was a "v" beside the majority of the numbers. There was nothing but "v's" from five thousand to eighty-eight thousand. I looked through several pages and rarely came across a "ü" *(überstellt)*. Often, all transports of up to several dozen people had only a "v".

The following night I was working on the cards of my own transport. No. 55907—*verstorben*, No. 55909—*verstorben*. Every number in front of me and after me was dead. I could not understand why I had to skip my own number. How did it happen that I was still alive?

I stopped writing. The hospital, typhus, sores and corpses beside the barracks—everything stood before my eyes. That was a year ago. That was when Zosia and many others died. That was when I had thought that I would not live another day. And I had survived a year.

The radio blared through the open door of our chief's office:

> *Es geht alles vorüber,*
> *Es geht alles vorbei,*
> *Nach jedem Dezember*
> *Kommt wieder ein Mai.*[216]

I walked out. It was snowing. White flakes of snow covered the barracks and crematories. They clung to the wire fence and melted on my forehead. Dark huts, set in even rows, slumbered in the white snow. I wasn't alone in the sublimity and serenity of the winter night. With me,

---

[216] Everything passes. Everything goes away. After every December comes back again May.

The wooden barracks at the BIIa sector of Auschwitz II-Birkenau.

next to me were all the *verstorben*. They hovered with their naked, emaciated bodies. They look with their burning eyes into the imperturbable whiteness. They stretched out their hands imploringly. Those from Pawiak and those from the quarantine, they surrounded me. There were more and more of them. I heard their commanding whisper: "Do not ever forget us. Do not forget us and let others not forget us either. Let them avenge us. They must avenge us because otherwise neither during the winter night nor during the spring day we will let them go peacefully. Freedom is approaching. Those who find happiness of freedom, let them never..."

"I will not forget!" I speak as an oath. "I am not able to forget."

Hunched over from the cold, a *posten* was standing sentry in his box. Surprised at the sight of a lone figure walking at night he shouted:

"Was machst du hier?"[217]

[217] What are you doing here?

"*Ich warte*"[218], I answered.

"For what?" the guard called.

"*Auf die Freiheit...* for freedom, understand?"

A laugh floated above the wire fence. I returned to the barrack. The chief wanted to see me. I entered, full of hate.

"Do you have much more to do?" he asked without lifting his eyes from the letter he was writing.

I looked over his shoulder. "*Meine allerliebste Eva...*"[219]

The radio was playing a Gypsy tune... *Ekh, ras yeshtcho... yeshtcho mnogho, mnogho ras...*[220] So my chief is writing love letters while we are compiling death lists. So he can love and long for Eva. She must love him, too. He looks so human right now—he's even pleasant... I felt

I felt repelled. There was a paperweight on the desk. I restrained myself from lifting my hand.

"*Na, was?*"[221] he raised his head. "Do you have much more to rewrite?"

"There's not much left, *Herr Chef!*"

He lit a cigarette and looked out of the window, "Oh, it's been snowing."

"Yes."

I looked at him carefully. His reaction to the snow had been just like ours. He also rose and walked out. He stopped near Basia. Both of them felt the charm of the snow. The SS man spoke, "How lovely and quiet."

Basia did not answer. I knew what she must have been thinking. Was it also beautiful and quiet when he had been the crematory chief?

"It doesn't look like a camp," he continued as if to himself. "All the traces have disappeared."

I moved back and sat at the typewriter. He was right.

[218] I am waiting.
[219] My dearest Eva...
[220] (Russian) Eh, once again... many, many times again...
[221] Well, what?

322

All the traces had been erased. And I at this moment was also eradicating traces. All the clues to the crime will go to Buchenwald[222]. The army of liberation will find only snow.

* * *

On the 4th December we congratulated Basia on her birthday. We decided not to work. I explained to the *kapo* that we had so little fun in life and that such a holiday should be celebrated. Discipline had truly become very lax because of the change in the attitude of the authorities toward us.

The *kapo* stared with surprise at our impertinence. Her eyes condemned us: "You seem to forget where you are."

At that moment, Irene rushed in and announced sadly, "The boys are leaving today. All of them."

"Ours, too?"

"All the Poles. The camp authorities are afraid of uprisings. They are afraid the boys are organized."

I knew that given our situation, if the beaten, humiliated *häftling* next to us is a man or a woman, it's all the same. But I understand the sadness and grief which overwhelmed us was based not only out of our sympathy. The knowledge that the men were close by had given us courage. The knowledge of their silent protection and help just "in case" had made us feel safe.

"We shall be alone," Irene said tearfully.

I went out to look for Wacek. The men from Birkenau were rushing about. The air was filled with the fever of departure—"We're leaving today"—that was frightful. Cyprian, one of our friends, shook my hand right under the nose of a passing SS man.

"Good-bye Krysia. We will meet in Lodz in front of the Grand Hotel on Piotrkowska Street."

[222] Perhaps the author is referring to documents the prisoners working in the camp offices were told to prepare for removal. In practice, most of them were burned on the spot.

"When?"

"One year from now at noon. I will come for sure."

Wacek was saying goodbye to Zosia. I stood in the doorway. He came up to me. We stood without saying anything. It was nearly dark. A mass of gray bags hung over us. We were standing in a narrow passage between the shelves. We didn't know what to say. Finally, Wacek smiled nervously, "One never knows what to say at such moments. I trust this is not our last meeting."

You couldn't plan ahead for a situation like this. We had lived through a very strange period and couldn't change that.

"Yes."

"We alone shall be able to appreciate to the fullest, the miracle of a home, silence and the ticking of a clock."

"Yes."

"I shall try to survive... I know you will remember."

"Yes.'

"You're only saying 'yes'. Say something in farewell."

"Keep well, Wacek. Everything you've said and done here was beautiful."

All the men gathered on a large field. The shivering stripes with ashen grey complexions were stamping their frozen feet. A man suddenly doubled over. A stream of blood flowed from his mouth and stained the glittering snow. He wiped his mouth with his sleeve. Lucyna opened the window and threw out a clean handkerchief.

Someone else picked it up. Lucyna motioned frantically that the handkerchief had been meant for the man who had the hemorrhage.

The *häftlings* began to line up. Nobody had to issue the command. Everybody knew that sooner or later they would have to stand in fives. There were those who had grown accustomed to the barrack, to the pallet, those who had friends in the *Essenkolonne*[223], and had learned how to

[223] Food column.

get extra portions of soup. There were those who had been fortunate enough to work under a roof. Now they were going to a strange place, to a new, crowded concentration camp. Here they knew whom they should watch out for. And there, they might die before they could learn.

The only thing that sustained them was the thought of the approaching front.

Our boys from Birkenau were passing by. They wore coats and hats and looked like normal people. Familiar faces, familiar features. Smiling, they waved to us in farewell. Beautiful Genia was crying. Her Bolek was leaving with his accordion.

"Button your coat," she called. Shy Pawel looked at Ziuta who stood next to me with a last loving gaze. Wacek passed by. Wacek—I saw his dark blue coat, glasses and his hard-set mouth. I threw him a pair of earmuffs.

"Put them on. You'll freeze," I tried to speak calmly.

Wacek caught the earmuffs, took off his cap and bowed.

"If I don't return try to find my mother. Tell her that I was happy here."

The columns of five moved away, this time irrevocably.

Nella began to cry.

"Don't you cry," she begged. "I must... I must think that my son might have been here."

Genia ran out of the hut. I followed her. She shouted after Bolek.

"Remember my address—Bydgoszcz!"

I repeated after her to Wacek, "Remember Lodz."

Wacek nodded with a smile.

"Chin up!" he called.

A raucous laugh, coming from the rear, startled both of us. The SS *hauptscharführer*, drunk as always, was laughing at us.

Our boys disappeared from our sight. The columns of stripes stretched far in the distance. A terribly thin young boy marching in the last column turned his head and shouted, "See you when we're free!'

* * *

The camp was empty and quiet. We finished copying names from the last, the thirteenth women's transport list. Ten thousand women still remained in the camp. The others had been sent to Flosenburg, Bergen Belsen, Ravensbrück and Buchenwald. We were wondering what would become of these transports at the end, because we were still not leaving,

We began to feel uneasy. "They plan to wipe out those who remain" was the current rumor.

The crematories were disappearing. One day, *zugangs* arrived whom we hadn't seen for a long time. They were from Czestochowa. They told us that they had been evacuated from the prison. Other *zugangs* began to arrive from the prisons in the vicinity of Czestochowa. These *zugangs* were made up of all kinds of people. There were those who had received sentences or were under investigation, as well as those who had been caught in street round-ups or locked up for one night. It looked as if all prisons had been ordered to evacuate immediately.

Then Jewish women from armament factories in Pionki and Plaszow came. They looked well fed and were dressed warmly. They all went to the *lager* without there being a selection. All of them were young and healthy. They took the place of those sent away.

The camp was becoming filled up again. Food parcels didn't arrive so frequently. There was nothing from the crematories. The camp portions remained the same. We were again very hungry. We ate the *lager's* bread with margarine with appetite, but there was always too little of it. Someone took liberties with a macabre joke, turning to a Jewish girl from *Canada* saying. "We could use a transport for the 'gas.'"

The girl bit her lip and turned away.

Chapter Three

The Last Christmas

Our last Christmas in Auschwitz was drawing near. We knew that. We had put away apples and candy from our food parcels. The kitchen served cabbage and potatoes. We put on dresses especially prepared for the occasion and arranged the tables in the form of a horseshoe. Our chiefs allowed us to stay up all night; they permitted everything we asked. The Christmas tree arrived. Bedarf, who suddenly began to talk to us and who was even seen to smile once, ordered a Jew to carry the tree into our barrack. The Jew answered something and walked away.

A few minutes later we heard shouts and a struggle. I peered into our chief's office through the crack in the door. Bedarf was punching the Jew and swearing, "*Verfluchter Jude, verfluchter Jude!*"

The man was down on his knees. Bedarf was beating him in the face.

Blood flowed from his nose and ears. The man tried to say something. Bedarf began to kick him with increasing fury. Wurm and the Blind Man were standing a few paces away. Wurm, a little paler than usual, looked at the scene with approbation. Bedarf finally stopped kicking and collapsed into a chair. The Jew rose with difficulty and took a few steps toward the exit. The Blind Man ran after him and kicked him.

We learned from one of the girls that the Jew had refused to carry in the tree because he had been summoned by the SS *hauptscharführer*. Bedarf told him to go to the SS *hauptscharführer* and return.

The Jew returned.

Zosia had received a letter from home with her sister's photograph. She had not seen her sister for three years. We placed the picture at her place. Each one placed a family picture at her place. I introduced my mother to Basia's mother—in the photograph of course. From then on everything became unreal. We resolved that we would pretend to be at home that night. Zosia picked up the only picture at her place:

"Oh God!" she called, "Where did you get that? That's my sister!"

"I knew that you'd cry," Basia, unshakable, noted.

How much this Christmas differed from last year's! How I astonished was I, that the nurses in the hospital were are able to dissociate themselves from the surrounding death—that they were in a solemn mood, as if rejuvenated.

* * *

I looked at my friends. They were all very pretty that night.

Their eyes shone, they moved somewhat distinctively, and they gesticulated and talked like civilized people. And yet everywhere around us were hunger, lice, diarrhea and dark berths and with cold, shivering, unhappy *musselmen*. I tried not to think about it. I looked at the Christmas tree in the corner. It was wonderful, beautifully decorated in accordance with the traditional snow, stars and candles. Only our hut had a Christmas tree and such a star.

Again memories of last year flooded back. How I had begged Elzunia to retrieve a bit of the "drinking" snow from outside of the hut. Elzunia had explained to me that the snow was dirty outside the barracks. I begged her, "You can find clean snow between the corpses."

328

"Krysia, read something!" they asked.

I began to read the poem I had written that morning. The poem was sad. I spoke of the future which seemed so unreal to us... Only today, only this one... evening:

> Resentment, hatred and grief will pass,
> In the holy brotherhood of unity will come true,
> The desire to silence will unite us all,
> All suffering in the same captivity,
> The dream of peace will reconcile us all...
> God is being born...

Next to me, Basia sighs deeply. Zosia looks at her and has her revenge, "I knew you would cry."

I keep reading:

> And here we are locked in a wire cage
> We have our Christmas Eve, we have the sacred tree,
> Victimized by longing, sadness and poverty,
> Today we break our wafer together,
> With you, who are fighting away from their homeland,
> Whose African sun heat burns,
> Siberian frost chills, the north wind cools,
> Take a break you all... Today, God is being born...

> And with children who may have the gifts,
> But are sitting pathetically in the shade of the Christmas
> tree
> Without the loving care, without their mothers' caresses,
> And with you... That you like us are in the cage,
> You who know the depths of poverty and the despair of
> man
> And you, my Mom, you only one, far away.
> In the brightness of this star, which rises for everyone,
> We salute you... Today, God is being born.

We shared the wafer, we kissed each other, we cried. All the words, all the whishes have one thing in common: the desire for "freedom."

We lit the candles on the tree and put out the lights[224]. Irene stood in front of the tree and recited a poem. The poem was beautiful.

"What are our loved ones doing now?" whispered Zosia.

"They are thinking of us," said Basia thoughtfully.

After supper we sang Christmas carols. The night fell. Through the window we could see the shadow of the *posten* moving back and forth. Nella rose from the table. She filled a plate with cabbage and potatoes and took it out to the *posten*. We saw him take the plate and say silently: "*Danke schön.*"[225]

We stopped singing when Nella returned. She was flustered by our accusing silence.

Nella, embarrassed, explained, "He's a human being and he's cold. It's not his fault that he's German. And besides, this is Christmas." Nobody spoke.

The *kapo* then rose to speak. Janda had asked her to wish us a Merry Christmas. That brought the party to an end. We were allowed to sing one more song.

Ziuta started us off and we joined in a joyous chorus:

Our Native Land, We'll not abandon Thee.

Our chief appeared in the doorway. He was a little drunk. We held hands and sang:

No German shall spit in our face.

---

[224] The entire preceding paragraph, including the poem, which follows the words: "Krysia, read something!" was removed from later editions of the book (starting with the third one in 1951), most likely because it refers to "God being born".

[225] Thank you very much.

He knitted his brows for a second and then his face relaxed in a smile. He did not understand a word of Polish. Or, if he did, he preferred not to show it. We went back to the block.

* * *

A car stopped in front of the *sauna*. Two Germans jumped out of it. They took out a huge box and a strange looking apparatus. I strained my eyes but I could not see what it was. We became apprehensive. What did they intend to do now?

Irene ran in breathlessly:

"They've brought a film!"

"For whom?"

"For us." Indeed, they were screening a movie for us in the *sauna* room.

The film was about Soviet agents and their underhand methods in attracting "innocent"

Nazis[226] to work against their own country. The story was laid in a neutral country. The poor, honest victims[227] with angelic faces fought against the sullen Bolshevik agents. And the poor[228] SS men who had personally conducted so many selections in this very same *sauna* where the film was being shown, who murdered millions of innocent Soviet prisoners of war, these poor SS men[229] knew how aimless and paradoxical it was to show us this film to us prisoners waiting for the Soviet army to liberate us. They dared to show us this anti-Soviet propaganda film in the place where they had burned hundreds of thousands of people in front of our eyes after so many years of suffering, when every fiber in us breathed

---

[226] In the first edition from 1946—*Germans*. All the changes were introduced in the third edition from 1951. See footnote 173 (p. 260).

[227] In the first edition, 1946, *Germans*. See footnote 173.

[228] In the first edition,1946, *German—SS men*. See footnote 173.

[229] In the first edition, 1946—the *poor Germans understood it well.* See footnote 173.

hate and pulsed with a desire for retaliation and dreams of revenge[230].

Toward the end of the film we began to laugh. We decided to treat the film as a comedy. When one of the actors fell we rolled with laughter. The lights went on. The new camp commander Klausen[231] turned his steely gaze at us. We stopped laughing. We left the "cinema" in an excellent mood. "And when they will take us to a dance?" Nella wondered.

* * *

The sun became warmer at the beginning of January and the mountains stood out clearly against the bright sky. The crematories in Birkenau had disappeared. Only one crematory remained in Auschwitz[232]. The Germans could always explain that this crematory had been used for cremating those who had died a natural death.

It was strange to walk over the smooth, snow-covered ground. The temperature was very low and the snow crunched under our feet. We could not forget that we were walking over the ashes of millions of people. We trampled the beautiful Italian girl with the face of the Madonna and Polish, Hungarian, French, Dutch and Gypsy children. Each step on this piece of land brought memories of the procession of death, someone's painful smile, someone's eyes opened wide in fear, an imploring gesture, someone's last groan, final harrowing cry.

Here laid the ashes of my closest, dearest Zosienka,

[230] See footnote 173 (p. 260).

[231] In fact, SS Hauptsturmführer Josef Kramer was the Commandant of KL Auschwitz at that time.

[232] Crematorium I in the main camp Auschwitz I, actually ceased operation in mid-1943, after the crematoria in Birkenau had been made operational. The last of the crematoria to be destroyed was Crematorium V on January 26, 1945.

along with those of Hania, Janka, Nata and many other girls from Pawiak. Time rolled like a wheel of torture and crushed, making our hearts indifferent and weakening even our memories.

We walked in the sun over their ashes, over the disappearing traces of the most monstrous crime—we walked as if nothing had happened here. I myself had begun to doubt that it had all taken place. And what will all those who will come after us say?

On the 5th January, I listened in to a German communiqué from the front:

Oberkommando der Wehrmacht *reports that the long-*
-expected Russian offensive has started along the
whole length of the front.

They had finally moved again. This meant that they should reach Auschwitz within a few days. We tried to figure out how long it would take them to get through to us—a week at most, we thought. Our fate would be decided within that week. They would not be stopped now.

The chief sent a few women to the men's camp in Auschwitz. I was among them. We were to receive new transport lists from the Political division. We walked happily, certain, this time, of the liberation offensive.

"I have a strange premonition," Ziutka confided to me, "That those who are still alive will be saved. I can't imagine how it will feel to be free after so many years." She broke off and fell into deep thought. I knew she was trying to recall all those years of captivity. She had spent five years being moved from one prison to another and from concentration camp to concentration camp. Her mother had died here. Those five years of torment had etched an imprint on her face. She had horribly sad eyes, visible with grief and melancholy. I knew that together with the hope of approaching freedom she was troubled by a fear of the unknown. Would we know how to lead a normal life, how to find a place for ourselves in a strange world, without a home or close relations?

"I'm afraid I shall lose courage," Ziutka added. "I feel frightfully alone." I interrupted her, "Don't say that. You have showed enough fortitude through all these years. There's no need to startle freedom. Let's just hope it will come. Outside the camp you'll find yourself. You'll know what to do. Desire will return and you will find the purpose of life."

We entered the men's camp. We had to wait for the evening roll call to be dismissed. We sensed that this was not a normal roll call. The rows of five were stunned. The prisoners stood tensely. In the numb stillness emanating from the hostile throng, we noticed a gallows and four women hanging by the neck[233].

Four Jewish women from Poland had admitted that they had supplied gunpowder to the *Sonderkommando* from the factories in which they worked. They had been hung during the roll-call so that everyone could see and remember this act of justice. Before they died they called out: "Long live independent Poland! Death to the criminals!"

"Death to the criminals," said Ziutka, regarding the swaying figures sadly. She shook her head. "And they could have been free in an hour!" she muttered.

When we returned to Birkenau in deep dejection we were greeted by Basia who ran up to us greatly excited.

"Guess what! They've thought up something new again!" she called. "We're going to the theatre."

[233] Three days after the revolt had been put down, on the 10th of October, three female prisoners, Polish Jews from the *Union Kommando*, were arrested for supplying explosives to the *Sonderkommando* prisoners: Ala Gertner of Sosnowiec, Regine Safirsztain of Bedzin and Estera Wajcblum of Warsaw. Roza Robota, of Ciechanow, who delivered this material, was also arrested. The Union Werke was located in the vicinity of Auschwitz I. On the 6th of January 1945 they were hanged in the women's camp in Auschwitz.

The Auschwitz gallows.

"What are you talking about?" Ziutka asked, unable to comprehend Basia's enthusiasm.

"The theater. We're going right now. The men and women from *Canada* are going to give a play in the *sauna*."

"I'm not going," Ziutka said as she glanced at me.

"I'm not going either," I repeated. "I can't after the gallows."

I realized, however, that both of us would go. It would be senseless to sit in an empty barrack and think of the hanging. We had laughed and joked when they had been burning thousands of people.

Benches had been arranged in rows and a stage had been built in the *sauna*. We sat on the hard benches. The lights went out and the curtain parted. A man wearing a black suit and carrying a funeral wreath came on to the stage. Staggering slightly, he began to narrate his impressions of a funeral from which he was just returning. The monologue started with the words: "They buried one single man." The crowded hall burst into laughter. A funeral for one man, a black suit, a hearse, wreaths, a casket, an obituary—but that was not all. There would be a tombstone... The actor choked with laughter when he came to the climax of the narration.

The author of the monologue had lost his entire family in the crematories. He, the Jew, might be burnt or hanged at any moment. The ashes of the dead had been scattered over unknown fields and he suddenly remembered a funeral held for one man. How could he help but laugh?

The SS men laughed too. The whole audience laughed hysterically.

The next number on the program was a dance. A beautiful Greek dancer, Olga, in an Easter dance called *Tabu*. Her eyes slid softly over our upturned faces, her young, shapely body swayed. We were enchanted by the rhythmical movement of her hips surrounded by a cloud of green gauze. Olga was really *Tabu*. She was unattainable, proud and distant through the magic of her dance. She was removed beyond the reach of baseness and crime. I completely lost the sense of time, place and identity.

I turned abruptly and looked at the SS *hauptscharführer*. He was enraptured.

Other numbers followed. We were deeply moved. Olga, the dancer, returned to the block with us. She sobbed fitfully.

"What is it, Olga?" I asked.

"My only friend left with a transport today. And now I am completely alone... no one... nowhere... and now they took her away... and then they told me to dance... Why did I dance?"

"Don't cry, Olga. You danced beautifully. It was a beautiful dance. We shan't forget it quickly. Don't blame yourself. We all may be free soon. I saw four Jewish women hanging today. You are alive. Remember, that is most important. Don't cry. You'll live and you'll meet your friend again." I spoke confusedly, as if with a fever.

A bird's eye view of Auschwitz II-Birkenau, January 1945.

The desire for freedom overpowered me with a force I had not experienced before. I believed in it and my faith was communicated to Olga. She threw her arms about me and whispered with passionate entreaty, "To live! Oh my God, to live!"

Chapter Four

Auschwitz Ends

The day after the performance, the Germans took blood from the Jewish girls from *Canada* for transfusions. They were very polite. Ludka, a very resolute Jewish girl from Poland, refused to donate blood. "Why should I? If they want it let them shoot me outright. They can take all the blood they want when they kill me."

The German doctor was surprised at her attitude:

"You refuse to give *Blut für Vaterland* ?[234]"

"You never know how far they will go," Ludka later said to me. "I, the despised, down-trodden Jew, I who mean less to them than trash, I who come from an unclean race—I am to give my blood to the wounded Nordic soldier of the *herrenvolk*... and he dares to call it "blood for the fatherland?"And he was surprised that I refused?"

The daily communiqués gave the names of the liberated cities. New orders came every day. The *lagerkommandant* made a speech in which he emphasized that Germany was bleeding, the situation was at the moment very critical but the new weapon was almost ready and a great Germany would rise again—a more powerful Germany. He turned to the Jews. He told them that he was satisfied with their work and for that reason they would receive prizes and their stars would be exchanged for *winkels*. The *winkels* were in the

[234] Blood for the fatherland.

Richard Baer, the third commandant at Auschwitz (from May 1944 to January 1945). He followed R. Höss and A. Liebehenschel.

form of red triangles with a narrow white band on the top bearing a number. This unusual disposition, the aim of which was to eradicate all racial differences, came as quite a revelation to us.

The discipline in Birkenau was completely relaxed. The SS no longer paid attention to the couples that walked arm in arm in front of the *sauna*. They were occupied by their own thoughts, and were surprisingly gentle.

The parcel post came very rarely now. Finally, we received news that the Oswiecim post office no longer received parcels. That day I got the last enormous package from my most faithful, beloved friend. They were lemons in it. "Bolek always thinks of something special!" Basia said with delight. "It's so nice to consume a lemon before death!"

Now that the outcome was hanging in the air, the discussions of "what they would do with us" had stopped. All of us had come to the conclusion that "we did not need to invent anything."

On January 17th we suddenly got the news that Cracow had been liberated. We were all convinced that this was not a false rumor, besides, we could hear the distant explosions, the sounds for which we had waited so hopefully.

"Well, something's happening at last," Nella declared. I'm not undressing tonight." Basia retorted calmly, "If you want to die in your dress, go right ahead. That's your own affair. I'm undressing. It's all the same to me what I wear when I die."

"All joking aside!" someone opposed indignantly, "The situation is really serious!"

We argued until midnight whether we should undress or not.

I decided to undress. I folded my things carefully so that I could find them quickly if anything should happen.

Irene had found out that Auschwitz was to be evacuated on foot. We did not believe her. "Nonsense, they won't lead sixty thousand people on foot right across the battle line. They'll either kill us or escape and leave us here." These two possibilities seemed more plausible with each passing hour.

I finally fell asleep in a whirlpool of conjectures.

Someone rapped at the window. I sprang up, my heart pounding with apprehension. The others sat up in their beds.

"Maria?"

We recognized Wurm's voice. Maria ran to the window in her nightgown.

We strained our ears for the words that came muffled through the closed window. Wurm spoke slowly and clearly, "Maria, take ten girls and come to my office. We must get ready slowly." He emphasized the word "slowly" so that we would not be alarmed. He was encouraging himself.

We did not need to be told twice. Hardly had he finished the sentence and we stood ready to go. There were more than ten of us. Maria joked, "You got up just like for the *zugangs*."

From that moment on we were like in a fever.

Wanda and I were packing things into trunks.

"No one will get these things back," Wanda declared. "We are to send all these things to the Gross-Rosen camp. We will probably go there too."

They then told us to fetch empty suitcases from *Canada*. Three of us went to the closed barracks with "Slovak." He

340

jingled his keys. His handsome face was distorted by fear. He kept glancing back. We were enjoying this situation immensely. *Canada* was no longer working at night. The night shift was no longer necessary. The camp was silent, soft and white. We walked in silence between the barracks leaving traces on the unmarked snow.

Slovak opened the seventh hut. It was filled with furs. "But we came for suitcases," I informed him. "Pick out a fur coat for yourselves," he said. "What do I care now? They've put me in a hell of a hole!"

I looked at the SS uniform and asked, "Who are 'they'?"

"The Germans. I have nothing to do with them. They brought me here by force and they think I'll let them slaughter me. Not me. I'll go with the gold transport that is going with you. I'll go as an escort. They won't take me alive. Wurm or the SS *hauptscharführer* can stay here to the end. He's smart. He's got everything ready to beat it and he wants to leave us here. The damn Bolsheviks and that offensive. Who would have expected that they would come so quickly?"

"They can't be very close," Ziutka tried to draw him out. "It's not possible."

"Not very close?" he shouted irritably. "They're right under our nose! And they," he pointed toward Hahn's room, "They told me to stay here."

"We don't need fur coats," I said. "We would appreciate a few knapsacks. Do you know what they intend to do with us?'

"They don't know themselves. One way or another, I envy you."

I could have shouted with joy. That Nazi shrimp envied me. Even now he could liquidate me with one move, but he did not do it because he himself was in danger. One more or one less meant nothing to him! But he wanted to talk to someone, because "they" were unjust to him, because each one of them was only thinking of himself. Suddenly, in these last hours he remembered that he had come from Slovakia.

He realized that he was behaving stupidly, but he talked to us about it, knowing that we dared not protest because he was still master here. I could not deny myself the satisfaction of having a little fun. I said in a very serious tone:

"No harm will come to you if you stay. No one will hurt you. Why should they?"

Ziutka pinched me and gave me a warning glance. She added, "Yes, why should they?"

Slovak was uncertain for a second but then he looked at us with a friendly smile and said, "Yes, that's true. Why should they?"

We worked all that night, packing photographs, *kennkarten*[235] and the *karteikarten* of the living in trunks and valises—all according to the numbers from the list.

* * *

At ten o'clock in the morning a group of girls went out to load the trunks onto freight cars. They returned half an hour later. Genia shouted from the truck, "The first transport of the *häftlings* has marched out of the camp. We saw them with our own eyes." So it had happened.

We ate our last dinner in Zosia's hut. There were still a number of sacks in the hut. Some of the sacks had been taken to the train. We knew that nothing would reach its destination. We received communiqués every half hour:

"Camp B is leaving." "They're evacuating sector C." "They're leaving Rajsko."

We expected to be evacuated at any moment. Zosia had cooked all of the food we'd hidden for a rainy day. We ate the noodles with great appetite. Then we began to pack all the essentials into our knapsacks. We didn't expect to reach another concentration camp. Our good spirits were heigh-

[235] Identification Cards.

tened by the beautiful sunny day and the long-faced SS men.

"If they do not liberate us then I'll give them the slip," I announced with determination. "I'm taking the knapsack in case they liberate us."

The girls agreed with me. I felt a flow of added energy. Suddenly, we heard an explosion somewhere in the vicinity. We ran out of the barrack.

"They're here!" I thought joyfully.

A Jew from the *sauna* explained, "You need not be so happy. They are only dynamiting the foundations of the crematories."

To the accompaniment of explosions, we packed food into the sacks. I realized how much more lucky we were than the other women in the camp. We had shoes and warm clothing. Thousands would march barefoot, dressed in thin stripped dresses.

Chapter Five

The Hay Cart

We set out from the camp at 3:30 p.m., feeling strange at leaving Birkenau. I knew that whatever might happen to us, this cursed place would cease to exist. No longer would any transport "to the furnace" arrive here. "Jumping Jacks," kneelings and beatings would cease, the groans of the tortured would be silenced. The hopeless roll calls, fights for a spoonful of the frozen turnip or the bone of a horse would end. Selections, plundering of gold, the smell of corpses, blood and human sweat would pass. Auschwitz would end.

Irene, with a heavy knapsack on her back, her cheeks aglow, looked at the empty wasteland where the crematory had stood.

"There will come a time when grass will grow here," she said thoughtfully.

Elated and greatly moved by the significance of the moment, we passed through the camp gate. We did not feel the weight of our knapsacks and no one thought where the road was taking us. We marched with a light even step. Our feet sped forward. Disregarding the pickets, we burst into a camp song about freedom.

> *The liberation day has come,*
> *a joyful frenzy came upon us.*
> *No longer wandering like a shadow*
> *on Lagerstrasse at Birkenau.*

344

So take off your clogs dump the stripes,
no hair, so what, lift up your head!
Happy like that return home,
with a freedom song on your lips!

As I turned back to take a last look at Auschwitz, an image I will never forget, I could see Wurm wandering between the barracks.

The *sauna*, the roll call field, our barracks, the men's barracks, the path to the third and fourth crematory, and beyond, the forest and Birkenau—and around all this a wire fence. The "lofts" rose high above the fence. The lofts were empty. All the *postens* were with us. There was no one in the camp to watch. Our singing continued:

Goodbye, horrible Auschwitz
and you, terrible Birkenau.
In your empty huts in the winter
pitiful wind will blow...

Papers were burning in all the sectors of the camp. In front of the *blockführerstube*, SS men were stamping out the burnt paper and throwing on other documents. They were destroying every trace of evidence. They did not search us today. The more we carried the better. We were carrying it to another camp. There we would be deloused and everything would be taken away. We knew all about that. But I would not be trapped this time. I would not go to another prison. They might kill me, or I would escape.

Evacuation groups joined us from all sectors of the camp. The columns of five stretched in an unending train. We passed the women's camp. Hustek was standing at the gate. We clenched our fists at the sight of him.

Then we passed through the city of Oswiecim. I looked back on the bend behind the bridge and observed the long, weaving procession of exiles. The trains whistled at the station. We walked as in a dream. The knapsack began to press hard. In Oswiecim we saw the families of the SS men evacuating in great haste. Children, suitcases and bedding were piled on wagons. They too—I was overjoyed. They, too, into the unknown, on the front line. Finally!

It was easier to walk again. I abandoned my knapsack after the fifth mile. Basia laughed at me:

"Are you tired already?"

"I'd rather do it now than on the twentieth mile. Besides, I'm escaping."

A *posten* with a dog walked near every third column. The trained dogs panted at our feet. We could not even dream of escape. Sixty thousand people left the camp, among these, thirty-five thousand men from the Buna-Werke ammunitions factory[236]. Behind every group of four thousand rode a dog sleigh. Machine guns were set on every sleigh. Members of the *Vernichtungskommando*,[237] the extermination squad, surrounded the sleighs. There were dogs everywhere.

I asked the *posten* nearest us whether he knew how far we were going. He answered that we were to go three hundred miles[238]. Then I asked him when we would stop.

---

[236] The ratio had to be slightly different. On the 17th of January 1945 there were 10,223 prisoners in the Monowitz sub-camp which was established next to the chemical plant constructed by IG Farben Industry.

[237] Extermination (death) unit.

[238] As historical documents show, this march (undertaken on the orders of the SS headquarters), called the "death march," had about 15,000 casualties (more than 25% of those who started out). The prisoners, after five days of the murderous walk in the snow and cold, reached Wodzislaw Slaski (German name: Loslau) on January 22nd 1945. The whole vast operation had no rational goal and was merely an expression of the insane German *Ordnung muss sein* (must have order) as if order was the determinant of being. The authorities of this "order" (SS, Gestapo) had reached a high level of autonomy in the country and despite the visible collapse of the Third Reich, continued to perform their functions in a compulsive pathological way, as if the collapse of the country had not affected them.

February 1945. The main gate at Birkenau ("The Gate of Death.").

"I don't know. Maybe late at night."

"What if someone drops out?" I asked.

"She'll get it with the butt end of the gun."

"With the butt end?" I was surprised.

"Why should we shoot at you? Why waste bullets?'

The happiness with which we had left the camp disappeared without a trace. We were again overcome by despair. Our feet grew heavy, three-hundred miles. I had just walked seven miles. Snow-covered fields stretched on both sides of the road. There was no trace of a human being. Basia, Zosia and I clung to each other. The columns had broken a long time ago. We moved in a chaotic mass, prodded on by the *postens*: "*Los!... aufstehen... schnelle... schneller, Schweine!*"[239]

[239] Go!... get up... fast... faster, pigs!

Sighs could be heard with increasing frequency. Now and then someone would fall back and mix with another group. Polish women lost among the French Jewish women could no longer catch up with their own.

The first shots sounded. The sleigh bells of the *Vernichtungskommando* jingled with the melody of death, constantly accompanying us. The light began to fade. Darkness seemed to enter our very hearts. Everything became mercilessly tiring. Every step created pain.

We dragged our feet—three hundred miles, three hundred miles. We had just made nine miles and I felt as if we had walked a whole year... three hundred miles... the first stop at night... butt end over the head... three hundred miles. Would I even get there? Roll calls... hunger... fleas...

No! I knew that I would never reach...

We were passing a village. A couple was walking through the square. Civilians—he and she. He held her arm. She was wearing a fur coat. She was smiling up at him. I wished I could go after them.

Nonsense! A cross on my back, number, no documents...

It was completely dark now. We stumbled over the first corpses. It was very difficult to walk.

Listen," Nella said, "If I should die, look for my son and tell him..."

"I know what to tell him. And you know what to tell my mother, my sister and Bolek. Remember the address?'

Nella repeated the address.

"I'm afraid no one will survive this march."

I did not answer. I was too weak to speak. I felt like all my viscera were going to be torn away.

My hands hung like lead. My throat was parched. I breathed with difficulty. My heart was beating unevenly. I could not understand what the others were saying. Basia's voice came to me faintly.

"Krysia, I can't go a step further. I can't."

"*Los!... Aufgehen!*"[240] the *posten* shouted in my ear.

The woman walking beside me was hit with the butt end of the gun and fell on the snow.

I dragged my feet. All around us—bare, empty fields. Basia threw everything out of her sack. The whole road was scattered with shoes, sweaters, blankets and coats. We stepped over these things in dull resignation. Nothing was important. We did not remember anything. We strained every ounce of energy to make just one more step, a few more steps, perhaps one more mile, this one mile for your mother because you've suffered so, because you are waiting. Maybe at this mile they will jump out of the ditches and rescue us.

I can't fall here... only one more step...one more mile.

I suddenly noticed a capsized hay wagon lying on the road. I made a swift decision. The *posten* had just passed me. Another one was about ten steps behind.

"Now!" I caught Zosia by the hand. "Now! You too!" I added in a commanding voice.

I fell on the straw. Zosia grasped the situation and quickly covered me with some straw.

Oh, what bliss! I lay still. I did not have to walk any longer. I wanted to die. I knew that in a moment someone would strike me over the head. That would be all right—I would not have to walk.

Then I began to gather my scattered thoughts. The picket had passed. That meant he had not noticed. The dog did not smell me either. But there were so many more dogs! My heart pounded faster and faster, my muscles relaxed. I was resting, only my stupid heart beat faster. I fell into a stupor.

The procession was passing.

It seemed that I had been lying thus an hour when I heard Basia's voice:

"Krysia, their dogs are sniffing. I'm going."

[240] Go!... Rise!

My lips moved soundlessly.

"Keep well, Basia."

And the parade moved. Women's voices, pickets shouting, the sleigh as it passed me. I breathed again. So I was still alive...

Now the men approached.

I heard a Polish voice.

"Here—we'll hide here."

I grew weak.

I knew I should not be too concerned because I would die shortly anyway. If a dog did not find me, then someone else would hide here and they would get both of us.

But they did not hide. Another sleigh came by. Then came women's voices, tragic voices: "*Je suis malade* [241], I can't go a step further." The echo of suffering in all languages and always that one language: "*Los! Weiter!*"[242] It was so near, so close to my head.

The straw got into my eyes and mouth. I lay on my back. My head fell back. I felt an acid taste in my mouth.

I lost consciousness several times. Someone sat directly on top of me. "Oh," I heard a sigh.

"Get off!" I growled.

The girl started and got up immediately.

I heard her warn a friend:

"Don't sit there that's taken."

In spite of my fear, I smiled in my thoughts at the girl who had saved me.

"*Los! Weiter! Du wolltest dich hier verstecken?!*"[243] I heard next to me hateful words.

Well, here it comes! I prepared myself. I heard someone being pushed, a struggle, a shout. "Oh, God!"

They moved on.

[241] (French) I am sick.
[242] Keep moving!
[243] Keep moving! You wanted to hide up here?!

They had not found me. Suddenly, I felt a chill and realized that I was lying in a very uncomfortable position. I wondered how long I'd been lying this way—five minutes, an hour, or maybe all night.

A *posten* sat on my head. I heard the dog sniffing in the straw. His nose must have been a few inches from my head. I was certain that I was lost. In a second!...

The picket who was sitting on my head began to curse: "*Verfluchte Schweine, verfluchter Weg.*"[244]

There was another one with him. They talked for some time. I fainted again. He got up and moved on. I knew how I would die. They would stick me with a bayonet. But I was still alive. How was that possible? My body was numb. I could not feel my legs. I tried to move. My heart beat evenly. If I could only press my hands to it so that it would not beat so loudly. But my arms were spread out. I could not move them. They are still walking...

Something heavy dropped next to me. Someone began to dig into the straw. A shot sounded. The woman who had wanted to hide gave out her last tragic sigh.

I tried to think where the bullet had passed. Perhaps it had gone through me. But I felt nothing. I had been lying there such a long time and they had not found me. A glimmer of hope, again, maybe.

There was a moment of silence.

I decided to lean out. I stretched my fingers and bent one arm. Just then I heard wheels.

A car stopped right next to me. The sounds of conversations in German...

"*Komm hier!*"[245] The clang of tin buckets and then someone lifting the straw. Now they'd find me. But this must be the Wehrmacht.

[244] Damn pigs, damned road.
[245] Come here!

They might not shoot; they were not responsible. I prepared a sentence in German and began to repeat it to myself: "Leave me, you are not responsible, please leave me."

The buckets moved away. The wagon wheels revolved.

I decided to get up. No sounds reached me. A German might be standing there. But I must.

I peered out. The way was clear. I sprang up swiftly and just then noticed two civilians on the road.

"Polish?"

One of the civilians crossed himself at the sight of a phantom rising out of the straw.

"Y-yes," he stuttered.

"Is there a Polish village near here?" I asked. Still frightened, he pointed his finger.

"Over there. A little less than two miles from the road," he said.

I ran across the fields, sinking into the deep snow, pulling my feet out of the drifts with great difficulty. Behind me, I heard the transport again, and continued to run away from the road followed by the sounds of an approaching column, shots and sleigh-bells. Stopping for a moment, I tore the number off my coat, and looked back, I had left the road far behind now, and they couldn't see me.

I stumbled forward until in front of me I could see a quietly slumbering village. There were no more wire fences around me, instead, a peasant farmhouse, a fence and the sound of bells in the distance. A small funny mongrel on a chain began to bark. I wanted to shout, to dance with joy.

"I am free! I am free! I shall live!"

Krystyna Zywulska before the war.

Epilogue

Tadeusz Andrzejewski[246]: Our mother, Krystyna Zywulska, died August 1st 1993 in Düsseldorf, Germany, where she had lived since 1970. Her real name was Sonia Landau. She was born in Lodz, on September 1st 1914. After escaping from the Warsaw ghetto, she used false papers and during the arrests reported to be Krystyna Zywulska, also born in Lodz, but on May 28th 1918. She used this identity from that point on. Her real identity documents were lost. The Gestapo caught her and put her in Pawiak prison as a Resistance activist, not a Jew.

Describing all these events in the book had for her a dual purpose: it was both therapy and testimony, therapy by giving testimony. Convinced that she was the only one who survived Auschwitz-Birkenau, she broke her inherent relationship with the place only with the publication of the first edition of the book *I Survived Auschwitz* in 1946. Thus she freed herself from the responsibilities of being a solitary witness Since then, the book has had ten editions in Poland, each of between ten and thirty thousand copies. The book was translated into

---

[246] Tadeusz Andrzejewski, born June 4th 1949 in Warsaw, works in Information Technology. After starting as a student in Warsaw, he went to Gothenburg, Sweden, where he continued his mathematical studies. After his mother left Poland, he joined her in Düsseldorf, Germany, where he worked as a system analyst. There he met his future wife, Teresa, with whom he migrated to Paris a few years after their wedding. They have two daughters, Eve and Estelle.

English, French, Russian, Czech and German (in order of its appearance). Each issue has been sold out everywhere, including in Russia, where 600,000 copies were published.

Jacek Andrzejewski[247]: This book helped her endure the memory of Auschwitz. One could say that through this book, immediately after leaving the camp she was able to spew out everything that happened there, and thus afterwards was able to live a normal life. What's more, she lived via her wit, because it was, after all, humor and satire which were the source of her earnings after the war. In addition, it was after *I Survived Auschwitz* that her friends began to say that with her literary ability, she should write. Mom knew that she could effectively use the Polish language, because she had studied law before the war, but she never thought about being a writer. In fact, her whole life she had wanted to be a painter. And she passed this passion onto me. She herself did not realize the dream of painting until she was more than sixty years old. At that point her paintings started to appear at an amazing pace. During a single year she probably painted more than I have throughout my whole life, and everybody liked all of these paintings. They are likable, although, those who are familiar with mom's life can quickly discern their relationship with the nightmares that she endured. And in reality those nightmares were coming out of hiding at night, as I quickly realized how difficult it was for her was to sleep peacefully.

TA: In 1965 mother published a second book, *Empty Water* in which she describes her life in the Warsaw ghetto,

---

[247] Jacek Andrzejewski, born January 14th 1947 in Warsaw, is a painter and sculptor. He graduated from Kenar School in Zakopane and Grafik-Design in Krefeld, Germany. He has showed works at many exhibitions at home and abroad (Düsseldorf, Cleves, Cologne, Paris). Since 2004 along with his wife Natalia, he has run the studio-gallery Kamienikon in Warsaw. His son David, is like his father, an artist.

her escape from there, subsequent Resistance activity, arrest by the Gestapo and her first days after Auschwitz. That book ends with what happened after liberation from the concentration camp. *Empty Water* was translated into French, Italian, German Japanese and English. Between these two books dealing with the war, Krystyna Zywulska wrote satirical texts and song lyrics. To live you must know how to laugh and sing. The reason why she came back to the subject of the war was as follows. During one of the parties to which she was often invited, a man told a story concerning the war. When going over the bridge between the two parts of the ghetto, he noticed a child, clearly Jewish, who wanted to jump and commit suicide. He ran to the little one and saved his life. At this point they were approached by a German policeman who ordered the man to pass the child back through the railing, saying that if he did not, they would both be shot. Here, the person telling the story asked his audience: "So what would you do in my place?"

Mom immediately interrupted, asking everyone not to answer the question because nobody could accurately predict what his / her reaction would be. After all, the bravest people can sometimes be afraid, just as the greatest cowards can suddenly manifest superhuman courage. The weak can be strong and the strong may have moments of weakness. The question was simply inadequate. The real issue is: What can be done so that a human being will never again be brought before this kind of alternative?

We can therefore draw a very important message, carried by most of the survivors of the extermination camps—a specific form of optimism earned by those who have been granted a second life: who won. Every day is an extra one, gained, in the context of the death sentence issued by the Nazis. For this to never happen again, it is necessary to create a world of tolerance and rejection once and for all of prejudice, of any spark, which could be the beginning of racism.

After reading an excerpt from one of the books at a school while in Germany, my mother was approached by a 14-year-old student, "Madame, but you must hate us Germans." She replied, "Hate you? But why would you deserve that? I may hate Nazis and at the same time not recognize their ideas of *Ubermenschen*[248] or *Herrenrasse*[249] nor its opposite, *Untermenschen*[250], but there are as many characterological differences between Germans as there are Germans. No two people are alike. If everyone was always aware of this, also with regard to other nations, the Holocaust would have never have happened.

However, it is conceivable that some people, after having survived the war may have a specific aversion to the language in which they heard: *Los, Raus, Schnell, Verfluchte Schweine,*[251] etc. When it is said that I do not like the German language it does not mean: 'I do not like the Germans as a nation.' It is easy to make generalizations such as, 'But most of them are...' There is an easily crossed and subtle boundary that separates us from unjustified (or at least in the vast majority of cases from unjustified) discrimination. And the next step is then much easier.

JA: The strongest influence mom's story had on me was what gave her the strength to survive the war years in the ghetto, then at Pawiak, and then in Auschwitz and Birkenau. And she survived them so actively. In the ghetto she helped keep her family alive. Then there was the underground organization and also in the camp. The thing that gave her the strength, was simply the love she got from her family. She grew up in an atmosphere of enormous love. She was adored and treated like a real treasure. It was thanks to this that she

[248] Overhuman.
[249] Master race.
[250] Subhuman.
[251] Come on, Get out, Quick, Damn pigs!

(and not the children of drunken fathers, those neglected and thrown out into the snow, which one might think should harden up from that and be much more resistant) survived hell, holding onto memories, knowing that in addition to what was happening here and now, there was something else out there. It gave her strength. Not only did she live on, but she wrote poetry, which was memorized by many fellow women prisoners. She had become someone important in the camp, because she had given strength to the others. For example, she helped illiterates by writing letters for them.

TA: In all of her books she showed a mixture of good and evil, regardless of differences in skin color, nationality or religion. It is precisely this kind of educational *credo* that our mother gave us. She eventually left Poland to join us. Maciek, our adoptive brother, "chose freedom" in 1966. Jacek and I left in 1969 with documents on which it could be seen printed in six languages: "The holder of this travel document is not a Polish citizen."

Originally we stayed in Sweden. Our mother (speaking fluent German), because of her work as a writer, did not want to start learning a new language, so she asked us to join her in Germany. Having arrived there, I married a Frenchwoman, and thus added to my German citizenship, a second one, French. In 2002 I got back my Polish citizenship, so now I have three of them. I wish I had two hundred to show everyone that nationality does not matter!

JA: It seems to me to be symbolic that my mother is buried in a German cemetery in Düsseldorf. It is a sign of how she lived, neither as a Pole nor as a Jew, but as an ordinary person, in one or another country. Once a group of young people came to us and one of the girls suddenly asked: "How after all that you have gone through, can you live in Germany? If I were in your place, it certainly would not have been possible." My mother replied, "You know, if I *had* my place, I would not have come here either..." I quoted this exchange on several occasions when I heard some people pretending to be wise, "I am a better Jew, because I live in France, and this one is worse, because he lives in Germany," and so on...

TA: How to say something against racism and be clearly understood? How to say in a simple way that hatred creates hatred, that of racism is racism born, that distrust creates mistrust? I am proud of my daughter who at age eleven said to me: "Dad, I am so lucky! I am the granddaughter of a former prisoner of Auschwitz. How bad would I feel if I were the granddaughter of one of the executioners from Auschwitz! And this wouldn't be my fault, just as it isn't on my merit that I am the granddaughter of the victim..."

I think in this way she confirmed what can be best expressed by the slogan of the former prisoners of Auschwitz: *This* must happen "never again"—no more hatred.

It makes no sense to think in terms of revenge. If we are to be guided by the principle of "an eye for an eye, a tooth for a tooth," after all, Mahatma Gandhi said, all men would already be blind and toothless.

JA: There is something else. One day my mother said that she did not regret what she had lived through. Seeing that she has shocked me, she added that certainly she would not want to relive it all again, but what she has experienced there taught her immensely important things about people. Because, despite all of the atrocities in Auschwitz, there were also a lot of things very beautiful happening. A simple human gesture in those extreme conditions had dimensions difficult to imagine today. For example if an extremely exhausted prisoner got up and gave another, even more emaciated person, water. Today, for new generations who live many years after the war, it is difficult to even imagine what she said—how big a measure of humanity this testimony is.

German to English Dictionary

This dictionary contains all the German words and phrases used throughout the book. As the author mentioned in the text, after spending such a long time in the camp, everybody started to use certain *lager* slang, Polonized versions of German words, for example *zugangs* instead of entrants, *lager* instead of camp, *aussen* instead of *outside*. This made the book sound more real and to not include this in the English language version would have resulted in much being "lost in translation." Note that in German nouns are always capitalized. To have Americanized versions of German nouns we decided to use *italicized* lower case nouns throughout the book, unless the noun was used in a phrase.

Abgang — Departure
Achtung — Attention
Alle verfluchte Juden Zählappell! — All damn Jews, roll call!
Anweiserin — Instructor
Arbeit macht frei — Work makes you free.
Arbeiten — **Schweine, los! schneller** — Work, pigs, go! Faster!
Auf Freiheit — For freedom
Auf Tod — On death
Aufseherin — Overseer
Aufstehen — Get up
Aussen — Outside
Aussenkommando — Outside unit
Aussteigen — Get Out
Baracken schliessen! — Close the barracks!
Baracken schliessen! Schneller, du dumme Gans, du blöde Kuh!
  — Close the barracks! Faster, you fool, you stupid cow!
Bekleidungskammer — Cloakroom; Dressing Room
Blockälteste — Block elder
Blockführer — Block leader
Blockführerstube — Block leader's office

Blut für Vaterland?— Blood for the Fatherland?

Brave Mädels — Brave girls

Bündel — Bundle, package

Danke schön — Thank you very much

Das Dreck — The dirt

Die Damen von Effektenkammer — The ladies of the property store

Die schöne Irma — The beautiful Irma

Dirne — Prostitute

Dolmetscherin — Interpreter; translator

Durchfall — Dysentery; Starvation, bloody diarrhea

Du Arschloch! Du traurige Mistbiene! Du — You asshole! You sad dung bee! You!

Du dummes Arschloch! — You stupid asshole!

Dumme Mädels — Stupid girls

Effektenkammer — Stockroom; property storage

Ein Befehl — A command

Eine Halskette, eine Armbanduhr gelb, ein Ringweiss — One necklace, one yellow wrist watch, one white ring

Ein Rock... Eine Bluse... Eine Kittelschürze... — One skirt... One blouse... One apron.

Ein Rock... Ein Büstenhalte... — One skirt... One bra...

Eine schöne Nacht haben wir heute, nicht wahr? Schön ist das Leben! — Today we have a beautiful night, isn't it true? Life is beautiful!

Endlösung — The Final Solution

Endlösung der Judenfrage — The Final Solution of the Jewish Question

Entlassen — Discharged, released

Erziehungs häftling — Education, "correctional" prisoner

Es geht alles vorüber, — Everything passes,

Es geht alles vorbei, Everything goes away,

Nach jedem Dezember After every December

Kommt wieder ein Mai May comes back again.

Essenkolonne — Food column

Familienlager — Family camp

Frau Aufseherin — Madame, Warden

Frauenkonzentrationslager — Women's concentration camp

Frech — Impudent

Fressenbaracke — Food barrack (literally: grub barrack)

Funktionshäftling — Function prisoner; Prisoner with supervising assignments.

Generalplan Ost — General Plan East

Häftling — Camp prisoner

Hauptscharführer — Head/Chief Squad Leader

Hast du Brot? — Do you have bread?

Herr Chef — Mr Chief

Herrenvolk — Master race

Herrenrasse — Master race

Hier! Los! Stehen! Gehe! — Here! Go! Stand! Go!

Ich bin ein Sonderhäftling — I am a special prisoner

Ich brauche keine Millionen — I do not need millions

Ich warte — I am waiting

Ich warte auf dich — I wait for you.

Ihre Mutter hat... — Her mother has...

Ja, was schaust du dort, ist was interessantes? — Yes, is there anything interesting out there? What are you looking at?

Jawohl, Frau Oberaufseherin — Yes, Madame, senior overseer

Kapo — Camp prisoner who had authority over others

Karteikarten — Index cards

Kartei-mässig — Index card-worthy

Kennkarten — Identification Cards

Komm, komm, du alte Zitrone — Come on, come on, you old hag (literally: you old lemon)

Komm hier! — Come here!

Komm zurück — Come back

Kommando Effektenkammer — Property storage unit

Kommando Effektenkammer, antreten! — Property storage unit, line up!

Konzentrationslager — Concentration Camp

Krätze — Scabies

Kriminalpolizei — Criminal Police

Kultukampf — Culture fight

Kulturträger — Culture carrier

Lager — Camp

Lagerälteste — Camp Senior

Lagerführer — Camp commander

Lagerkommandant — Camp commander

Lagerkapo — Camp Kapo; Kapo overseeing the organization of work in the whole camp

Lagerruhe — Camp Silence

Lagersperre, Lagersperre, alles auf Block — Closing the camp, closing the camp, everybody inside the huts

Lagerstrasse — Camp road

Lass diese alte Zitrone! Geh arbeiten! Los! — Leave this old lemon! Go to work! Go!

Läufer— Runner; messenger

Läuferin — Female runner; Female prisoner serving as a messenger.

Leichenkommando — Corpse unit

Links, links, links und links — Left, left, left and left

Los! Auf! Schnell! Laufen! Los! Auf! — Go on! Up! Quick! Move! Go on! Up!

Los!... Aufgehen! — Go!... Rise!

Los!...aufstehen...schnelle...schneller, Schweine! — Go!... get up... fast... faster, pigs!

Los! du blöde Kuh — Go! You stupid cow

Los, Raus, Schnell, Verfluchte Schweine! — Come on, Get out, quick. Damn pigs!

Los! Schnell! — Go! Quick!

Los! Weiter! — Keep moving!

Los weiter ab! — Keep moving ahead!

Los! Weiter! Du wolltest dich hier verstecken?! — Keep moving! You wanted to hide up here?!

Los weiter, verflucht, noch einmal — Keep moving, damn you, one more time

Mädels — Girls

Mein Liebchen, was willst du noch mehr? — My darling, what more do you want?

Meine allerliebste Eva — My dearest Eva

Meiner allerliebsten Mutti, Hans. Kijew 1943. — My dearest mom, Hans. Kiev 1943.

Meiner allerliebsten Sophie — ein Erinnerung an die schönen Tage in Saloniki... Sommer 1942 — My dearest Sophie — a reminder of the beautiful days in Thessaloniki... Summer 1942.

Morgen gehen wir nach Birkenau — Tomorrow we go to Birkenau.

Na, Krysia, gehen wir weiter, nicht wahr? — Well, Krysia, we move on, right?

Na, was? — Well, what?

Na, was, dumme Schweine, lustig, nicht wahr? — Well, what, stupid pig. Funny, isn't it?

Na, was, warum so spat? — Well, what, why so late?

Nachtwache — Night watch

Nebelwerfer — Rocket launcher

Namenskartei — Name Index

Nein, ich wollte das Fenster zumachen — No, I was about to close the window.

Nein, Maria, sie sind vergast.... — No, Maria, they were gassed...

Nicht wahr? — Isn't it true?

Nicht wahr? Verfluchte Juden! — Isn't it true? Damn Jews!

No... lass, Maria, genug... — No...leave it, Maria, enough...

Oberaufseherin — Senior overseer

Oberkommando der Wehrmacht — High Command of the Armed Forces

Oberkommando der Wehrmacht gibt bekannt... — The High Command of the Armed Forces announces...

Oberscharführer — Senior Squad Leader

Ordnung — Order

Ordnung muss sein — Must have order

Pflegerin — Nurse

Politische Abteilung — Political Section

Posten — Guard

Puff — Brothel

Reichsdeutsch — Ethnic German living inside Germany with German citizenship.

Rapportführerin — Report leader; Head reporting officer

Rapportschreiberin –Reporting clerk

Räumungskommando — Cleaning unit

Ruhe! — Be quiet!

Schade! — Too bad!

Schade, das war ein wertvoller Mensch! — Too bad, this was a valuable person!

Scheisskommando — Shit unit; unit engaged in latrine cleaning and litter

dumping.

Schön — Beautiful, lovely

Schönes Wetter haben wir heute. Nicht wahr, Joasia? — Nice weather we have today. Isn't it true, Joasia?

Schmuck — Jewelery

Schnell — Quickly

Schreiberin — Writer, Clerk

Schreibstube — Office

Selbstmord, schade — Suicide, shame

Sie ist verrückt! — She's crazy!

Sofort, Herr Chef... — Immediately, boss...

Sonder Behandlung — Special treatment

Sondergericht — Special Court

Sonderkommando — Special unit; the Jewish prisoners who are working in the crematorium.

Sonderwagen — Special cars

SS (Schutzstaffel) — Protection squads of Nazi NSDAP (National Socialist German Workers' Party)

Strafenkommando — Punishment unit

Streifen — Streak; line

Stubendienst — Office services

Torwache — Gate guard

Totenliste — List of the dead

Transport aus Breslau — Transport from Wroclaw

Übermenschen — Overhuman
Überstellt — Transferred
Überstellung — Transfer
Unterkunft — Accommodation
Untermenschen — Subhumam
Unterscharführer — Junior Squad Leader
Verfluchter Jude — Damn Jew
Verfluchte Judinen — Damn Jewish woman
Verfluchte Schweine — Damn pigs
Verfluchte Schweine, verfluchter Weg — Damn pigs, damned road
Vernichtungskommando — Extermination (Death) unit
Vernichtungslager — Death camp
Verstanden — Understood
Verstorben — Deceased
Vertreter — Assistant
Volksdeutsch — Ethnic German
Vorarbeiter — Foreman
Vorarbeiterin — Forewoman
Vorne — Front
Warum, Herr Chef, sie waren doch so jung und hübsch? — Why, boss? They were so young and pretty.
Was? Du dummes Arschloch! — What? You stupid asshole!
Was machst du hier? — What are you doing here?
Was machst du, Mala? — What are you doing, Mala?
Was machst du, stehe! — What are you doing? Don't move!
Waschraum — Washroom
Wasser! — Water!
Wie lange wird der Dreck noch dauern? Wie lange noch? — How long will this shit take? How long?
Wiener Schnitzel — Viennese Schnitzel
Wiese — Lawn
Winkel — Triangular badge showing the prisoners' number, nationality and reason for internment.
Wo ist der kleine Wołodia? — Where is the little Volodya?
Zählappell — Roll call
Zu fünf anstellen, los! — Set up five abreast, go!
Zugang — New prisoner brought into the camp.
Zulage — Food bonus for harder working prisoners.
Zwölf Zugänge — Twelve Additions

Pronunciation and Equivalents of Names

Andrzej — Male Polish name pronounced [AHND-zhay], Polish equivalent of Andrew.

Aniela — Female Polish name [ahn-YE-lah], Polish form of Angela.

Ada — Female Polish name [AH-dah], Short form of Adelaide.

Alina — Female Polish name [ah-LEE-nah].

Alinka — A diminutive of Alina [ah-LEEN-kah].

Ania — Female Polish name [AHN-yah], Polish diminutive of Anna.

Antos — Male Polish name [AHN-tos], Diminutive of Antoni [ahn-TAW-nee], Polish form of Anthony.

Basia — Female Polish name [BAH-shah], Diminutive of Barbara.

Bolek — Male Polish name [BAW-lek], Diminutive of Boleslaw [baw-LE-swahf] — English equivalent, William.

Czesia Female Polish name [CHE-shah], Diminutive of Czesława [ches-WAH-vah].

Cyprian — Male name [SIP-ree-ən].

Elzunia — Female Polish name [el-ZHUNYAH], Diminutive form of Elżbieta [elzh-BYE-tah], Polish form of Elizabeth.

Ewa — Female name [E-vah], Polish form of Eve.

Genia — Female Polish name [GEN-yah], Diminutive of Genowefa [ge-naw-VE-fah], Polish form of Genevieve.

Hania — Female Polish name [HAHN-yah], Diminutive of Hanna [HAHN-nah], Cognate of Hannah.

Hanka — Female Polish name [HAHN-kah], Diminutive of Hanna [HAHN-nah], Cognate of Hannah.

Irena — Female Polish name [ee-RE-nah], Latinate form of Irene.

Irka — Female Polish name [EER-kah], Diminutive of Irena.

Jadwiga — Female Polish name [yahd-VEE-gah], English equivalent: Hedwig or Harriet.

Janka — Female Polish name [YAHN-kah], Diminutive of Janina [yah-NEE-nah], it is the Polish feminine form of John. The English equivalent is Janine.

Joanna — Female Polish name [yaw-AHN-nah], English and Polish form of Latin *Iohanna*.

Joasia — Female Polish name [yaw-AH-shah], Diminutive of Joanna.

Jozka — Female Polish name [YUWZ-kah], Diminutive of Jozefa [yuw-ZEF-ah], Polish feminine form of Joseph.

Jurek — Male Polish name [YUW-rek], Diminutive of Jerzy [YE-zhi], the Polish equivalent of George.

Kasia — Female Polish name [KAH-shah], Diminutive of Katarzyna [kah-tah-ZHI-nah], the Polish form of Katherine or Catherine.

Katia — Female Russian name [KAH-tyah].

Krysia — Female Polish name [KRI-shah], Diminutive of Krystyna, [kris-TI-nah], English equivalent, Christina.

Krystyna — Female Polish name [kris-TI-nah], English equivalent, Christina.

Lucyna — Female Polish name [luw-TSI-nah].

Lucja — Female Polish name [LUWTS-yah] or [WUWTS-yah].

Magda — Female Polish name [MAHG-dah], Short form of Magdalena [mahg-dah-LE-nah].

Marta — Female Polish name [MAHR-tah], Cognate of Martha.

Maryla — Female Polish name [mah-RI-lah], Diminutive of Maria.

Maria — Female Polish name [MAHR-yah].

Marysia — Female Polish name [mah-RI-shah], Diminutive of Maria [MAHR-yah], Mary in English.

Mela — Female Polish name [ME-lah], Diminutive of Melania [me-LAHN-yah], English equivalent, Melanie.

Pawel — Male Polish name [PAH-vew], Polish form of Paul.

Sabinka — Female Polish name [sah-BEEN-kah].

Stasia — Female Polish name [STAH-shah], Diminutive of Stanislawa [stah-nee-SWAH-vah], feminine form of Stanislaw, of which English equivalent is Stanley.

Stasio — Male Polish name [STAH-shoh], Diminutive of Stanislaw, [stah-NEE-swahf], English equivalent is Stanley.

Stefa — Female Polish name [STE-fah], Diminutive of Stefania [ste-FAHN-yah], feminine form of Stefan [STE-fahn], English equivalent, Steven.

Stenia — Female Polish name [STE-nyah], Diminutive of Stanislawa [stah-nee-SWAH-vah], feminine form of Stanislaw, of which English equivalent is Stanley.

Tania — Female Russian name [TAHN-yə], Diminutive of Tatiana, [tah-TYAH-nah].

Tadeusz — Male Polish name [tah-DE-uwsh], Polish form of THADDEUS.

Todzia — Female Polish name [TO-dyah], Diminutive of Teodora [TEO-dorah].

Wacek — Polish male name [VAH— tsek], a diminutive of Wacław, [VAHTS-wahf]. Female Polish name pronounced

Wanda — Female Polish name [VAHN-dah].

Wiesia — Female Polish name [VIE-shah], Diminutive of Wieslawa [VIESLA-fyah].

Wisia — Female Polish name [VI-shah], Diminutive of Wislawa [VISLA-fyah].

Ziuta — Female Polish name [ZYUT-ah], Diminutive of Jozefa [yuw-ZEF-ah], Polish feminine form of Joseph.

Zosia — Female Polish name [ZAW-shah], Diminutive of Zofia [ZAW-fyah], Polish form of Sophia.